URSYN.COM

I0802253

NATURE APPRECIATION
KNOWLEDGE AS ART

URSYN.COM

URSYN.COM

Cover design and images Symbols in Nature and Swirl © 2025 by Anna Ursyn

First published 2026
by CRC Press
2385 NW Executive Center Drive, Suite 320, Boca Raton FL 33431

and by CRC Press
4 Park Square, Milton Park, Abingdon, Oxon, OX14 4RN

CRC Press is an imprint of Taylor & Francis Group, LLC

© 2026 Anna Ursyn

Reasonable efforts have been made to publish reliable data and information, but the author and publisher cannot assume responsibility for the validity of all materials or the consequences of their use. The authors and publishers have attempted to trace the copyright holders of all material reproduced in this publication and apologize to copyright holders if permission to publish in this form has not been obtained. If any copyright material has not been acknowledged please write and let us know so we may rectify in any future reprint.

Except as permitted under U.S. Copyright Law, no part of this book may be reprinted, reproduced, transmitted, or utilized in any form by any electronic, mechanical, or other means, now known or hereafter invented, including photocopying, microfilming, and recording, or in any information storage or retrieval system, without written permission from the publishers.

For permission to photocopy or use material electronically from this work, access www.copyright.com or contact the Copyright Clearance Center, Inc. (CCC), 222 Rosewood Drive, Danvers, MA 01923, 978-750-8400. For works that are not available on CCC please contact mpkbookspermissions@tandf.co.uk

Trademark notice: Product or corporate names may be trademarks or registered trademarks, and are used only for identification and explanation without intent to infringe.

Library of Congress Cataloging-in-Publication Data

ISBN: 9781041025054 (hbk)
ISBN: 9781041025030 (pbk)
ISBN: 9781003619574 (ebk)

DOI: 10.1201/9781003619574

Typeset in Times New Roman and Herculanum

Publisher's note: This book has been prepared from printer-ready copy provided by the author.

Firtu: always ready for a party.

For M and M, with Much Love.

Frozen Fractal. © 2025 by Anna Ursyn

A SERIES OF BOOKS: KNOWLEDGE THROUGH THE ARTS
PLAYFUL BOOKS ABOUT SERIOUS THINGS

This series consists of the following volumes:

- Dance Code: Dance Steps as a Code, Taylor & Francis
- New Storytelling: Learning through Metaphors, Taylor & Francis
- Code Appreciation: Reshaping Knowledge, Taylor & Francis
- Nature Appreciation: Knowledge as Art, Taylor & Francis

Several common threads are running through all four volumes. These books offer elemental information concerning coding and ever-present connections between coding and most branches of knowledge, areas of specialization, courses of study, and many subjects of interest. In a playful way, the books talk about novel areas of knowledge and technologies in the context of everyday situations encountered by characters, humans, and imagined individuals, and their attempts to explain their issues by coding. The books also discuss worldwide changes, ecological balance, and our common care for Nature. In all volumes, texts and illustrations are matched up by presenting the author's artworks, visual outputs of computer programs, and a great number of sketches drawn by the author, showing imaginary characters. This time, the codes are embedded into short texts to have the reader see them as a language.

Twist. Output from the computer code. © 2025 by Anna Ursyn

Water Falling. © 2025 by Matylda Czarnecka. (Used with permission).

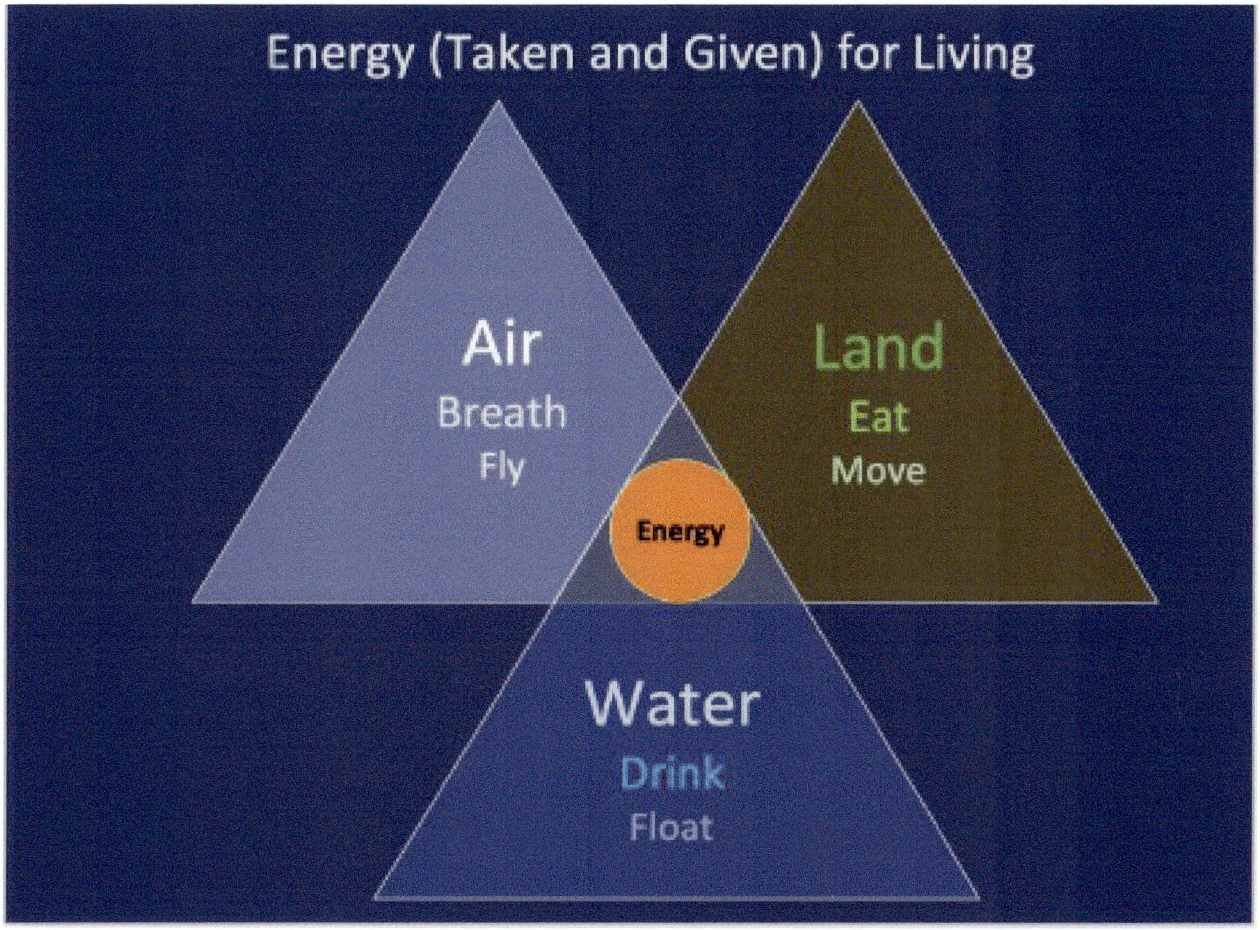

IF THERE IS ONE THING
WE ALL CAN AGREE ON
IT'S OUR LOVE FOR
NATURE

Shadows. © 2025 by Matylda Czarnecka. (Used with permission).

Tacho: keeps it all in his pocket.

Water. © *2025 by Matylda Czarnecka. (Used with permission).*

WALK, SWIM, FLY, STAY, WAVE
A PLAYFUL BOOK ABOUT SERIOUS THINGS

TABLE OF CONTENTS

This book comprises chapters focused on ways we move in various environments. Short stories have embedded codes, so the reader can read them without any fear of coding.

A bird. © *2025 by Matylda Czarnecka (Used with permission)*

Hutago: is happy, sad, or just is.

INTRODUCTION

If asked what everyone can agree on, we can see one answer: we all love Nature, in one way or another.

In this book, impossible creatures playfully deliver computer codes, with an underlying notion that everything is connected in nature, materials, sciences, techniques, computing, and the arts. In this innovative space, these characters introduce programming. With codes in Python intertwined into simple facts and events, the book shows how we appreciate nature and thus helps us learn in a playful, nonjudgmental way. When employees do not shy away from coding, it speeds up communication with the ever-present coders. It also helps with prompt writing.

Knowledge is divided into subjects and classes at schools, colleges, then universities. Facts, processes, and rules are not divided in our life. Facts, processes, and rules are all connected: biochemistry, product materiality, changes from matter to energy and vice versa, bonding and dispersion, and conversion of one state into another. In this book, they are considered as ways of living in different environments, such as:

GEO, earth, soil, minerals, and natural resources are experienced when walking on the ground.
WATER, transportation, ecosystems, leisure time, and energy-related to water environs.
AIR, transportation, space and planets travel, galactic objects, space junk. One can fly or carry materials and devices through it.
WAVES, communication, transformation, energy, music, color – everything related to light, electromagnetic waves, oscillation, and vibration.
There are also DEEP UNDERWATER space and COSMIC SPACE explorations.

MANY WAYS OF MOVING

Earth's inhabitants move. They use and produce energy. Some animals create colonies and follow as if they would have a group brain. Those are called swarm animals. Some walk, some swim, some fly, and others can do all the above.

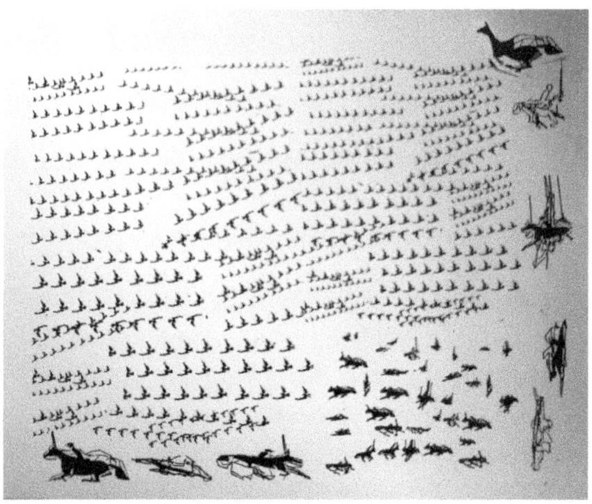

Some creatures are black and white. Some possess the unique ability to swim, fly, and walk through the stages of their lives. Many belong to various birds, from a small seabird, guillemot, albatross, pelican, penguin, mallard ducks, and other waterfowl found across many continents, which are excellent swimmers and can dive for food. While their feet help them swim, some are not the best for walking. The Muscovy duck can swim well, and the nesting in trees makes them fly. They are foraging for fish and aquatic plants but are less efficient flyers than mallards. Gannets are seabirds reaching speeds up to 100 km/h when hunting for fish. They excel at diving up to 15 meters, with their air sacs softening the impact. Puffins are good at flying, flapping their wings 400 times a minute, and they excel at diving up to 60 meters to catch fish. Moorhens swim in freshwater, fly, and move on land. There are also insects, such as dragonfly which gracefully flies and can walk on water surfaces hunting in aerial and water environments. Mosquitoes fly and they like being near water to lay eggs. A reptile, a flying lizard gecko moves between trees by gliding and can walk, move across water by swimming underwater, or move fast across the water's surface by slapping their feet for the air bubbles that help them stay afloat. Even fish can swim, walk, and fly, such as garnai, the rare breed of flying fish, the flying gurnard. Also, there are mammals, such as flying squirrels, which can glide, swim, walk, or run. There are scores of variations regarding locomotion, and they differ depending on many factors. People examine them and apply solutions for their needs to improve them later by incorporating new knowledge, tools, and materials.

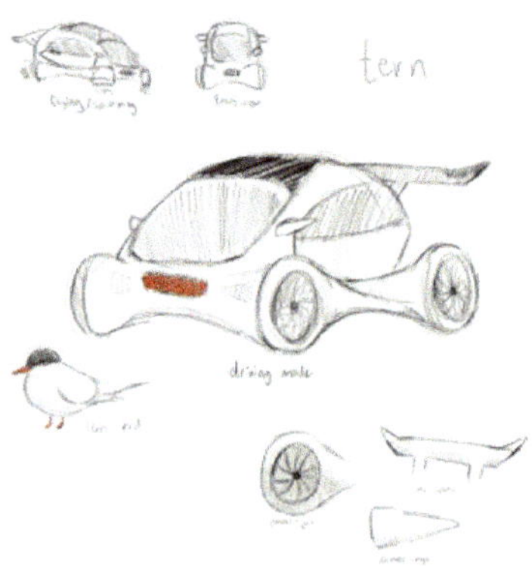

A car designed after a bird. © 2025 by Eunice Lee. iArt Institute, NYC. (Used with permission).

IMITATING NATURE

We mimic nature in various ways. We try to understand some patterns and widen our approaches with new technological solutions. We pose many questions, form problems, and try to find answers, even solutions. New tools help generate new questions. We try visual approaches to describe nature, from fractal graphics to visualizations, various diagrams, and multidimensional, interactive, and dynamic systems.

Our understanding of the electromagnetic spectrum may help us find some solutions when we are working on bio-inspired data by mimicking nature. As described by the National Research Council of the National Academies (2008, pp. 63-64), the three ways to create new materials and systems may include:

Biomimicry is when people design structures that function in the same way as living systems and create synthetic materials that respond to external stimuli. For example, certain cells such as T-lymphocytes can sense specific external stimuli and then deal with pathogens. The challenge is to design bio-inspired systems and devices for detecting hazardous biological and chemical agents and strengthen national security systems.

Bio-inspiration is when people strive to create structures acting in different schemes than living systems to perform the same functions. For example, the self-cleaning lotus leaf, and the fracture-resistant mollusk shell are examples of inspiring structures. The gecko's adhesive works like glue in a vacuum and underwater, leaves no residue, and is self-cleaning; adhesion is reversible, so geckoes alternatively stick and unstuck themselves 15 times per second as they run up walls. Mimicking this design involves synthesizing artificial polymers and bio-adhesives that match the magic of a gecko's "dry glue" with its reversible attachment. Scientists strive to create self-evolving, self-healing, self-cleaning, and self-replicating super-materials that could mimic the ability to evolve and adapt. The cutting-edge optical technology solutions can also be found in animals: multilayer reflectors, diffraction gratings that spread a beam of light waves, liquid crystals, and structures that scatter light. For instance, Morpho butterfly has an iridescence sparkle and blue color visible from hundreds of meters due to periodic photonic nanostructure in scales on wings that responds to specific wavelengths of light without any dye involved.

Bio-derivation, which means the incorporation of biomaterials into human-made structures. Using existing biomaterial to create a hybrid with artificial material. For example, it may involve exploring biologically derived proteins into polymeric (having many similar units bonded together) assemblies for targeted drug delivery. The eyes of higher organisms and the photosynthesis mechanism (in green plants and other organisms that use sunlight to synthesize carbohydrates as food from carbon dioxide and water) are examples of biological structures and processes that can support harvesting light and fuels (by converting cellulose polymer to ethanol). Deciphering force and motions in proteins driven by sub-cellular, molecular motors can advance clinical diagnostics, prosthetics, and drug delivery. Molecular motors convert chemical energy (usually in the form of ATP – adenosine triphosphate) into mechanical energy. Contrary to Brownian movements, they are not driven solely by thermal effects (National Research Council, 2008, pp. 63-64). With bio-inspired data, we expand technology and devices, from physical computing with Arduino boards, Makey Makey, and Raspberry Pi, or VR, AR XR, holograms, and machine learning, to 3D printing.

Humans inspire themselves with nature while creating art in different media, traditional and digital. Recently, the arrival of iArt – digital art that incorporates artificial intelligence (AI) opens new options in a wide spectrum of media. It can be the creation of visual artworks created with AI algorithms, interactive installations, producing images, music, video, and text-based art, and finding new forms of expression. Using big datasets collected by AI, people can mimic artistic styles, produce works with old and new materials, tools offered by many, such as ALL-E, Midjourney, or Stable Diffusion, and procedures, or create artworks in a new style.

But there is more and growing. The new tools and techniques allow us to record what was not seen before, bypassing old scales and levels up and down to beyond micro, nano, pico, etc. Artificial intelligence helps us discover the past. There is a discipline in coding known as swarm computing.

The changing role of coding impacts us with new tools and solutions. We need to understand how computers operate to write better prompts, feel more confident and current, and communicate better with coders on the job. This book is a set of situations where text is merged with concise codes in Python. By reading the codes embedded into the stories, the reader can grasp some major ideas. Coding is a language that can be understood to have some structure and rules one can comprehend.

Where the living things want to move determines how they move. Different environments create conditions, and natural laws change how we do things. Energy access determines our ways.
Many have experienced a story told in a particular linear fashion: a mailperson whose dog barked at the hairdresser, whose son met a… The set of creatures in this book playfully delivers serious facts with an underlying notion that everything is connected.

The book can be seen as illustrated biographies of impossible creatures. They can be seen as atoms, molecules, or anything the reader envisions fit. The book is divided into sections:
Locomotion (earth), Float (waters), Fly (air and beyond), Under the Ocean (not really explored), Space (travel and tools to explore it), Still (invisible travel), and Waves (rules, physical laws, signals, energy, communication). Space is considered here on Earth or may be also cosmic.

A SET OF ENVIRONMENTS

People love to travel. We want to see places, meet people, animals, plants, and more, which means nature. Our socialization, movie watching, conference and training participation, and gaming slowly shift toward online situations, without ever-present mighty small devices allowing for it. For example, the Paris Orchestra practiced online during the pandemic lockdown: (https://www.theguardian.com/world/video/2020/apr/04/french-orchestra-play-together-in-coronavirus-lockdown-video. https://www.rfi.fr/en/culture/20200401-covid-19-french-symphonic-orchestra-plays-ravel-s-bol%C3%A9ro-from-home-video). There is a culture of experimenting with new places made from one's place while sharing the experience. For that, we enhance virtual reality-based solutions and immersive technologies.

New ways of looking at things with new technologies and techniques, such as photonics and biophotonics, help us to see the unseen and experience online. Games help us exercise when playing them, and make the experience related to shifting places. A typical view in any museum is a group of people engaged in their phones, taking photos with them and selfies. Some people work to follow up with the trend of bringing museum experience to their homes, with all the possible technologies already employed to do so. The robots become DJs, artists, performers, and more. Some people develop a culture where the zoos and circuses are made as holograms, so the experience becomes immersive and sensual, and the whole group can enjoy it online with extended family and friends still offering revenue to the organizers, gain an opportunity to virtually mingle with those who inspire us. The format of this book offers a more interactive, indirect approach to experiencing ideas through art to see how we can appreciate nature, all with respect and without judgment while learning basic ideas behind coding.

EDUCATION WITH AND AGAINST AI

Many platforms are offered to manage learning and working projects. Autodesk offers free Autodesk University; Adobe MAX is free if attended online. It is a great opportunity to learn and network. Lynda.com is free if accessed through a local public library with a free membership. It is good to check which library offers that. Students can have assigned homework to solidify what has been taught. It saves them thousands of dollars during their studies and after graduation. There are also paid options, such as Udemy, Digital Tutors, and more. Many cities have Maker Spaces. We converted an old newspaper building into one (LINC). In most cases, it is open and free to anyone. Processing.org, developed by two MIT graduates to help artists understand coding, is free, intuitive, and available for any system (Unix, Windows, or Linux). There is a library with graphics, animation, and an interactive one, so once you download the program, you tweak the existing code, and the output changes. It is an intuitive way to learn basic coding, which also helps with prompt writing.

AI options are considered great assistants that can take away tedious work, so many see it as crucial to use new technologies. However, it is important to work on developing the individual skills of each student rather than promoting AI as a ready solution or inspiration. Adobe offers training for educators related to AI and promotes it across their platforms rapidly. Those are very useful tools for many tasks in various areas. Students are often afraid of AI. The ability to understand coding and creating novel content rather than copying ideas seems to be the best way to stay current and not that worried (which can block creativity and might not be healthy).

Understanding creative outcomes is now the most important part. Since various types of AI-aided solution design provide perfect suggestions and outcomes, probably creative thinking is the one to focus on. Students grow by acknowledging individual talents. Offering tasks related to spatial abilities helps students grow intellectually, as the research states. Also, knowledge visualization skills are very important in our interconnected world. Building some level of understanding of how disciplines are connected helps with the creative process. Thus, exposing students to various types of technology and asking them to use them actively to create something meaningful might help the creativity, mental health, and self-fulfillment of a student. It is fun for them if enough stimulation is provided, and collaboration is involved. We can say that most, if not all, jobs are collaborative, and parents want to make sure their children can find employment. With a problem-solving and problem-finding approach, students discover their niche, thus hopefully ending up with a successful career.

Strategies of supporting creative thinking versus design thinking of students have much attention. Creative thinking is focused on generating innovative ideas and free, open-ended forms without structured processes, not necessarily combined with practical implementations. Design thinking is described as user-centered, structured, step-by-step iterative thinking with clear stages, aimed at practical, user-centered, workable solutions, product design, and business strategies. To develop user-centered solutions, people combine creativity with pragmatic considerations (Mikro Grafeio, 2024; Harvard Business School, HBS Online, Business Insight, 2024; McKinsey & Company, 2023).

SYMBIOSIS AS COLLABORATION?

Symbiosis among many species is a key to many animals' survival or offers mutual benefits. In some cases, symbiosis is obligate when two organisms can't survive without each other. When two species live together by choice, they live in facultative symbiosis. The four main types of symbiotic relationships are mutualism, commensalism, parasitism, and competition. The question is if those who live in different habitats can still benefit from collaboration. There might be many answers to these questions.

Characters present in this book can be seen as random creatures. They may represent minerals, atoms, molecules, or elements residing in nature such as carbon and its allotropes, e.g., fullerenes. They say that everything is made of carbon. They appreciate looking at carbon isomers, diamonds, graphite, and more while producing new technologies. Novelties are based on the past thought. An ancient Greek philosopher, Plato, a primary thinker and philosopher through his dialectic forms, worked with geometrical forms. Platonic forms were those being flawless. Characters discuss these forms in people, animals, plants, and resources. In the 17th century, Johannes Kepler, an astronomer, mathematician, astrologer, and natural philosopher led the Scientific Revolution, and developed laws of planetary motion. He considered that cosmic space consisted of platonic forms.

Natural resources are organized as elements in the Periodic Table of Elements named after Dmitri Ivanovich Mendeleev who developed the periodic table. They are seen in nature in people, animals, plants, and other living organisms and are examined in ecological terms. Soil gives us various types of resources for our survival. We discuss soil, and other elements (e.g., particles' assimilation by plants and animals). Inorganic and organic chemistry can hardly be seen independently from physics, math, health, and more perspectives. Energetical resources are vital in the economy, e.g., in chip production. We admire and benefit from rocks, making semiconductors, chips, fuel, and more. We focus on water and what's in various types of water resources, such as rivers, lakes, swamps, seas, and oceans. Water as states of matter: liquid, solid, gas, and plasma fascinates us but also helps us deal with new ideas. We can stay on the surface, swim, or go above the water's surface.

HOWARD GARDNER AND HIS THEORY OF MULTIPLE INTELLIGENCES

Joy Paul Guilford, Robert Sternberg, and Howard Gardner have independently described individual peak performance as dependent on differences in abilities. Howard Gardner is renowned for his theory of multiple intelligences, which classifies human abilities and emphasizes learning in ways that respect individual interests and strengths. He defines intelligence as the capacity to solve culturally valued problems. Gardner's multiple intelligences include:

1. Linguistic intelligence – the ability to use language effectively.
2. Logical/mathematical intelligence– proficiency in logic and mathematics.
3. Spatial intelligence– the ability to understand spatial relationships and navigate environments.
4. Musical intelligence – the capacity to recognize musical patterns.
5. Bodily-kinesthetic intelligence – skillful use of the body for problem-solving or creation.
6. Interpersonal intelligence – understanding and interacting effectively with others.
7. Intrapersonal intelligence – self-awareness and self-reflection.
8. Naturalistic intelligence – the ability to recognize and categorize natural elements.

Gardner later suggested adding existential and moral intelligences to this list. His theory remains relevant, reflecting the idea that individuals often draw on multiple types of intelligence, as evidenced by interdisciplinary activities in fields like art and engineering. Gardner later stated, "existential and moral intelligences may also be worthy of inclusion" (Gardner, 2000, 2011b, 2016), as he "considered several new candidate intelligences, including naturalistic, spiritual (however later on, Gardner did not want to commit to a spiritual intelligence), existential, and moral ones" (Gardner, 2011b, p. 4).

Howard Gardner's theory of multiple intelligences still holds, but more and more one person feels a need for more than one type of intelligence. The concept of left and right brain changes as well. It might be all affected by the options offered by artificial intelligence. When visiting art departments, we see students coding, while going between electrical engineers or computer scientists we see them sketch and create art. Many students select a major and a minor, or even two majors to combine curiosity, and creativity with abstract thinking, skills, and knowledge.

FINDING AN OWN NICHE IN THE WORLD

There is a void between a classroom and the beginning of a professionally active life. Creativity, abstract, and cognitive thinking foster skills in meaningful images, concept art, animation, video, storytelling, and character development for the visual delivery of a meaningful story-based visual knowledge-based task. Many current industries and their audiences expect novelty, and the arrival of new tools challenges us. It all comes easier to those who are not afraid of coding. Short stories focus on promoting the understanding of technology and coding, building creativity and inventiveness, and the ability to convey these skills through visually oriented education.

We live between the species and plants and share the same environment. Those on the ground walk. The ground can also be underwater. Some swim, while some fly. Some can do all of the above. Many kinds of waves rule our world. They affect us on many levels. They guide us and inform us. We cannot survive without water, air, or minerals in a broad meaning. We walk on the ground or move with other means. We swim in the waters and fly in various spaces. We learn and communicate. We share, build, or destroy.

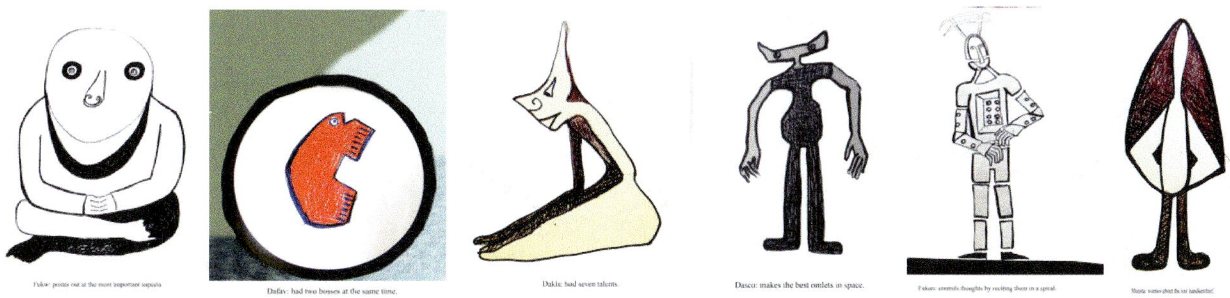

KEYWORDS

Art, Coding, Storytelling, Programming, Mathematical Art, Art and Science Connection, Professions, Computer Graphics, Digital Media, Knowledge Visualization, Knowledge Transfer through Art, Characters, Character ..Creation, Concept Art and Digital Illustration, Cognitive and Abstract thinking, and Talents.

Boats. © 2025 by Matylda Czarnecka. (Used with permission).

Growth. © 2025 by Matylda Czarnecka. (Used with permission).

CHAPTER 1
LAND – LOCOMOTION
MOVE (WALK), EAT
ALIGNMENT

We move. Like time does, but we stop. We develop styles and ways of moving while considering speed, fashion, method, and elegance. We do it by alternating. All creatures have rituals. We correct and adjust surfaces to move better, often making it harder for other creatures. We move plants; we think we cannot travel. We build up and wide to move accordingly. We research, learn, play, relax, produce, develop, exchange, and conquer. We enjoy sports and recreation.

Xafu: sells flowers after midnight.

Xafu spreads information on how walking benefits a person. His task is to make people grow interactively:

```
def walking_benefits(minutes_walked):
    calories_burned = minutes_walked * 5  # Approximate calories burned per minute
    improved_mood = minutes_walked * 2   # Mood improvement scale (arbitrary units)
    heart_health_points = minutes_walked // 10  # Heart health points earned for every 10 minutes

    print(f"Walking Benefits for {minutes_walked} minutes:")
    print(f"- Calories burned: {calories_burned} kcal")
    print(f"- Improved mood: {improved_mood} units")
    print(f"- Heart health points: {heart_health_points} points\n")

def track_walking(days):
    total_minutes = 0
    for day in range(1, days + 1):
        minutes = int(input(f"Day {day}: How many minutes did you walk today? "))
        total_minutes += minutes
        walking_benefits(minutes)

    print(f"Total benefits over {days} days:")
    walking_benefits(total_minutes)
# Example usage
days = int(input("Enter the number of days you want to track your walking: "))

track_walking(days)
```

Kakalico, his couch changes it shapes when being carried.

Kakalico kept saying that Xafu's job was considered a healthy one.

Ranyho: wise, but can be handled.

Ranyho pondered how to fulfill our work-free time when artificial intelligence (AI) handles tasks for us.

```
import random

def suggest_activities(interest):
    activities = {
        "arts": ["Painting", "Sculpting", "Playing musical instruments", "Singing", "Writing", "Visiting a museum", "Photography"],
        "sports": ["Hiking", "Yoga", "Cycling", "Swimming"],
        "learning": ["Reading a book", "Taking an online course", "Learning a new language", "Attending a workshop"],
        "social": ["Volunteering", "Spending time with family", "Hosting a dinner", "Joining a club"],
        "relaxation": ["Meditating", "Taking a nature walk", "Gardening", "Listening to music"]
    }

    return random.choice(activities.get(interest, ["Exploring new hobbies", "Traveling", "Creative writing"]))

def fulfill_free_time():
    print("Welcome to your AI-powered work-free life!")
    print("What are you interested in today?\n")

    interests = ["arts", "sports", "learning", "social", "relaxation"]

    for i, interest in enumerate(interests, 1):
        print(f"{i}. {interest.capitalize()}")

    choice = int(input("\nSelect an interest (1-5): "))

    if 1 <= choice <= 5:
        selected_interest = interests[choice - 1]
        activity = suggest_activities(selected_interest)
        print(f"\nSuggested activity: {activity}")
    else:
        print("\nInvalid choice. Please select a valid interest.")
# Example usage
fulfill_free_time()
```

Based on the interests and choices, it randomly showed activities when AI handles all the work!

Fafura: often taken for a walk.

Fafura shared his code but forgot to mention AI suggested all the activities.

Munsta: worries about the lost handkerchief

Munsta was perceived as selfish for having strong opinions, which made him wonder how to learn thinking from other people's perspectives by asking questions and reflecting on alternatives.

```
def ask_questions(scenario, character_a, character_b):
    print(f"Scenario: {scenario}\n")

    print(f"What might {character_a} think?")
    perspective_a = input(f"Enter {character}a's perspective: ")

    print(f"\nWhat might {character_b} think?")
    perspective_b = input(f"Enter {character_b}'s perspective: ")

    print("\nConsidering both perspectives:")
    print(f"{character_a} might think: {perspective_a}")
    print(f"{character _b} might think: {perspective_b}\n")

    print("How might this change your original perspective?")
    new_perspective = input("Enter your revised perspective: ")

    print(f"\nYour new perspective: {new_perspective}")
# Example usage:
scenario = "Two friends disagree about patterns in weather changes."
character _a = "Munsta"
character _b = "Bob"

ask_questions(scenario, character _a, character _b)
```

Munsta started his journey by defining different perspectives to ponder what each character might think. After knowing both perspectives, he changed his viewpoint so his mind could consider different angles.

After that, his friends complimented him on his empathy, communication, and problem-solving.

Gyter: has no doubt where to go when.

Gyter, as always, was just doing what he thought was the best for everyone. There is no "everyone," Munsta said.

Muster: can send the leaves back to a tree

Muster thought that people return to roots where they started, as leaves fall from a tree and return and nourish the tree. Reconnecting with one's past, closure, and completion of a cycle is similar to how leaves complete their life.

```
def journey(steps):
    position = 0  # Start at the origin (position 0)
    history = [position]  # Track the path taken

    # Simulate the journey
    for step in steps:
        position += step
        history.append(position)

    print(f"Journey path: {history}")

    # Returning to the starting point
    return_to_roots = -position
    history.append(history[-1] + return_to_roots)

    print(f"Returning to roots: {history[-2]} -> {history[-1]}")
    print(f"Final path: {history}")
# Example usage
steps = [3, 2, -1, 4, -2]  # Simulated steps (can be positive or negative)
journey(steps)
```

Renewal and growth metaphor for experiences (leaves) to return to a source (the tree): wisdom/strength. The position 0, represents the "roots" or starting point as position tracking. The movement starts away from the origin with a list of steps. Positive steps move forward, and negative steps move backward. The steps to return to the starting point, the roots, and this final move to history, show metaphorically how one ventures away from their origins and returns, reflecting on the path and experience gained.

Guteron: makes big jumps, then stays still.

So did Guteron.

Segas: has legs for walking and legs for running.

Segas thought that from a biological perspective, legs are a common anatomical structure with bones, muscles, and joints, that allow us to move.

```
class LegMovement:
    def walk(self):
        print("Walking: Alternating leg movements to propel the body forward.")

    def run(self):
        print("Running: Rapid alternating leg movements with a brief airborne phase.")

    def jump(self):
        print("Jumping: Both legs push off the ground simultaneously to propel the body upward.")

    def hop(self):
        print("Hopping: Using one leg to push off the ground and land on the same leg.")

    def skip(self):
        print("Skipping: A combination of a step and a hop, alternating legs.")

    def climb(self):
        print("Climbing: Lifting legs to ascend a surface like stairs or a ladder.")

    def squat(self):
        print("Squatting: Bending the knees and lowering the body while keeping the feet flat on the ground.")
# Example usage
leg = LegMovement()
leg.walk()
leg.run()
leg.jump()
leg.hop()
leg.skip()
leg.climb()
leg.squat()
```

The efficiency and speed at which an individual can walk, or run may depend on factors such as muscle composition, bone structure, and biomechanics. Some individuals naturally excel at running due to factors like muscle fiber type distribution thus while others may prefer walking. As a long-distance runner, Segas focuses on practice endurance training, while Liny, a sprinter prioritizes explosive strength and speed.

Liny: whistles while walking.

Liny used his bed as an office to write his theories down in it.

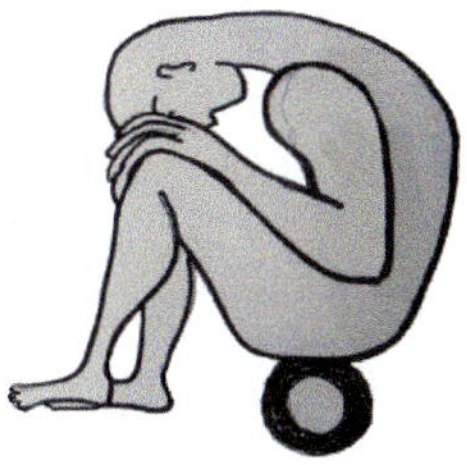

Metu: rolls through the life thinking about life.

Metu enjoyed a reflective and contemplative approach to life, where he navigated through his experiences and thoughts.

```
class RollingThroughLife:
    def __init__(self):
        self.position = 0
        self.momentum = 0

    def start(self):
        self.momentum = 1
        print("Starting to roll through life...")

    def roll_forward(self):
        self.position += self.momentum
        print(f"Rolling forward... Current position: {self.position}")

    def encounter_obstacle(self):
        if self.momentum > 0:
            self.momentum -= 0.5
            print("Encountered an obstacle. Slowing down...")
        if self.momentum <= 0:
            print("Stopped by an obstacle.")
            self.momentum = 0

    def gain_momentum(self):
        self.momentum += 1
        print(f"Gaining momentum! Current momentum: {self.momentum}")

    def reflect(self):
        print(f"Reflecting on the journey... Current position: {self.position}, Momentum: {self.momentum}")
# Example usage
life = RollingThroughLife()
life.start()
life.roll_forward()
life.encounter_obstacle()
life.gain_momentum()
life.roll_forward()
life.reflect()
```

He faced challenges, overcame them, and reflected on progress, formed goals, values, relationships, and personal growth to make decisions, appreciate the present moment, and find meaning in his journey.

Safade: draws shapes when dancing.

He even learned not to collide with his girlfriend, Safade's rolling journey.

Igaren: very fast, but careful.

Igaren knew to approach pressing issues with speed and care. Due to the interconnected nature of worldwide issues, actions in one area may have cascading effects elsewhere. His key was to bike, whenever stressed out, while balancing the urgency of the response considering the worldwide context, potential consequences, and the need for preserving solutions.

```
class Preserving Solution:
   def __init__(self, name, region, environmental_impact, social_impact, economic_benefit):
      self.name = name
      self.region = region
      self.environmental_impact = environmental_impact  # Positive values indicate benefits
      self.social_impact = social_impact              # Positive values indicate benefits
      self.economic_benefit = economic_benefit        # Positive values indicate benefits

   def evaluate universal_impact(self):
      universal _impact = (self.environmental_impact + self.social_impact + self.economic_benefit) /
      3  return universal _impact
# Example of preserving solutions
solutions = [
   ReceptiveSolution("Renewable Energy Program", "Africa", 8, 7, 9),
   ReceptiveSolution("Reforestation Initiative", "South America", 10, 6, 7),
   ReceptiveSolution("Water Conservation Project", "Asia", 7, 8, 6),
   ReceptiveSolution("Circular Economy Model", "Europe", 9, 7, 8)
]

# Evaluate and display the universal impact of each
solution  for solution in solutions:
   impact = solution.evaluate_ universal _impact()
   print(f"{solution.name} ({solution.region}) - Universal Impact Score: {impact:.2f}")
```

Glikten: uses multiple modes of transportation

He shared it all with Glikten, who biked to work, finished all his meals from his vertical garden and prepared on a solar cooker, recycled everything 3D-printed, reused friends, refused to pollute, renewed his subscriptions in a digital format, and traveled on the internet for his vacations, but could not stop drinking mineral water bottled at the source then packed in small plastic containers.

Mestal: protects all writers.

Mestal supported writers, adding to their voices and their well-being.

```
class Writer:
    def __init__(self, name, effect_of_ universal _change):
        self.name = name
        self.effect_of_ universal _change = effect_of_ universal _change

    def describe_effect(self):
        return f"{self.name} is influenced by universal change: {self.effect_of_ universal
_change}"  # Example writers and the effects of universal change
writers = [
    Writer("Mestal", "Now writes about atmospheric conditions changse due to its growing impact."),
    Writer("Maduraho", "Faces challenges in creative expression due to societal shifts."),
    Writer("Clara", "Draws inspiration from universal movements for her stories.")
]

# Displaying how universal change affects each
writer  for writer in writers:
    print(writer.describe_effect())
```

Maduraho: knows the diference between a part and a whole.

Hufes: makes things look easy.

Maduraho and Hufes preferred writing about *Amanita muscaria*, commonly known as the fly agaric or fly amanita.

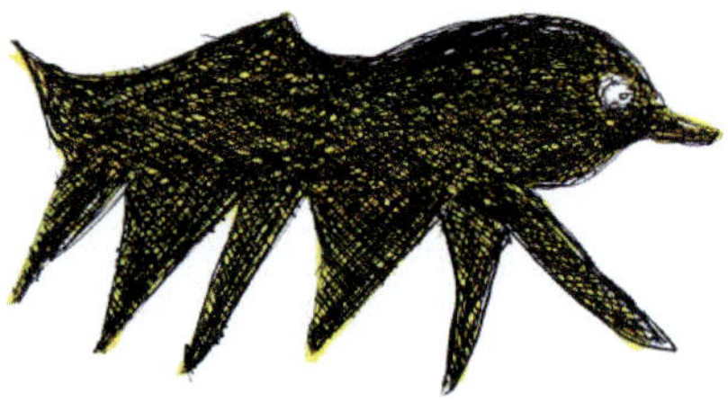

Lavarac: oferrs rides to everyone who needs to go someplace.

Lavarac offered rides to help people enjoying nature.

```
# Define carbon emissions per kilometer (in grams of CO2)

emissions = {

    "car": 120,    # average car

    "bus": 68,    # average bus

    "train": 28,    # average train

    "bike": 0,    # biking emits no CO2

    "walking": 0    # walking emits no CO2

}

# Define the distance of the trip in kilometers

distance_km = 15
```

```
Calculate total emissions for each mode of transport

total_emissions = {mode: emissions[mode] * distance_km for mode in emissions}

# Find the most eco-friendly option

eco_friendly_option = min(total_emissions, key=total_emissions.get)

# Display the results

print(f"For a trip of {distance_km} km, the most eco-friendly option is {eco_friendly_option}.")

print(f"Total CO2 emissions by mode of transport (in grams):")

for mode, total in total_emissions.items():

    print(f"{mode}: {total} g CO2")
```

Through these practices, his rides aligned with eco-friendly transportation.

Bulga: has very straight priorities.

In his office, Bulga, with everybody else was walking to work. They all saw it as a healthy way of transportation.

Lorkagon: makes the least amount of steps within a certain distance.

Lorkagon used “Walk or Bike” for better contact with nature and supporting well-being.

```
def promote_walk_or_bike(distance_km):
   if distance_km <= 5:
      return "For a short trip like this, consider walking or biking! It's great for your health and the environment."
   elif distance_km <= 15:
      return "Biking is a fantastic option for this distance. You'll reduce the toxins and get some exercise!"
   else:
      return "For longer distances, consider a hybrid approach: bike part of the way or use public transportation. Every little bit helps!"
# Example usage
trip_distance = 7  # distance in kilometers
message = promote_walk_or_bike(trip_distance)
print(message)
```

He planned efficient routes, combined errands, utilized public transportation, carpooled or ride-shared, chose preserving vehicles, avoided peak traffic times, implemented remote work or virtual meetings, supported local businesses to contribute to his community, used eco-friendly transportation services, encouraged walking as a way of transportation, and considered electric skateboards, scooters, or other innovative mobility solutions to maximize the number of steps for health, and optimize travel within a certain distance while making an impact on health.

Puf: keeps everything well hidden.

Puf delivered his winning candidacy speech on his skateboard.

Htera: throws balls every day.

Htera saw energy and materials as connected.

```
    # Dictionary of contexts and corresponding materials
healthy_life = {
    "Energy": ["Solar Panels", "Wind Turbines", "Hydroelectric Power", "Energy-efficient Appliances"],
    "Transportation": ["Electric Vehicles", "Bicycles", "Public Transportation", "Carpooling"],
    "Food": ["Organic Produce", "Plant-based Diet", "Local Farmers' Markets", "Composting"],
    "Construction": ["Recycled Steel", "Bamboo", "Cork", "Stable Concrete", "Green Roofing"],
    "Water": ["Rainwater Harvesting", "Low-flow Fixtures", "Greywater Systems", "Water-efficient Landscaping"],
    "Waste Management": ["Recycling", "Upcycling", "Biodegradable Products", "Waste-to-Energy Technologies"],
    "Fashion": ["Organic Cotton", "Recycled Fabrics", "Second-hand Clothing", "Natural Dyes"],
    "Personal Care": ["Natural Soaps", "Biodegradable Toothbrushes", "Organic Skincare", "Plastic-free Packaging"]
}

# Function to display the preserving life contexts and materials
def display_healthy_life():
    print("Key Contexts and Materials Involved in Preserving Living:\n")
    for context, materials in healthy_life.items():
        print(f"{context}:")
        for material in materials:
            print(f" - {material}")
        print()  # Blank line for readability
# Example usage
display_healthy_life()
```

Figim: hides what's really important.

Figim talked about material composition, waste management practices, and daily activities by choosing options mindful of resource use and waste generation while being playful, thus people followed her and the trends they both set.

Gysa: drives fast

Gysa knew fast driving impacts the costs and affects other people:

```
def cost_impact_of_speed(speed_mph):
    # Define the general impacts of driving fast
    if speed_mph > 90:
        return ("Driving at very high speeds significantly increases costs, "
                "it puts other drivers at risk. "
                "Additionally, higher speeds lead to increased tire wear, which makes the life of tires shorter.")
    elif speed_mph > 65:
        return ("Driving above moderate speeds increases fuel consumption. "
                "Even slight speed increases the danger to the pedestrians. "
                "It's safer to drive at or below the speed limit.")
    else:
        return ("Driving at or below 65 mm/h is more fuel-efficient. "
                "Maintaining a steady, moderate speed also minimizes wear and tear on your vehicle, which further reduces dangerous impacts.")
# Example usage
current_speed = 95 # speed in miles per hour
message = impact_of_speed(current_speed)
print(message)
```

She always walked back home after winning endless car racing competitions, just like her friend,

Pikutun: can adjust his tempo.

Pikutun, who's dog always preferred walking, so they all pleasantly benefited from it.

Lazacepa: always carries all her friends.

Lazacepa understood the role of the community support:

```
# Define a dictionary of community actions that promote ecological balance
community_support = {
    "Organize": ["Community Clean-up Initiatives", "Tree Planting Events", "Neighborhood Recycling Drives"],
    "Educate": ["Workshops on Healthy Living", "Educational Campaigns on Reducing Waste", "Energy-saving Tips for Households"],
    "Support": ["Local Farmers' Markets", "Community Gardens", "Supporting Local Businesses", “Sharing experience and resources”],
    "Collaborate": ["Carpooling Networks", "Tool-sharing Programs", "Community Projects"],
    "Advocate": ["Help Your Neighbor", "Support for Local Farmers", "Participation in Waste Collection", Voting"]
}

# Function to display community support actions for ecological balance
def promote_community_community():
    print("Ways Community Support Can promote healthy lifestyle:\n")
    for action, activities in community_support.items():
        print(f"{action} Initiatives:")
        for activity in activities:
            print(f" - {activity}")
        print()  # Blank line for readability

# Example usage
promote_community_support()
```

Her always-carrying friends reflected their commitment to building supportive, and interconnected communities to prioritize the well-being of individuals and the environment as a way of friendship.

Pucero: always carries a ball in case someone would like to play.

Pucero solved all the problems through playful kindness.

Ftu: carries imaginative water when visiting friends.

Ftu learned that heavy lifting strengthened him, so he followed by carrying heavy water from a nearby pond.

```
advantages = [
    "Builds physical strength",
    "Promotes hydration",
    "Encourages mindfulness",
    "Supports daily exercise",
    "Saves money on gym memberships"
]

for advantage in advantages:
    print(advantage)
```

Byrb: makes short connections long.

Byrb and

Muteo: can be very fast when he needs to.

Muteo

noticed that whoever invited him received two full buckets of pond water. When returning home, his buckets were filled with soil from his friends. This made him bring more water for the new plants he shared with his neighbors. They all fertilized their gardens with the shells after eating their hefty breakfasts. Soon, Ftu built a pond in his backyard, and thus, more water was needed. For this, he started a company. This is how important water is in one’s life, he kept saying. He was especially popular during droughts.

Darasta: knows where to go.

Darasta wanted to be able to control the rain for her garden

```
class RainController:
    def __init__(self):
        self.rain_status = "off"

    def start_rain(self):
        self.rain_status = "on"
        print("Rain started. 🌧️")

    def stop_rain(self):
        self.rain_status = "off"
        print("Rain stopped. ☀️")

    def set_rain_intensity(self, intensity):
        if self.rain_status == "on":
            print(f"Rain intensity set to {intensity}/10.")
        else:
            print("Rain is off. Turn it on to set intensity.")
# Example usage
controller = RainController()
controller.start_rain()
controller.set_rain_intensity(7)
controller.stop_rain()
```

After submitting her invention to the patent office,

Vasta: can change her opinion fast for your own good.

Vasta told her she wrote a program for a sprinkler system.

Jodurno: his face was young, but his eyes were old.

Jodurno took good care of his eyes.

```
def eye_health_tips():
    tips = [
        "Take regular breaks from screens (20-20-20 rule).",
        "Blink frequently to keep eyes moist.",
        "Eat foods rich in vitamins A, C, and E.",
        "Wear sunglasses to protect against UV rays.",
        "Maintain proper lighting when reading or working."
    ]
    for tip in tips:
        print(f"Tip: {tip}")

eye_health_tips()
```

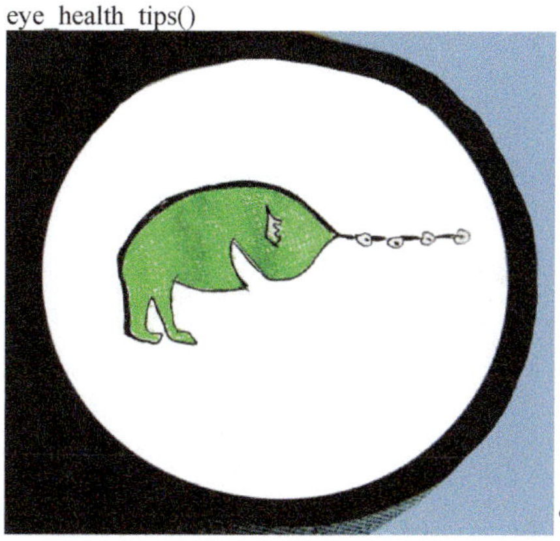

Tuhadzu: knows his way around mosquitos.

Tuhadzu took good care of his body.

```
def promote_healthy_body():
    tips = [
        "Exercise regularly for at least 30 minutes a day.",
        "Eat a balanced diet rich in fruits and vegetables.",
        "Stay hydrated by drinking plenty of water.",
        "Get 7-9 hours of quality sleep each night.",
        "Practice stress management techniques like meditation."
    ]
    for tip in tips:
        print(f"Tip: {tip}")

promote_healthy_body()r
```

Ihuso: creates stories on a bus.

Ihuso commuted to and from work. Since he stopped riding his car in heavy and stressful traffic, he used the time to write about what surrounded him.

```
def bus_ride_inspiration():
    reasons = [
        "Observing diverse characters and interactions.",
        "Witnessing unexpected events and conversations.",
        "Experiencing the rhythm and flow of the city.",
        "Time for reflection and daydreaming.",
        "Exposure to different environments and scenery."
    ]
    for reason in reasons:
        print(f"Reason: {reason}")

bus_ride_inspiration()
```

After receiving the Best Community Writer's award, his stories became even better, and so did his health and mood.

Wiv: always sings while walking.

Viv added the missing entertaining part to that wholeness.

Odeles: gets angry when there is no sunshine.

Odeles was very practical and saw the benefits coming out of the sunrays

```
def sunshine_benefits():
    benefits = [
        "Boosts vitamin D production.",
        "Improves mood and reduces stress.",
        "Supports healthy bone development.",
        "Regulates sleep-wake cycles.",
        "Enhances immune system function."
    ]
    for benefit in benefits:
        print(f"Benefit: {benefit}")

sunshine_benefits()
```

He knew his limits:

```
def sunshine_disadvantages():
    disadvantages = [
        "Increases risk of skin cancer with excessive exposure.",
        "Causes sunburn if unprotected.",
        "Leads to premature skin aging.",
        "Can cause dehydration if not careful.",
        "Triggers sun-induced headaches in sensitive individuals."
    ]
    for disadvantage in disadvantages:
        print(f"Disadvantage: {disadvantage}")

sunshine_disadvantages()
```

Every time he visited a doctor, they told him they would like to have him take control of his health.

Pelo: hard to follow.

Pelo was moving very fast to limit the exposure of the sun.

Wasaluko: very handy when moving out.

Wasaluko was known for her ability to send 3D models of furniture to be printed at the destination place of those moving to faraway places. She knew how to select the materials to make the items look like before the move. It involved using libraries like OpenSCAD, Blender, or PyOpenGL for 3D modeling and a 3D printing library like pySTL to export models for printing. She used the solidpython library (which is a wrapper for OpenSCAD) to generate basic 3D models of furniture. After installation: `pip install solidpython` she followed with a code:

```
from solid.utils import *

def generate_table():
    # Create a simple table
    tabletop = cube([100, 60, 5]) # Top surface of the table
    leg = cube([5, 5, 50])        # One table leg

    # Position legs at the corners of the tabletop
    legs = [
        translate([0, 0, -50])(leg),
        translate([95, 0, -50])(leg),
        translate([0, 55, -50])(leg),
        translate([95, 55, -50])(leg),
    ]

    return union()(tabletop, *legs)

def generate_chair():
    # Create a simple chair
    seat = cube([40, 40, 2])    # Seat surface
from solid import *
    leg = cube([2, 2, 40])      # One chair leg
    backrest = cube([40, 2, 40]) # Backrest of the chair

    # Position legs at the corners of the seat
    legs = [
        translate([0, 0, -40])(leg),
        translate([38, 0, -40])(leg),
        translate([0, 38, -40])(leg),
        translate([38, 38, -40])(leg),
    ]

    # Position backrest
    backrest = translate([0, 38, 0])(backrest)

    return union()(seat, backrest, *legs)

def save_models():
    table = generate_table()
    chair = generate_chair()

    scad_render_to_file(table, 'table.scad')
    scad_render_to_file(chair, 'chair.scad')

save_models()
```

After running her code, she had a table.scad and chair.scad files. She then opened these .scad files in OpenSCAD, where she'd render and export them as .stl files for 3D printing. She donated the left-behind furniture to charities for those who prefer traditional materials. She posted his 3D scanned models online for those wishing to try their furniture. One day, after the daily news, she started a 3D recycling business.

Pazeto: can see in any scale, any direction.

Pazeto was faster and made furniture from biodegradable materials.

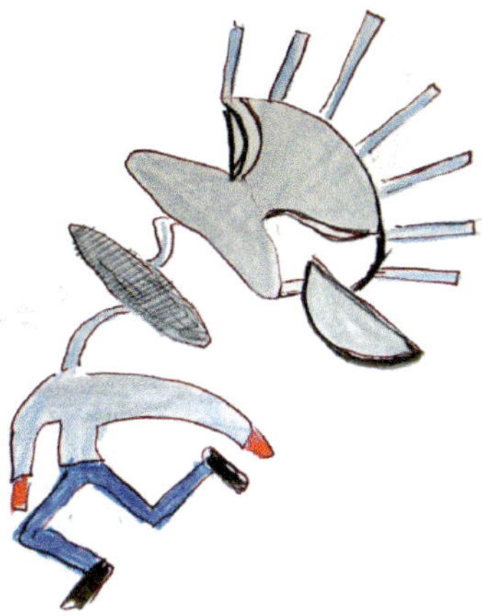

Heregendy: feels sorry for everyone that is sorry.

Heregendy is known as the one who acts passively.

```
def act_or_weep(feeling_sorry, solving_problem):
    if feeling_sorry:
        return "Feeling sorry achieves nothing."
    elif solving_problem:
        return "Solutions bring change."
    else:
        return "Decide to act."

print(act_or_weep(True, False))  # Example usage: feeling sorry
print(act_or_weep(False, True))  # Example usage: solving problems
```

Vahalas: flies, swims and runs.

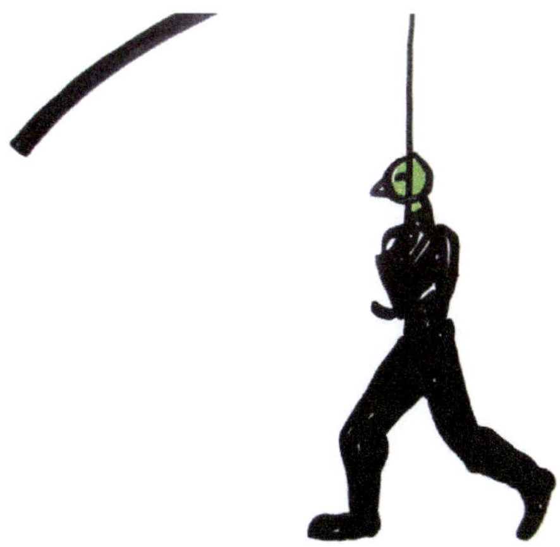

Kaoru: has a solution for any problem.

Vahalas and Kaoru solve problems. Together, they all decide where to detect the issue needing attention and find a source of joy to address it properly with no blaming or singling out anyone.

Eduro: always hangs out.

Eduro and

Helra: developed new dance steps.

Helra both believed

in friendship. They were trustful

```
def friendship_or_facts(friendship, fact_checking):
    if friendship:
        return "Friendship values trust."
    elif fact_checking:
        return "Fact-checking values truth."
    else:
        return "Balance trust and truth."

print(friendship_or_facts(True, False))  # Example: friendship
print(friendship_or_facts(False, True))  # Example: fact-checking
```

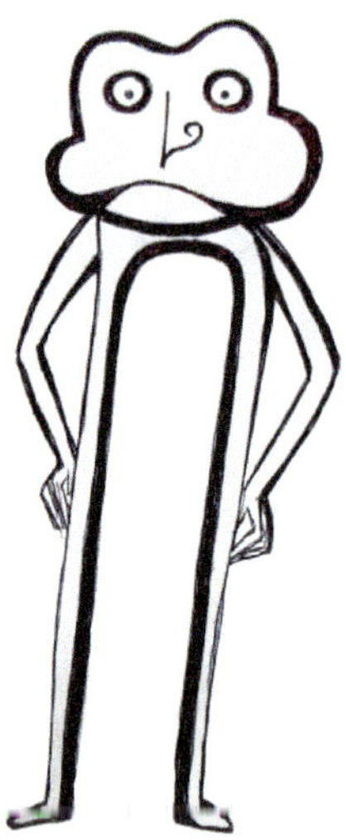

Geyax: has a pen in each pocket, no matter what.

Geyax and

Kaktasa: has a point.

Kaktasa

focus everything on facts. Balance trust and truth kept them together.

Kanda: sings and whistles at the same time.

Kanda and

Nutco: can see you!

Nutco

use their special skills to make sure the gatherings are safe and productive. In case of problems, they call

Henderelo: handsome, friendly, and supportive.

Henderelo who shows up whenever needed

```
def safe_gathering(skills, help_available):
    if skills and help_available:
        return "Skills ensure safety, help boosts productivity."
    elif skills:
        return "Skills enhance safety."
    elif help_available:
        return "Help makes things productive."
    else:
        return "Both are needed for success."

print(safe_gathering(True, True))  # Example: skills and help available
```

Gudu: always was making it harder than it had to be.

Gudu had the best intentions but always had questions.

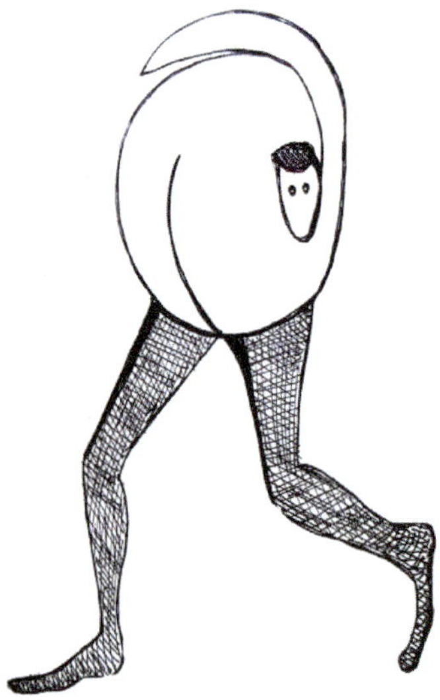

Alazuro: all confused, but knows where he's going.

Du: feels too slow.

Alazuro and Du had to be there to support him and ensure his well-being.

```
def too_many_questions(questions):
    if questions > 5:
        return "Too many questions can overwhelm others."
    else:
        return "Asking is fine, but balance is key."

print(too_many_questions(6))  # Example: too many questions
```

Hanalo: became a friend with flies when they need him.

Hanalo studied balance within the ecosystem.

```
def importance_of_flies(present):
    if present:
        return "Flies recycle nutrients and support the food chain."
    else:
        return "Without flies, ecosystems lose balance."

print(importance_of_flies(True))  # Example: flies are present
```

Gyi: never repeats himself.

Holop: can dance with anyone.

Gyi and Holop have different priorities as they are concerned with safety and focus on stopping any spread of harm. That is a difficult task as controlling and balancing may ensure safety, but they break so needed stability.

Gurady: runs fast when watching around.

Hadaso: thinks twice before acting.

Gurady and Hadaso enjoy exploring various paths while staying safe.

```
def cement_sidewalks(needed):
    if not needed:
        return "Unnecessary cement ruins the lanscaping."
    else:
        return "Use cement where truly necessary."

print(cement_sidewalks(False))  # Example: cement sidewalks not crucial
```

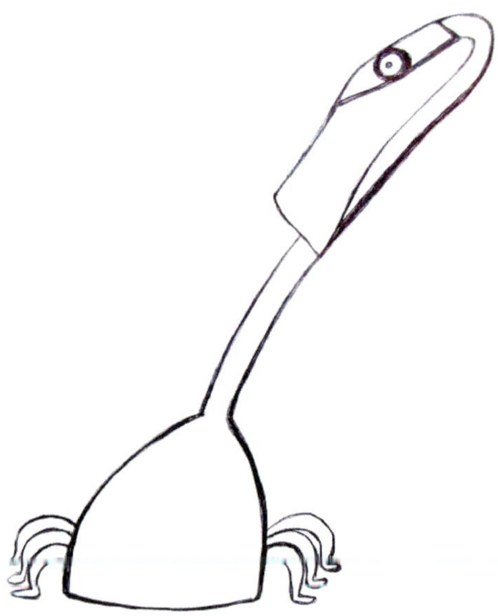

Alud: helps his legs walk when the terrain is uneven.

Alud tries to learn to move fast on uneven surfaces, but his legs are too short for the lawn.

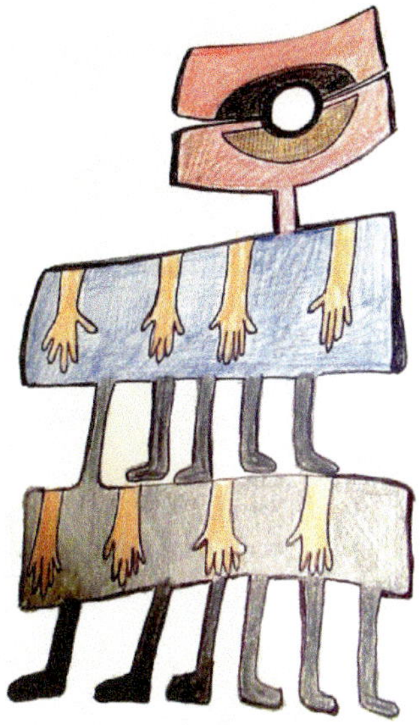

Firendo: very productive, fast, and happy.

Firendo and

Nuvago: never feels alone, no matter what.

Nuvago

saw happiness as comfort.

```
def happiness_comparison(personal_happiness, universal _care):
    if personal_happiness and not universal _care:
        return "Personal happiness is fulfilling but limited."
    elif universal _care:
        return "Caring for others and the world brings deeper, shared joy."
    else:
        return "Happiness grows with connection and care."

print(happiness_comparison(True, False)) # Example: personal happiness
print(happiness_comparison(False, True)) # Example: universal care
```

Adango: tries tosole the problem three years in a row.

Adango saw joy as caring for others.

Liku: brings food for the table.

Licu and

Lugatar: knows well where he goes.

Lugatar

know how to provide for their families.

```
def secure_food(safe_techniques, current_problems):
    if safe_techniques and current_problems:
        return "Apply safe techniques to adapt to current food challenges."
    elif safe_techniques:
        return "Techniques are safe, but problems remain."
    else:
        return "Without safety, food security is at risk."

print(secure_food(True, True))  # Example: using safe techniques, current problems exist
```

Fahuo: knows how to fly, but prefers walking.

Fahuo and

Gutco: holds some snakes in your pockets.

Gutco

emphasize the importance of safe techniques while considering ongoing food-related issues.

Dichma: waits till he's ready to jump.

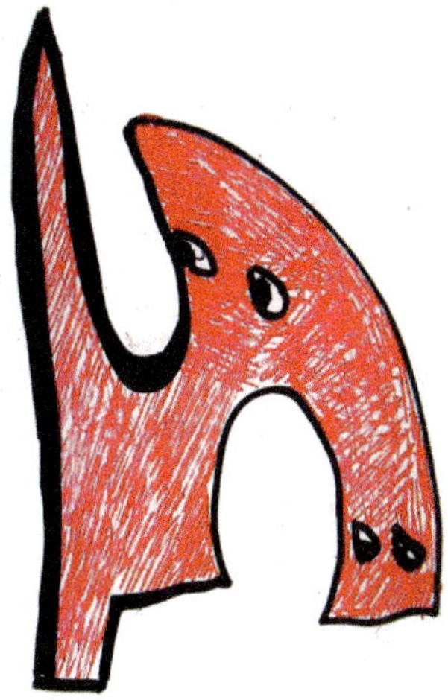

Cachudor: His aura was more importnt than he was.

Dickhma and Cahudor

Use instinct, logic, and consensus as decision-making approaches

Juiel: can dance very fast.

Enum: can dance at any moment and in any place.

Juiel Enum

use a spontaneous and playful approach to any situation, no matter what.

```
def decision_making(method):
    if method == "instinct":
        return "Instinct is quick but risky."
    elif method == "logic":
        return "Logic is reliable but slow."
    elif method == "consensus":
        return "Consensus involves others, ensuring balance."
    else:
        return "Choose wisely based on the situation."

print(decision_making("logic")) # Example: logical decision-making
```

Fohadu: always has a company.

Taparuka: she watches over the dogs at night.

F ohadu and T aparuka took care of the animals.

Tudusu: converts grass to herbs.

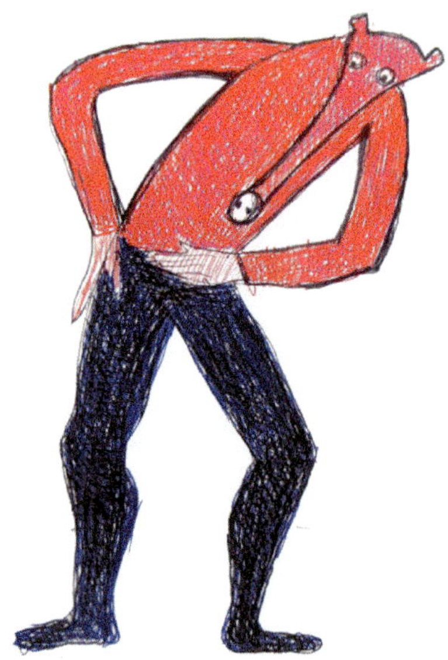

Ohasa: knows the name of each flower by heart.

T udusu and O hasa knew about the significance of plants for maintaining ecological balance.

```
def care_for_nature(animals, plants):
    if animals and plants:
        return "Caring for animals and plants ensures balance in the world."
    elif animals:
        return "Animals need care for ecosystem stability."
    elif plants:
        return "Plants sustain life."
    else:
        return "Both are essential for survival."

print(care_for_nature(True, True))  # Example: caring for both animals and plants
```

Burynos: punctual, but absent-minded.

Burynos and

Sulog: lives point to point.

Sulog

have different lifestyles.

Mesaro: very kind, but independent.

Mesaro and

Segyl: sits, but never shakes.

Segyl

have different mindsets. They all understand that both mindset and lifestyle are crucial for health and safety.

```
def compare_mindset_lifestyle(mindset, lifestyle):
    if mindset and lifestyle align:
        return "Aligned mindset and lifestyle protect safety."
    elif mindset:
        return "Mindset guides change, but action is needed."
    elif lifestyle:
        return "Lifestyle affects us, even without awareness."
    else:
        return "Both shape the future."

print(compare_mindset_lifestyle(True, True))  # Example: aligned mindset and lifestylehave different mindsets.
```

Fusegala: notices every slightest sound.

Ruganga: three legs are the most balanced.

Fusegala and Ruganga were very resilient.

Hadalemel: knits while she walks.

Rau: can juggle.

Hadalemel and Rau were very successful.

```
def person_advantages(skills, playfulness, support_knowledge):
    if skills and playfulness and support_knowledge:
        return "Skills, playfulness, and support knowledge lead to success and resilience."
    else:
        return "All three together create a balanced and adaptive individual."

print(person_advantages(True, True, True))  # Example: person has all three traits
```

Rodo: he was very fast.

Rodo and

Rogita: she can skate!

Rogita

liked to move fast to enjoy the speed.

Mroover: can make all food dissapear really fast.

Mroover and

Ogute: runs very fast, but sees it all around him.

Ogute

are fast to avoid collisions

```
def fast_action(support_life):
    if support_life:
        return "Fast action adapts to change and protects life."
    else:
        return "Delays increase risks for nature."

print(fast_action(True))  # Example: fast action supporting life
```

Marhize: he either walked or rolled.

Padyryko: knows the direction of rin when one approaches.

Marhize and Padyryko always knew where they were going.

Mutle: move fast by cutting corners.

Mutle and Mutle wanted to make an impact by measuring things while walking

```
def green_transportation():
    return ["Bicycling", "Walking", "Skateboarding", "No peddlaing or motor", "Skipping"]

print(green_transportation())  # Example: green transportation options
```

Yasala: goes rhythmically whenever he goes.

Tugosa: creates music by dancing, or by singing.

Yasala and Tugosa

used music for better movement.

```
def walking_advantages():
    return "Walking reduces stress, improves health, and preserves nature."

print(walking_advantages())  # Example: benefits of walking
```

Muzon: tiptoes effordessly.

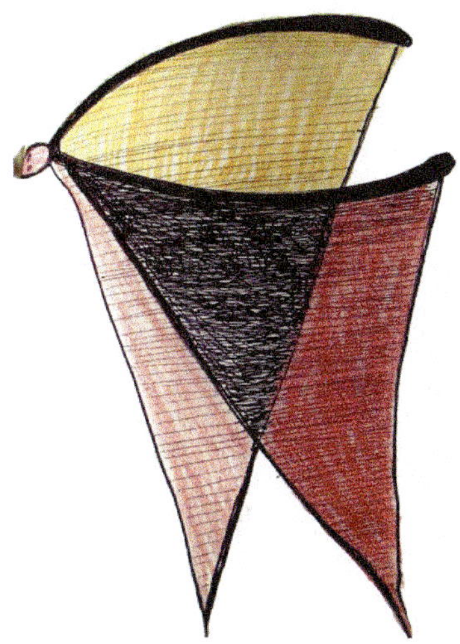

Ephremil: is fast; looks slow.

Muzon Ephremil

Use walking as a form of prestige

```
def walking_prestige():
    return "Walking reflects simplicity, health, and environmental awareness—true prestige."

print(walking_prestige())  # Example: walking as prestige
```

Tugo: calculates every descission he makes.

Tugo and

Sukeo: always watches his back.

Sukeo

are both very careful and calculated.

Vugana: moves by dancing.

Vaguna and

Wamaku: the fastest one around you.

Wamaku

are simply spontaneous

```
def compare_styles(style):
    if style == "careful":
        return "Advantages: Reduces risk, well-planned. Disadvantages: Slow, overthinking."
    elif style == "spontaneous":
        return "Advantages: Quick, flexible. Disadvantages: Risky, less predictable."
    else:
        return "Balance is key."

print(compare_styles("careful"))      # Example: careful and calculated
print(compare_styles("spontaneous"))  # Example: spontaneous
```

Muno: has more pockets he remembers about.

Xudango: dances to whispersing.

Muno and Xudango are resourceful and ready for anything

```
def compare_preparedness(style):
    if style == "resourceful":
        return "Resourceful: Ready for any weather, adaptable, but requires effort."
    elif style == "hopeful":
        return "Hopeful: Efficient in good conditions, but vulnerable to surprises."
    else:
        return "Balance preparation with optimism."

print(compare_preparedness("resourceful"))  # Example: being resourceful
print(compare_preparedness("hopeful"))       # Example: being hopeful
```

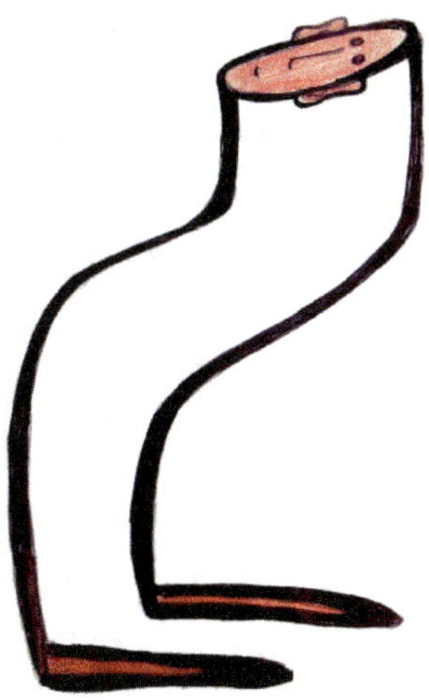

Undipag: always hopes for the best.

Uvarugr: makes it all going fast.

Undipag and Uvangur are hopeful and efficient.

Arunakono: goes to corn festivals.

Vachero: could not find what he lost.

Arunkono and Vachero enjoy their routines.

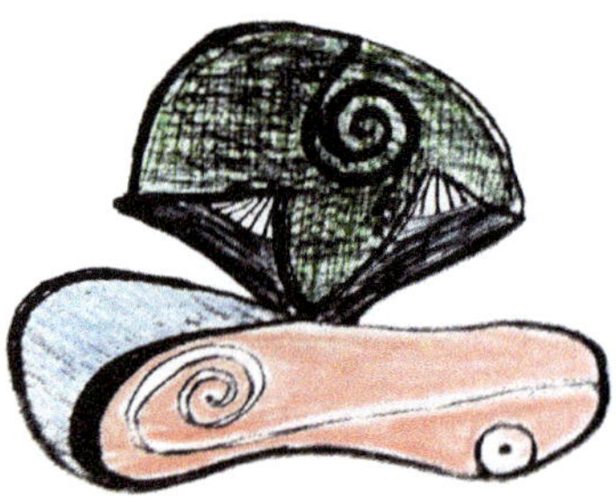

Futazo: goes where others cannot.

Futazo likes to explore things.

```
def sport(perspective):
    if perspective == "routine":
        return "Routine: sport, stable activities, but less discovery."
    elif perspective == "explorative":
        return "Explorative: Broader experiences, but higher physical activities through travel and exploration."
    else:
        return "Balancing routine and exploration maximizes helth impact."

print(sportroutine"))      # Example: enjoying routines
print(sportroutine("explorative")) # Example: being explorative
```

Bugerta: can drive on one wheel when nobody is watching.

B ugerta and

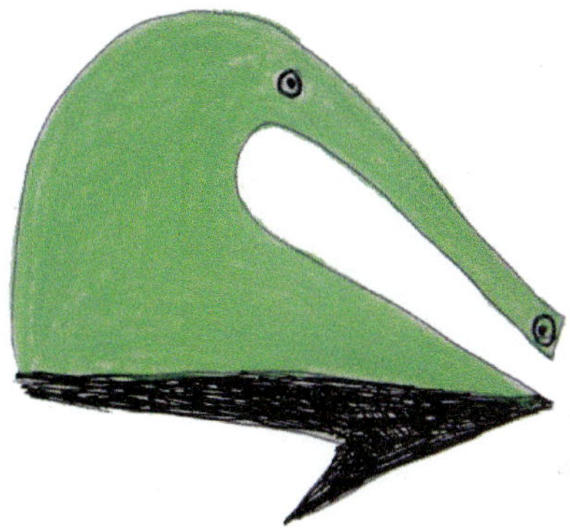

Davebura: cuts and moves.

D avebura

have their ways around them.

Nij: can see what's invisible for others.

N ij and

Firtu: always ready for a party.

F irtu

possess insight.

```
def help_others(knowledge, insight):
   if knowledge and insight:
      return "Knowing the way and having insight guide others effectively."
   else:
      return "Both are key to being helpful."

print(help_others(True, True))  # Example: having both knowledge and insight
```

Muchatar: never misses a chance.

Gufus: does everything with a stick.

Muchatar and Gufus

Both study physics, and thus understand nuclear fusion as a reaction of some nuclei, forming atomic nuclei and subatomic particles as neutrons or protons.

```
def nuclear_fusion(understanding):
    if understanding:
        return "Fusion offers limitless energy, but requires breakthroughs in technology and safety."
    else:
        return "Understanding fusion is key to unlocking its potential."

print(nuclear_fusion(True))  # Example: understanding fusion
```

Tusta: solves all the problems while waking.

Muchachuga: was known for his very long footsteps.

Tusta and Muchachiga

understand nuclear fission as a nucleus of an atom splitting into small nuclei and releasing energy.

Nunera: makes the longest jump.

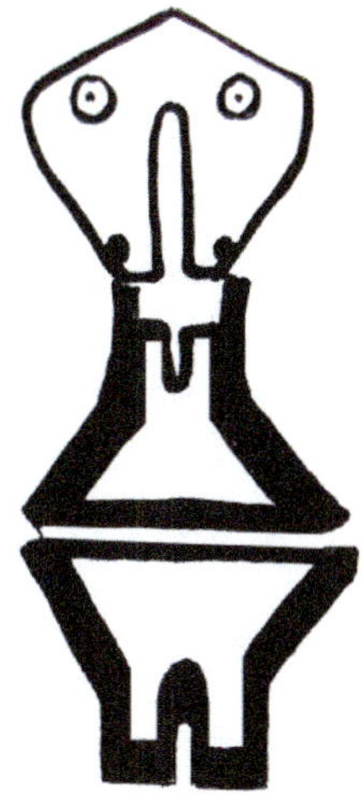

Yatumara: never over-decorated.

Nunera and Yutamara are very active and physically fit.

Mowgadani: always sets diections.

Nuduzeku: never solved his problems.

Mowgadani and Nuduzeku understood empathy and fitness as a form of good leadership.

```
def fitness_and_leadership(fitness, understanding_needs):
   if fitness and understanding_needs:
      return "Physical fitness boosts energy, while knowing others' needs sets clear direction."
   else:
      return "Both fitness and empathy are key for effective leadership."

print(fitness_and_leadership(True, True))  # Example: fit and understanding others' needs
know what most of us need.
```

Aturago: travels inside himself.

Alturago and

Gubor: is always aware of his surroundings.

Gubor

researched planets around them.

```
def distant_view():
    return "From afar, everything looked good for the planets, but up close, the problems were hidden."

print(distant_view())  # Example: distant perspective hides issues
```

Wakapa: always very careful.

Wakapa

Padalaj: moves carefully.

Padalaj

both knew that a distant view could obscure underlying problems.

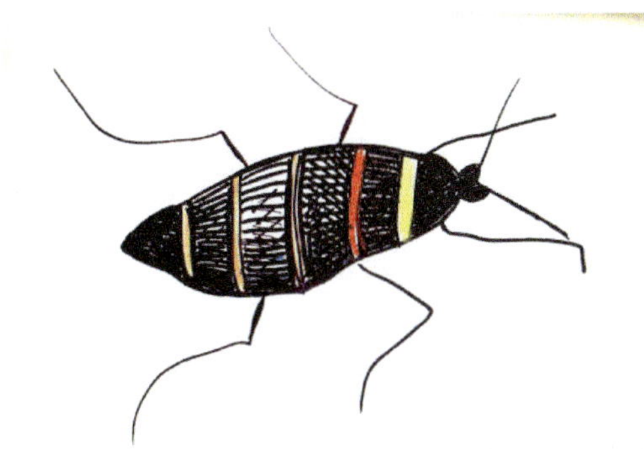

Baduzo: will cut your grass upon request.

Baduzo and

Buriega: very fast, very determined, but not decided.

Buriega

have their yards covered with various types of flowers.

Cuvetio: eats only pizza crust.

Cuvetio and

Fyzna: has more work to do.

Fyzma

cut grass regularly and use it for composting to make it all beautiful.

```
def grass_and_soil(beauty, method):
   if beauty and method == "cutting grass":
      return "Cultivated grass looks beautiful."
   elif method == "composting":
      return "Composting enriches the soil, promoting lasting beauty."  else:
      return "Choose composting for long-term benefits."

print(grass_and_soil(True, "composting")) # Example: beauty with composting
```

They give some of the compost to Baduzo and Buriega in exchange for their flowers.

Surinda: collects dirt to transform it into roads.

Avasag: never trusts what he sees.

Surinda and Avasag

research steel and wood.

```
def steel_vs_wood():
    return "Steel is strong and universal, wood is renewable and unique to Earth's life systems."

print(steel_vs_wood())  # Example: steel vs. wood
```

Triples - can walk on many legs to move faster.

Deka: always has more to say than she thinks.

Triples and Deka

research feathers and wool

```
def feathers_vs_wool():
    return "Feathers insulate and enable flight, wool provides warmth and durability."

print(feathers_vs_wool())  # Example: feathers vs. wool
```

Can we call our relationship with other living creatures “Symbiosis,” they kept asking.

Felugos: dances well to slow music.

Felugos and

Cudren: fights for the truth.

Cudren

studied measuring systems.

```
def measuring_systems():
    return "Measuring systems include metric (meters, liters) and imperial (feet, gallons) units."

print(measuring_systems())  # Example: measuring systems
```

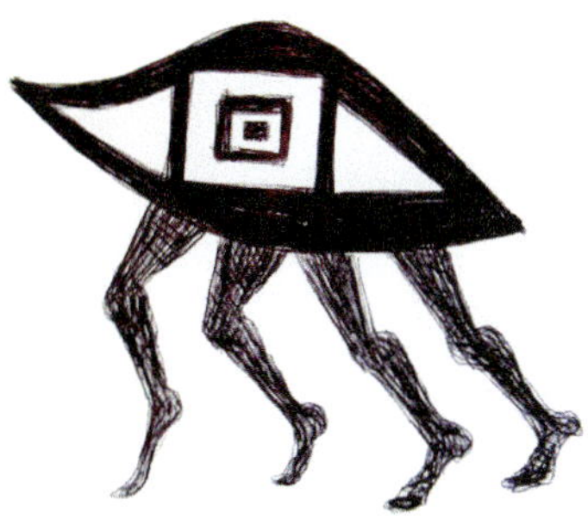

Faral: is looking, but does not see.

Faral and

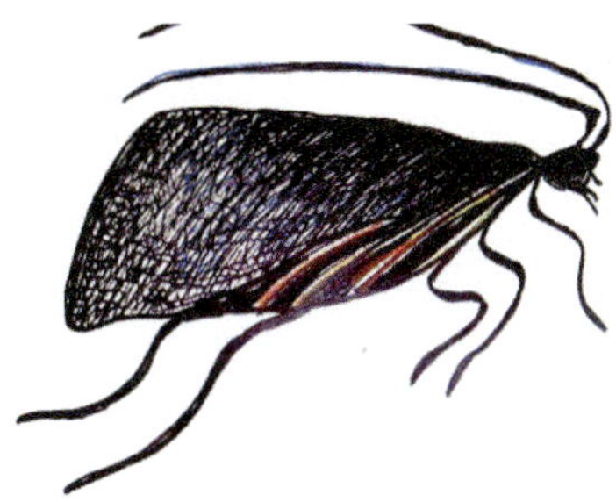

Kutug: senses the invisible

Kutug

explored measuring health through studying bones and teeth

```
def study_bones_teeth():
    return "Studying bones and teeth reveals health patterns, aiding in disease prevention and safety."

print(study_bones_teeth())  # Example: importance of studying bones and teeth
```

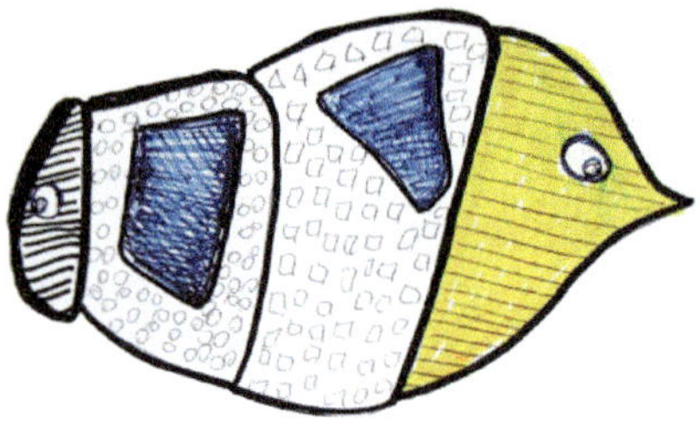

Bluo: goes either direction.

Yngus: whenever sad, dances to his own humming.

Bluo and Yngus

Were curious about the difference between Carbon allotropes and fullerenes

Bugater: all that's important is in-between.

Tikara: multiplies everything by four.

Bugater Tikara

knew, but one cannot stop learning, they kept saying

```
# Define carbon allotropes and fullerenes
allotropes = {"diamond", "graphite", "graphene", "amorphous carbon"}
fullerenes = {"C60", "C70", "C84"}

# Function to explain the difference
def explain_difference():
    print("Carbon Allotropes:", allotropes)
    print("Fullerenes:", fullerenes)
    print("Difference: Fullerenes are specific molecular structures of carbon, while allotropes are different structural forms of carbon.")

# Call the function
explain_difference()
```

Asagro: composes by singing.

Asagro and

Bungo: knows his way around.

Bungo

collected various calendars

```
# Define types of calendars
calendars = {
    "Gregorian": "Solar calendar used worldwide.",
    "Lunar": "Based on moon phases, e.g., Islamic calendar.",
    "Lunisolar": "Combines solar and lunar cycles, e.g., Chinese calendar.",
    "Julian": "Older solar calendar, less accurate than Gregorian."
}

# Function to display calendar types and descriptions
def display_calendars():
    for name, description in calendars.items():
        print(f"{name}: {description}")

# Call the function
display_calendars()
```

Busera: visits often.

Busera and

Suseldon: watches current events.

Suseldon

saw them as one of the systems of measuring, organizing, and recording of days, months, and even years.

Uket: watches for his watch.

Wabuda: makes right turns only.

Uket and Wabuda

studied bones and teeth to understand wider problems.

```
# Define a dictionary relating bones, teeth, and universal issues
issues = {
   "Osteoporosis": "Bone density loss, prevalent in regions with poor nutrition.",
   "Dental Decay": "Linked to access to dental care and nutrition.",
   "Malnutrition": "Affects bone and dental health worldwide.",
   "Access to Healthcare": "Disparities impact treatment of bone and dental issues."
}

# Function to display issues  def
display_ universal _issues():
   for issue, description in issues.items():
      print(f"{issue}: {description}")

# Call the function
display_universal_issues()
```

Geruga: has too many followers.

Puchuruchu: moves only when noone is watching.

Geruga and Puchuruchu

were more interested in the historical perspective

```
# Historical insights from bones and teeth
insights = {
   "Fossils": "Evidence of evolution and extinct species.",
   "Teeth Analysis": "Insights into ancient diets and health.",
   "Archaeology": "Dating human settlements and migrations.",
}

# Display insights
for topic, description in insights.items():
   print(f"{topic}: {description}").
```

Nykret: talks only when walking fast.

Yarusi: rents traveling flats by weeks.

Nykret and Yarusi

were interested in jetpack commuting.

```
class Jetpack:
    def __init__(self, fuel_capacity, weight_limit):
        self.fuel_capacity = fuel_capacity  # in liters
        self.weight_limit = weight_limit      # in kg
        self.current_fuel = fuel_capacity     # starts full

    def fly(self, weight):
        if weight > self.weight_limit:
            return "Overweight! Cannot fly."
        if self.current_fuel <= 0:
            return "Out of fuel! Please refuel."
        self.current_fuel -= 1  # consuming fuel per flight
        return "Flying!"

    def refuel(self):
        self.current_fuel = self.fuel_capacity
        return "Refueled!"

# Example usage
my_jetpack = Jetpack(fuel_capacity=10, weight_limit=100)
print(my_jetpack.fly(weight=80))  # "Flying!"
print(my_jetpack.refuel())         # "Refueled!"
```

Vasurta: knows thirty ways of walking.

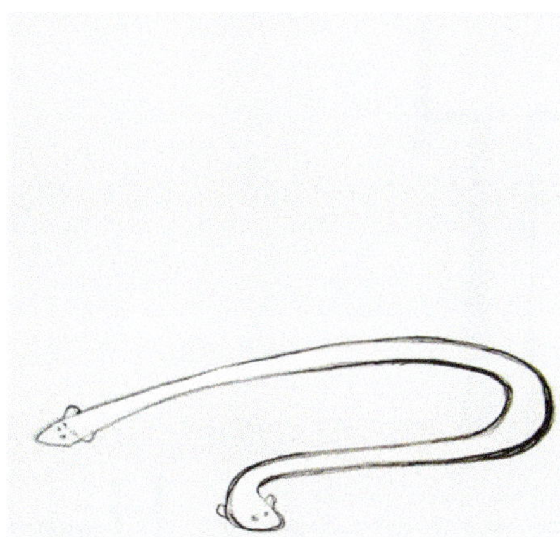

Zaruzudo: dances to own duo.

Vasurta and Zaruzudo

preferred drone-based communication, but it was not ready.

Busanati: has more flowers at home.

B usanti

Hibun: is very dependable, but has his days.

H ibun

were interested in the watering systems.

```
# Define watering systems
watering_systems = {
    "Drip Irrigation": "Delivers water directly to plant roots.",
    "Sprinkler System": "Distributes water evenly over a large area.",
    "Soaker Hose": "Allows water to seep out along the length of the hose.",
    "Flood Irrigation": "Inundates fields with water, typically for rice."
}

# Display watering systems
for system, description in watering_systems.items():
    print(f"{system}: {description}")
```

Hunfa: enjoys looking at his monument.

H unfa

Horel: knows where to go.

H orel

preferred traveling and visiting beautiful lakes. They installed small ponds in their backyards.

Tli: Solvs all the problems right after they occur.

Tli and

Harex: shows up when someone needs syrup.

Harex

were interested in vertical farming

```
# Define vertical farming explanation
vertical_farming = {
    "Definition": "Growing crops in stacked layers or vertically inclined surfaces.",
    "Benefits": [
        "Maximizes space in urban areas.",
        "Reduces water usage.",
        "Minimizes the presence of the insects.",
        "Enables year-round production."
    ]
}

# Display explanation
print(vertical_farming["Definition"])
for benefit in vertical_farming["Benefits"]:
    print(f"- {benefit}")
```

Heyan: sees double whenever confused.

Heyan and

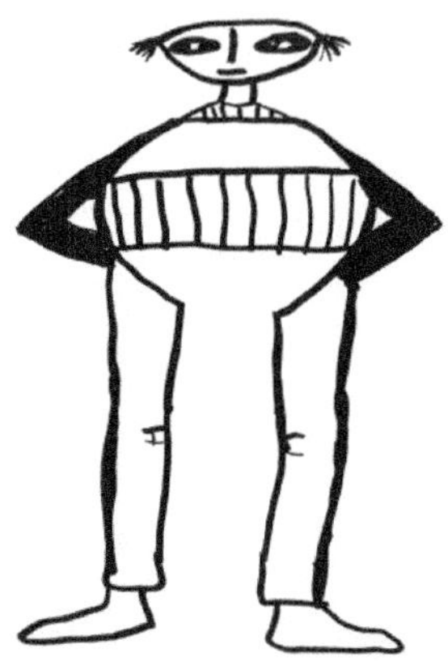

Ugalia: does not need any pockets, as she never carries any objects.

Ugalia

preferred having edible plants in pots in their kitchen windows.

Tumtatu: likes his own space.

T umtatu and

Kudarto: moves by dancing.

K udarto

wanted to experience self-flying planes

```
Explored self driving planes
# Define self-driving planes concept
self_driving_planes = {
   "Technology": "Autonomous flight systems using AI.",
   "Power Source": "Electric or hybrid engines to reduce emissions.",
   "Benefits": [
      "Lower operational costs.",
      "Reduced noise foulness.
      "Increased safety through automation."
   ]
}

# Display the concept
print("Self-Driving, Contamination-Free
Planes:")  for key, value in
self_driving_planes.items():
   if isinstance(value, list):
      print(f"{key}:")
      for item in value:
         print(f"- {item}")
   else:
      print(f"{key}: {value}")
```

Hyphra: dances while she bows.

H yphra and

Dagao: keeps all his belongings safe.

D agao

did not even trust self-driving cars.

Sudura: possesses equally sharp senses.

Sudura and

Daryge: controls everyone.

Daryge

asked how many species have white dots on red coatings

```
class Species:
    def __init__(self, name, has_white_dots_on_red):
        self.name = name
        self.has_white_dots_on_red = has_white_dots_on_red

# List of species
species_list = [
    Species("Ladybug", True),
    Species("Red Admiral Butterfly", True),
    Species("Frog", False),
    Species("Red Dragonfly", False),
]

# Count species with white dots on red coatings
count_with_white_dots_on_red = sum(1 for species in species_list if species.has_white_dots_on_red)

print(f"Species with white dots on red coatings: {count_with_white_dots_on_red}")
```

Huyerod: invents types of transportation.

Huyerod and

Vai: sometines feels hopeless, but the rest of the time acts.

Vai

suspected some trap.

Jukibon: supports your balance.

Lawade: composes music on the train.

Jukibon and Lavade

kept track of species with dot patterns on their coatings:

```
class Species:
    def __init__(self, name, has_dots):
        self.name = name
        self.has_dots = has_dots

# List of species
species_list = [
    Species("Frog", True),
    Species("Tiger", True),
    Species("Elephant", False),
    Species("Ladybug", True),
    Species("Shark", False)
]

# Count species with dots
count_with_dots = sum(1 for species in species_list if species.has_dots)

print(f"Species with dots: {count_with_dots}")
```

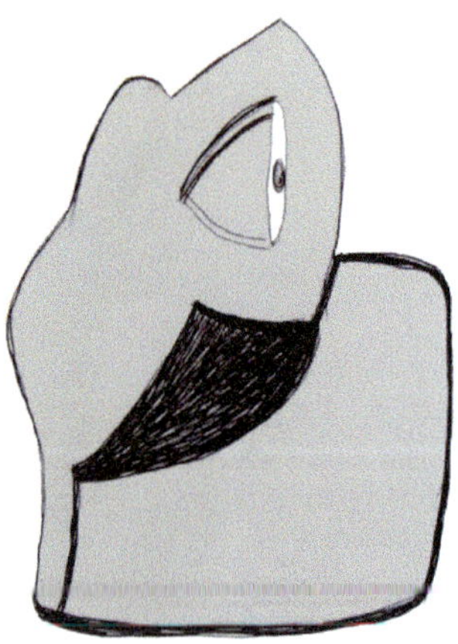

Hadura: always waits for her followers.

Sasado: likes to be close to everything that matters.

Hadura and Sasado

started to dress like that.

Tagasa: thinks with his hands.

Caseca: his pockets are endless.

Tagasa and Caseca studies art of Pompeii which only survived because of the disaster.

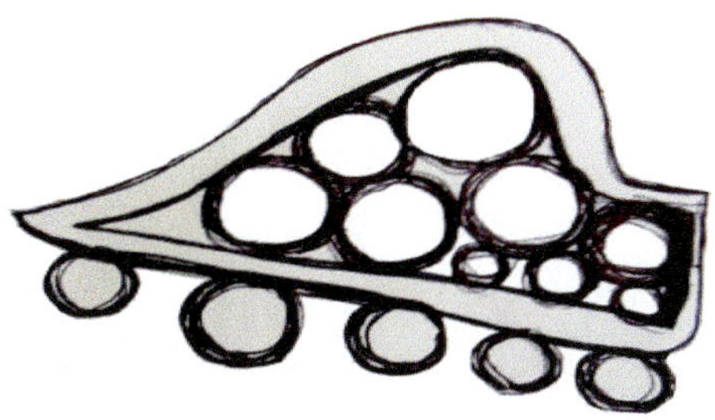

Sibhta: keeps her business open.

Litgo: never rode a bike, and was not interested.

Sibhta and Litgo researched other examples of things we do not appreciate but can have some positive outcomes

```
class Disaster:
  def __init__(self, name, positive_effect):
    self.name = name
    self.positive_effect = positive_effect

# Example disasters and their effects
disasters = [
  Disaster("Wildfire", "Regrowth of native plants"),
  Disaster("Flood", "Replenished aquifers"),
  Disaster("Earthquake", "Improved building codes"),
]

# Displaying positive effects
for disaster in disasters:
  print(f"After {disaster.name}: {disaster.positive_effect}")
```

Bahaduru: changes his walk frequently.

Bahduru and

Lavalo: the first thing he saw was a mirror.

Lavalo

were fascinated by the solar eclipse

```
def solar_eclipse():
    sun = "☀️"
    moon = "🌑
    for i in range(6):
        print(" " * i + moon + " eclipsing " + sun)

solar_eclipse()
```

Vutango: many wondered how he never gets tired.

Vutango and

Atasa: her look will melt your heart.

Atasa

watched the moon moving across, thus "eclipsing" the sun and passing in front of it during a solar eclipse.

Halake: moves object through surfaces.

H alake and

Vydago: can ride a bike upside down.

V ydago

studied under-the-ground cities and constructions

```
def reveal_underground():
    ground = "🌍"
    underground = ["🏰", "🏢", "🏟️", "🕌", "⛪"]

    print(ground + " Ground level")
    for structure in underground:
        print("⬇️ Excavating... Found:", structure)

reveal_underground()
```

Gego: always very precise.

G ego and

Arupa: carries any shape or weight.

A rupa

found about

```
def list_underground_constructions():
    underground_cities = ["Derinkuyu", "Nushabad", "Naours", "Burlington Bunker"]
    for city in underground_cities:
        print("Underground city:", city)

list_underground_constructions()
```

They already knew about some cities in Europe and the pipes that survived under Rome’s Trevi Fountain.

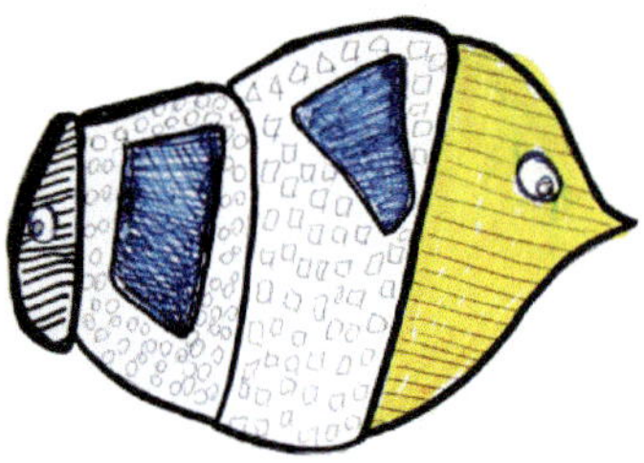

Bluo: goes either direction.

Mepe: always helpful.

Bluo and Mepe researched alchemy and ancient knowledge

```
def explain_alchemy_ancient_knowledge():
    alchemy = "Alchemy: The pursuit of turning base metals into gold."
    knowledge = "Ancient Knowledge: Early wisdom in philosophy, medicine, and astronomy."
    print(alchemy)
    print(knowledge)

explain_alchemy_ancient_knowledge()
```

Cusukl: knew it all in and out.

Melango: picks a flower daily all year round.

Cusukl and Melango were more interested in alchemy and ancient knowledge from a scientific perspective:

```
def alchemy_and_knowledge():
    insights = {
        "Alchemy": "Proto-chemistry, aimed at transforming matter.",
        "Ancient Knowledge": "Foundation for modern science, including astronomy, medicine, and math."
    }
    for topic, description in insights.items():
        print(f"{topic}: {description}")

alchemy_and_knowledge()
```

Anekar: no one can hear him approaching, but they sense it.

Anekar and

Makasap: dances to woodwork.

Makasap

wondered about the pressure points

```
def explain_pressure_points():
    print("Pressure Points: Specific body areas where pressure relieves pain or tension.")

explain_pressure_points()
```

Larode: has only good memories.

Larode and

Malusada: loves all those smaller then him.

Malusada

knew how to locate them

```
def list_pressure_points():
    points = ["LI4 - Hand Valley", "PC6 - Inner Gate", "ST36 - Leg Three Miles", "GB20 - Wind Pool"]
    for point in points:
        print("Pressure Point:", point)

list_pressure_points()
```

Sutego: His gestimate was not to fly.

Gax: dances to the daily news.

Sutego and Gax

wondered why there are so many different points of view on any given topic

```
def             explain_different_views():
   print("Different views arise due to:",
        "\n- Personal experiences",
        "\n- Cultural backgrounds",
        "\n- Education levels",
        "\n- Emotional perspectives")

explain_different_views()
```

Surau: cames with music.

Gendowe: composes music while walking.

Surau and Gendowe

listed some r:

```
def list_points_of_view():
   views = ["Personal", "Scientific", "Philosophical", "Cultural", "Political"]
   for view in views:
      print("Point of View:", view)

list_points_of_view(
```

Sutego: His gestimate was not to fly.

Denede: always feels the rush to help out.

Sutego and Denede

discussed various approaches to locomotion present in nature

```
class Locomotion:
    def __init__(self, method, example):
        self.method = method
        self.example = example

# List of locomotion methods
locomotion_methods = [
    Locomotion("Walking", "Humans"),
    Locomotion("Flying", "Birds"),
    Locomotion("Swimming", "Fish"),
    Locomotion("Crawling", "Snakes"),
    Locomotion("Gliding", "Flying Squirrels"),
]

# Display locomotion methods
for locomotion in locomotion_methods:
    print(f"{locomotion.method}: {locomotion.example}")
```

Vutel: runs after his on nose.

Sango: He was.

Vutel and Sango

preferred their own ways of moving.

Gy: Flowers grow better when he is around.

Gy and

Vaharasa: always knows when to leave.

Vaharasa

were fascinated by the ability to see things

```
eyes = ["Compound Eyes", "Simple Eyes", "Camera-Type Eyes", "Mirror Eyes", "Pinhole Eyes"]
print("Types of Eyes in Nature:")
for eye in eyes:
    print(eye)
```

Samtua: manages all her balances.

Samtua and

Rasatusa: stops only those who talk on the phone.

Rasatusa

studied hearing techniques

```
hearing_types = ["Ears", "Vibrations", "Lateral Line", "Tympanal Organs", "Sound Waves"]
print("Types of Hearing in Nature:")
for hearing in hearing_types:
    print(hearing)
```

Nu: he is.

Nu and

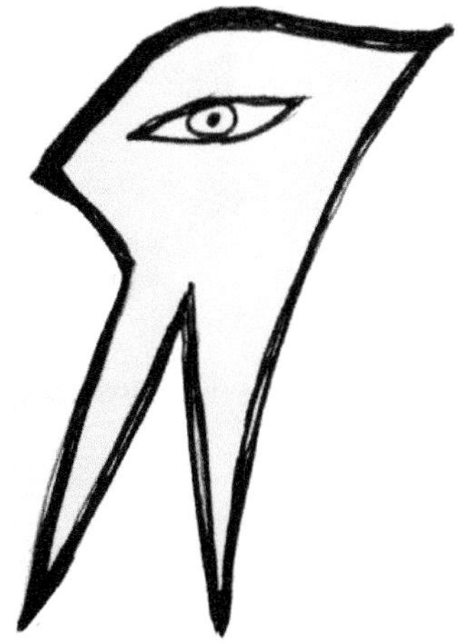

Tetan: knows too much.

Tetan

studied ways people get inspiration from nature

```
inspiration_sources = ["Art", "Poetry", "Science", "Meditation", "Architecture"]
print("Ways People Get Inspiration from Nature:")
for source in inspiration_sources:
   print(source)
```

Telifa: controls her own movement when going backward.

Telifa and

Fantado: can dance three danves and sing three songs.

Fantado

were more interested in the ways applied to industry and product design.

```
bio_designs = ["Biomimicry", "Longlasting Materials", "Natural Patterns", "Energy Efficiency", "Ergonomics"]
print("Nature-Inspired Ideas in Industry and Product Design:")
for design in bio_designs:
   print(design)
```

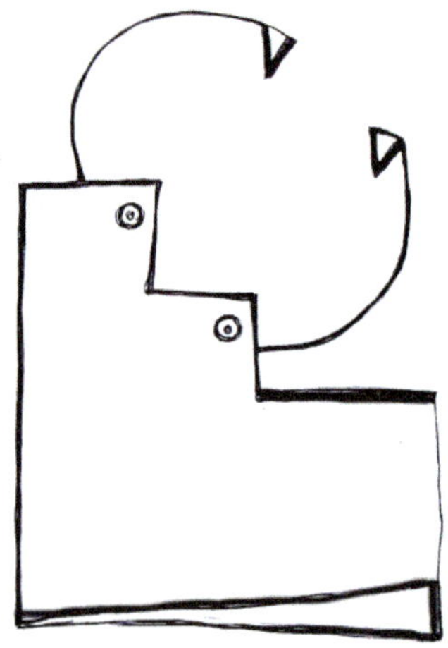

Tapalaka: captures flowers to replant them in a better spot.

T apalaka and

Sagufta: moves fast, but works slow.

S agufla

were awed by the secrets of Nature:

```
nature_secrets = ["Photosynthesis", "DNA", "Symbiosis", "Natural Selection", "Biodiversity"]
print("Prominent Secrets of Nature:")
for secret in nature_secrets:
    print(secret)
```

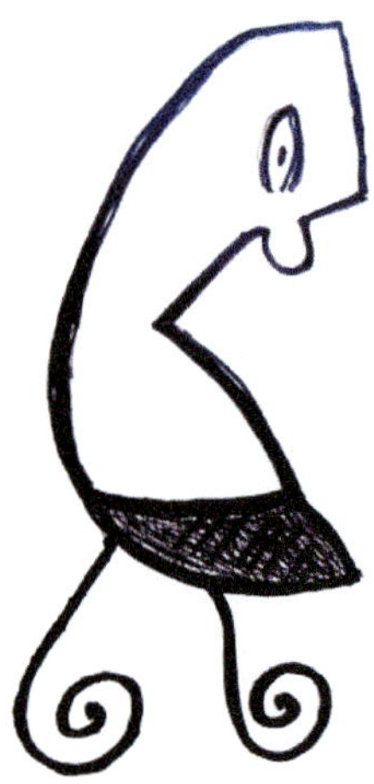

Pulgo: rocks as he walks.

P ulgo and

Punek: s always greeting everyone around him.

P unek

saw their hopes and goals differently

```
dangers = ["Health Issues", "Ethical Concerns", "High Cost", "Animal Welfare"]
print("Why Cloning Pets Might Be Dangerous:")
for danger in dangers:
    print(danger)
```

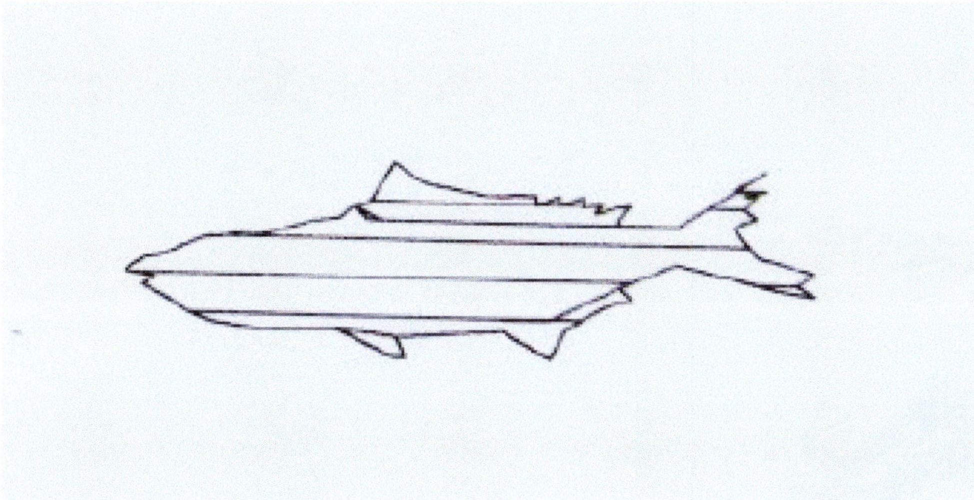

CHAPTER 2
WATERS – FLOAT
SWIM, DRINK
NAVIGATION

There are many types of water resources. They change. They move and act in various ways. The changing states of matter make it even more complex. We are learning to explore resources, some of them being way beyond our reach before the invention of specific tools. We are exploring water transportation, from the use of wind to advanced mechanisms. We use moving water to generate power and even control its flow for better or worse. This is probably the most crucial resource on many levels, as supportive as dangerous. Types of water generate different levels of coexistence.

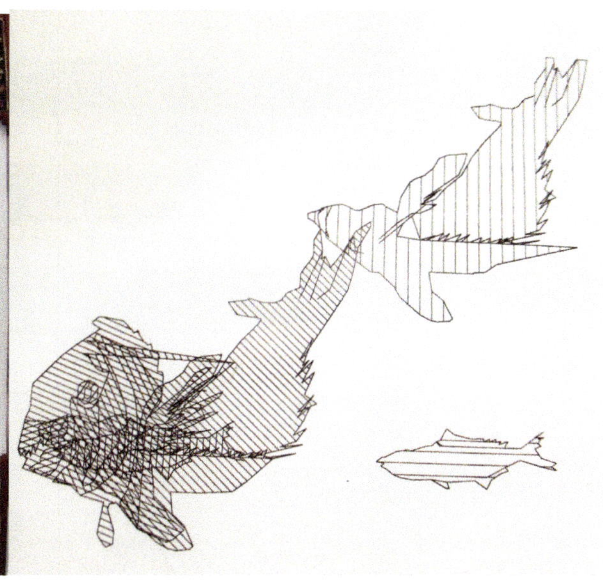

Jutero: uses his wings for swimming.

Jutero's family was known for their flying records. When the waters rose, the thought of swimming emerged. Using the wing class to represent different types of wings and their swimming capabilities helped him survive in the new environment

```
class Wing:
    def __init__(self, wing_type):
        self.wing_type = wing_type

    def swim(self):
        if self.wing_type == "flipper":
            return "Propelling forward with graceful strokes."
        elif self.wing_type == "feathered":
            return "Creating resistance to push through water."
        else:
            return "Wing type not suited for swimming."

# Example usage
flipper_wing = Wing("flipper")
print(flipper_wing.swim())

feathered_wing = Wing("feathered")
print(feathered_wing.swim())
```

The toughest thing for him was to meet all new friends down there.

Zarugo: knows when to start boxing.

Nachaha: jungles his matters with grace.

Wagazo: lkes to play "look and catch."

Nuhantra: follows good rules.

Nuhantra was concerned about the future.

```
class Life:
    def __init__(self):
        self.habits = []

    def add_habit(self, habit):
        self.habits.append(habit)
        print(f"Added preserving habit: {habit}")

    def follow_habits(self):
        for habit in self.habits:
            print(f"Following: {habit}")

# Example usage
life = PreservingLife()
life.add_habit("Reduce, Reuse, Recycle")
life.add_habit("Conserve water and energy")
life.add_habit("Support local products")
life.add_habit("Use public transportation or bike")
life.follow_habits()
```

Kumkudu: always watches you

Kamkudu developed systems that ensured it was all applied widely.

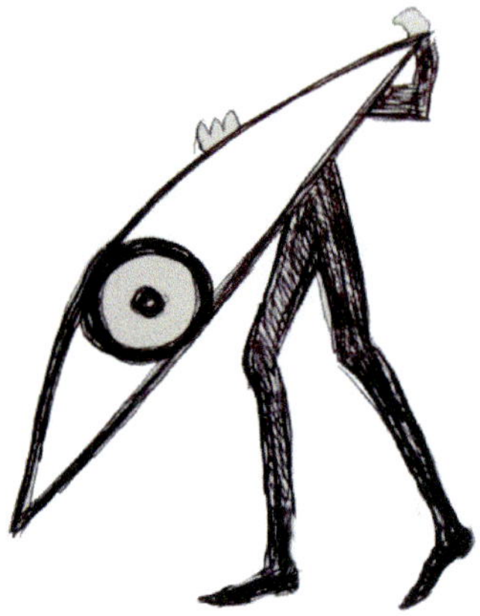

Gasa: his surfing board guides him.

Gasa understood water like anybody else.

```
class Surfboard:
  def __init__(self, length, width, volume, fin_type):
    self.length = length  # Length of the surfboard in feet
    self.width = width   # Width of the surfboard in inches
    self.volume = volume  # Volume of the surfboard in liters
    self.fin_type = fin_type  # Type of fins on the surfboard

  def guide_surfer(self, wave_height, wave_speed):
    if wave_height > 6 and wave_speed > 10:
      return "Use a longer board with more volume for stability."
    elif wave_height < 4 and wave_speed < 7:
      return "A shorter board with less volume will allow more maneuverability."
    else:
      return "A medium-length board with balanced volume is ideal for these conditions."

# Example usage:
my_surfboard = Surfboard(length=7.0, width=21.5, volume=45.0, fin_type="Thruster")
wave_height = 5  # in feet
wave_speed = 8   # in mph

guidance = my_surfboard.guide_surfer(wave_height, wave_speed)
print(f"Surfboard Guidance: {guidance}")
```

Jaralo: can swim, fly, or slide.

Jaralo on his board enjoyed flying, swimming, and sliding time.

Fuso: always surprised.

Fuso was surprised by the output of the code he wrote:

```
surprising_facts = [
    "The first computer mouse, built from wood was built in 1964.",
    "The first computer bug was a real bug (a moth).",
    "The first Gibibyte hard drive weighed five hundred pounds or more.",
    "The first website is still available: https://info.cern.ch/.",
    "There are more phones on the globe than people."
]

for fact in surprising_facts:
    print(f"Surprising Fact: {fact}")
```

```
Output:
Surprising Fact: The first computer mouse, built from wood was built in 1964.
Surprising Fact: The first computer bug was a real bug (a moth).
Surprising Fact: The first Gibibyte hard drive weighed five hundred pounds or more.
Surprising Fact: The first website is still available: https://info.cern.ch/.
Surprising Fact: There are more phones on the globe than people.
```

Hbas: confused, but full of hope.

Hbas could not believe that the output of the program looked almost the same as the code that generated it.

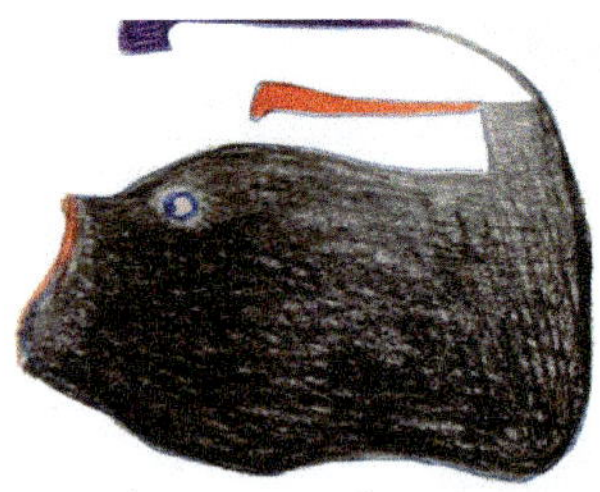

Kelbi: signals when turning any direction.

Kelbi was a leader but followed group actions

```
class UnderwaterCreature:
    def __init__(self, position, speed):
        self.position = position  # Position as a tuple (x, y)
        self.speed = speed        # Speed as a tuple (dx, dy)

    def avoid_collision(self, nearby_creatures):
        # Calculate average position and speed of nearby creatures
        avg_position = [0, 0]
        avg_speed = [0, 0]
        for creature in nearby_creatures:
            avg_position[0] += creature.position[0]
            avg_position[1] += creature.position[1]
            avg_speed[0] += creature.speed[0]
            avg_speed[1] += creature.speed[1]

        n = len(nearby_creatures)
        if n > 0:
            avg_position = [avg_position[0] / n, avg_position[1] / n]
            avg_speed = [avg_speed[0] / n, avg_speed[1] / n]

            # Adjust direction to avoid collisions
            self.speed[0] += (self.position[0] - avg_position[0]) * 0.1
            self.speed[1] += (self.position[1] - avg_position[1]) * 0.1

            # Align with the average speed of nearby creatures
            self.speed[0] += (avg_speed[0] - self.speed[0]) * 0.05
            self.speed[1] += (avg_speed[1] - self.speed[1]) * 0.05

# Example usage:
creature1 = UnderwaterCreature(position=(5, 5), speed=(1, 0))
creature2 = UnderwaterCreature(position=(6, 6), speed=(0, 1))
creature3 = UnderwaterCreature(position=(7, 7), speed=(-1, 0))

# List of nearby creatures
nearby = [creature2, creature3]

# Creature 1 adjusts to avoid collision
creature1.avoid_collision(nearby)

print(f"Updated Speed of Creature 1: {creature1.speed}")
```

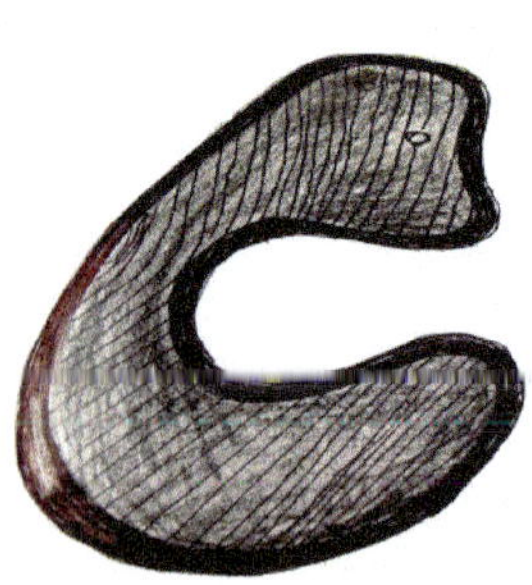

Cynem: sees across the ocean.

Cynen knew how creatures move within a group, and people mimic nature.

Fufkal: never wets his feet.

Fufkal learned his skills from the water strider (a pond skater), which can walk on the surface of the water due to the high surface tension of the water and their hydrophobic (water-repellent) legs covered with tiny hairs that trap air, gliding across the surface without sinking. This adaptation allows them to hunt and move around on water while staying completely dry

```
class WaterStrider:
    def __init__(self):
        self.feet_wet = False  # Initial state: feet are dry

    def stay_on_surface(self, surface_tension, leg_hydrophobicity):
        if surface_tension > 0.072 and leg_hydrophobicity > 0.9:
            self.feet_wet = False  # High surface tension and hydrophobic legs keep feet dry
        else:
            self.feet_wet = True  # If conditions aren't met, feet may get wet

# Example usage:
strider = WaterStrider()
strider.stay_on_surface(surface_tension=0.073, leg_hydrophobicity=0.95)

print(f"Water Strider's Feet Wet: {strider.feet_wet}")
```

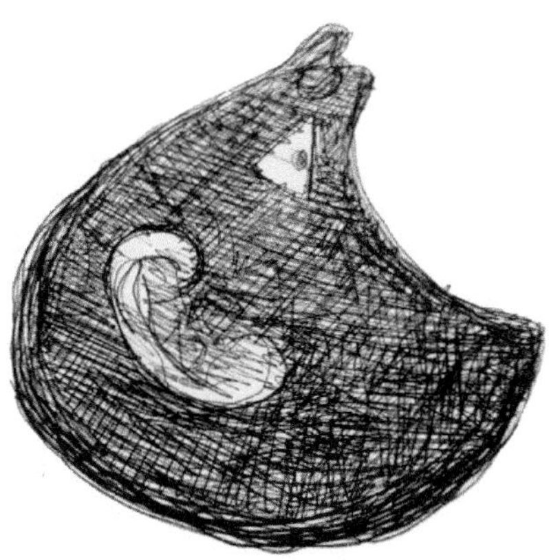

Hudaru: has a warning voice, but does not need to use it.

Hudaru never takes his socks out of his feet now.

Felango: can understand distributions.

Felango shared how distributions can be visualized

```
import numpy as np
import matplotlib.pyplot as plt

# Generate data for a normal distribution
data = np.random.normal(loc=0, scale=1, size=1000) # mean=0, std_dev=1, 1000 samples

# Plot the distribution
plt.hist(data, bins=30, density=True, alpha=0.6, color='blue')
plt.title("Normal Distribution")
plt.xlabel("Value")
plt.ylabel("Frequency")
plt.show()
```

He could be heard talking about data generation, where his code generated 1,000 data points from a normal distribution with a mean (loc) of 0 and a standard deviation (scale) of 1, and the plotting which used matplotlib to create a histogram, visually representing the distribution of the generated data.

Ebura: the funny one.

Ebura liked it without knowing what he was referring to.

Kirea: enjoys water.

Kirea understood the power behind the miracle of water

```
# Function to simulate enjoying water

def enjoy_water(water_temperature="cool", setting="nature", activity="relax"):
    print("You find a peaceful spot by the water.")

    if setting == "nature":
        print("The sound of a nearby stream calms your mind.")
    elif setting == "beach":
        print("Waves gently lap at the shore, inviting you to relax.")
    else:
        print("The stillness of the water mirrors your tranquil state.")

    print(f"The water is {water_temperature}, perfectly refreshing.")

    if activity == "relax":
        print("You dip your toes in, feeling the gentle ripples against your skin.")
    elif activity == "swim":
        print("You dive in, the water embracing you as you move freely.")
    elif activity == "float":
        print("You lay back, floating effortlessly, letting the water carry you.")

    print("You close your eyes, letting all stress melt away as you enjoy the moment.")

# Call the function with different parameters
enjoy_water()
```

Jasul: always protects hs buckets.

Jasul knew how to keep it clean.

Jasuky: always finds a way with his partners.

Jasuky and his team worked on water preservation

```
def clean_water_methods():
    methods = {
        "Boiling": "Heat the water until it reaches a rolling boil for at least 1 minute. This kills most bacteria, viruses, and parasites.",
        "Filtration": "Use a water filter to remove impurities and contaminants. Filters can range from simple cloth filters to advanced systems with activated carbon or ceramic elements.",
        "Distillation": "Boil water and then collect the steam in a clean container. The steam condenses back into liquid, leaving most impurities behind.",
        "Chlorination": "Add chlorine or chlorine-based tablets to water. This disinfects the water by killing pathogens, but requires careful dosing to avoid harmful byproducts.",
        "Solar Disinfection (SODIS)": "Place water in clear plastic bottles and leave them in direct sunlight for 6 hours. UV radiation from the sun kills pathogens.",
        "UV Purification": "Use a UV light purifier to kill bacteria, viruses, and other pathogens. This method is effective but requires access to electricity.",
        "Chemical Treatment": "Add chemicals like iodine or chlorine dioxide to water. These chemicals kill bacteria and viruses but may leave an aftertaste."
    }

    for method, description in methods.items():
        print(f"{method}: {description}\n")

# Call the function to display the water cleaning methods
clean_water_methods()
```

Lusek:very careful.

Lusek only drank water bottled at the source.

Furtugo: always wonders why there is no bottom right below him.

Furtigo did not know about life beyond water

```
def below_water_facts():
    facts = [
        "The water cycle leads to weather patterns such as  rainfall and droughts.",
        "Warmer ocean temperatures develop hurricanes and typhoons.",
        "Ocean marine ecosystems, impact water quality."
    ]

    for fact in facts:
        print(f"Water-Related Fact: {fact}")

# Call the function to display water-related facts
below_water_facts()
```

Gurafo: can suck into any surface and stay still for a minute.

Gurafo thought that everything requires patience.

Lineo: smiles when he eats.

Lineo used his baleen plates to filter small food items like krill from the water. That is what he enjoyed doing the most, but was not careful when eating

```
def eating_underwater_warning():
    reasons = [
        "Breathing and swallowing underwater can be difficult and may lead to choking.",
        "Water can mix with food, making it harder to chew and swallow properly.",
        "Food particles can attract fish or other marine animals, which might cause unexpected interactions.",
        "Eating underwater increases the risk of inhaling water, leading to potential drowning hazards."
    ]

    for reason in reasons:
        print(f"Be Careful: {reason}")

# Call the function to display reasons to be cautious when eating underwater
eating_underwater_warning()
```

Lerte: backs off twice a day.

Lerte alerts others, so they call him Lerte Alerte.

Gilf: measures as he walks.

Gilf turned unwanted objects into reusable forms

```
def recycle(objects):
    reused_objects = []
    for obj in objects:
        if obj['status'] == 'unwanted':
            new_form = f"Recycled {obj['type']}"
            reused_objects.append(new_form)
            print(f"{obj['type']} recycled into {new_form}")
    return reused_objects

# Example: List of unwanted objects
objects = [
    {'type': 'Plastic Bottle', 'status': 'unwanted'},
    {'type': 'Old Newspaper', 'status': 'unwanted'},
    {'type': 'Glass Jar', 'status': 'unwanted'}
]

# Recycle unwanted objects
recycled = recycle(objects)

# Output results
print(f"Recycled objects: {recycled}")
```

Lutenua: hides, then appears to collect what you have for him.

Lutenua was a collector. Not a usual one. She took discards to make art.

```
def create_art(objects):
    art_pieces = []
    for obj in objects:
        if obj['status'] == 'unwanted':
            art_piece = f"Art from {obj['type']}"
            art_pieces.append(art_piece)
            print(f"{obj['type']} transformed into {art_piece}")
    return art_pieces

# Example: List of unwanted objects
objects = [
    {'type': 'Old Tires', 'status': 'unwanted'},
    {'type': 'Broken Mirror', 'status': 'unwanted'},
    {'type': 'Scrap Metal', 'status': 'unwanted'}
]

art_collection = create_art(objects)
print(f"Art pieces created: {art_collection}")
```

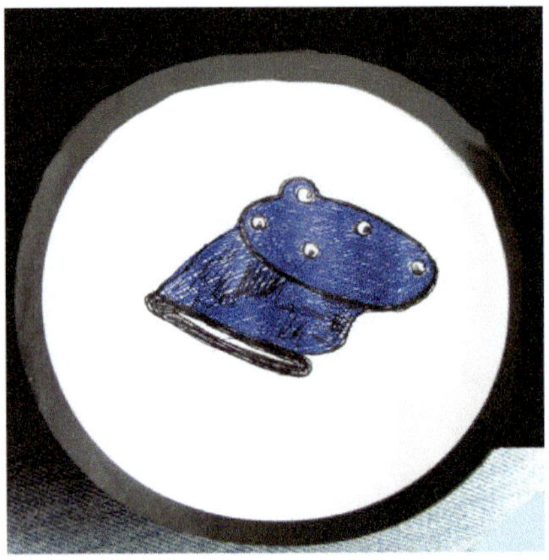

Bortengo: bought a house, sold it twice.

Bortengo kept selling his underwater house

```
def sell_house(house, times_sold):
    for _ in range(times_sold):
        print(f"{house} sold to a new owner.")
    print(f"Selling {house} {times_sold} times by reducing the need for new construction.")

# Example: Selling the same house multiple times
house = "Profitable House"
times_sold = 2

# Sell the house twice
sell_house(house, times_sold)
```

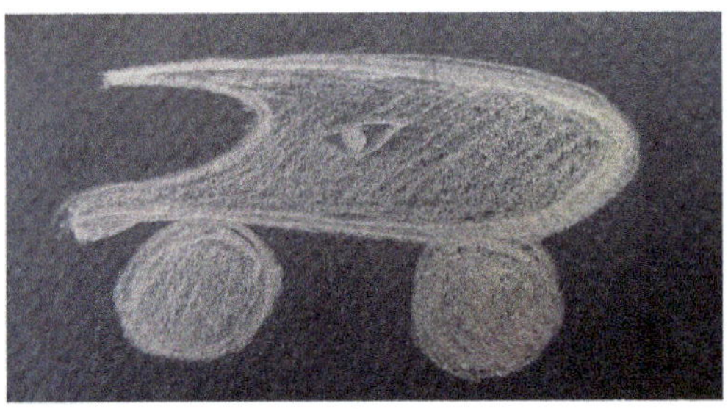

Latasa: cleans up the air and the water.

Latasa was a detective, and a good one

```
def catch_fraudulent_seller(sales):
    sales_tracker = {}
    for sale in sales:
        house = sale['house']
        seller = sale['seller']
        if house in sales_tracker:
            print(f"Detective: Caught {seller} for selling {house} twice!")
        else:
            sales_tracker[house] = seller

# Example: House sales records
sales = [
    {'house': '123 Maple St', 'seller': 'John Doe'},
    {'house': '456 Oak Ave', 'seller': 'Jane Smith'},
    {'house': '123 Maple St', 'seller': 'John Doe'}  # Illegal second sale
]

# Detective catches the fraudulent seller
catch_fraudulent_seller(sales)
```

Then, she realized that his house was regrowing on him. The Limpet created his homes from materials such as rocks and other debris. He was leaving the old shell behind.

Ilonget: we for them all.

Ilonget kept making sure everyone knew what to do

```
import datetime


def good_behavior():
    # Suggest enabling Do Not Disturb a creature during non-urgent hours
    current_hour = datetime.datetime.now().hour
    if 22 <= current_hour or current_hour < 7:
        return "It's late! Consider enabling Do Not Disturb mode to prevent unhappiness ."
    else:
        return "Keep your Do Not Disturb mode when you're focused to avoid distractions."

print(good_behavior())
```

Kusa: can see very far.

Kusa shared her long-term vision

```
import random


def better_behavior_long_term():
    # Suggest helping other creature on a random day each week
    days_of_week = ['Monday', 'Tuesday', 'Wednesday', 'Thursday', 'Friday']
    suggested_day = random.choice(days_of_week)

    return f"Consider helping other creature every {suggested_day} to reduce stress  in the long run."

print(better_behavior_long_term()
```

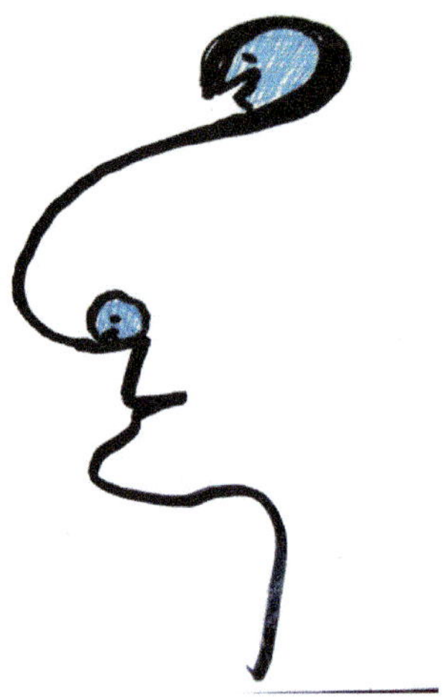

Megila: his people tell him everything.

Megila as an informed person, weighted his shipping options

```
class Shipment:

    def __init__(self, distance, weight, eco_friendly=True):
        self.distance = distance  # in kilometers
        self.weight = weight  # in kilograms
        self.eco_friendly = eco_friendly

    def calculate_waves(self):
        # waves per km per kg (average waves)
        waves_per_km_kg = 0.1
        return self.distance * self.weight * waves_per_km_kg

    def suggest_packaging(self):
        if self.eco_friendly:
            return "Use biodegradable packaging."
        return "Consider switching to see packaging."

# Example of shipping 10kg over 100km with see packaging
shipment = Shipment(distance=100, weight=10, eco_friendly=True)
print("Estimated waves:", shipment.calculate_waves), "kg")
print(shipment.suggest_packaging())
```

Faldu: swims fast, and flies fast.

Faldu was ready to deliver anywhere and anytime.

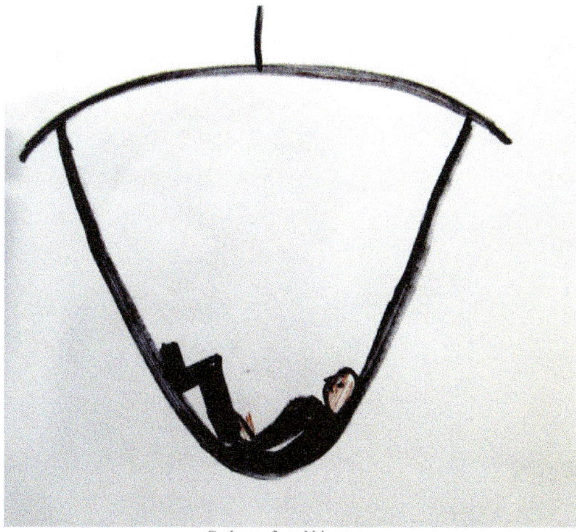

Guduras: found his spot.

Guduras used only paints he made himself and such as yolk for tempera painting, white cheese for casein-based painting, and walnut oil for oil painting. He used grounded vegetables and minerals for powdered pigment to be mixed with those binders.

```
def find_your_spot(choices, passions):
    for choice in choices:
        if choice in passions:
            return f"Your spot in painting: {choice}"
    return "Keep exploring, your spot is out there."

choices = ["tech", "art", "binders", "colors"]
passions = ["art", "self_production"]

spot = find_your_spot(choices, passions)
print(spot)
```

Colze: counts to three, but only four times.

Colze knew better. She used her computer, tablet, phone, or watch. Disposing of them properly underwater was another challenge.

Duskiol: gives what he gets

Duskiol believed that whatever resources you take, you should give back an equivalent amount to maintain balance in the world

```
def give_what_you_get(resource, usage):
    return f"Give back {resource * usage} units to maintain the balance."

resource = 5  # Example: energy, water, etc.
usage = 0.8   # Percentage of what you use

maintainable_giving = give_what_you_get(resource, usage)
print(maintainable_giving)
```

Hamadu: can swim and fly at the same time.

Hamadu often visited Duskiol in his new underwater castle.

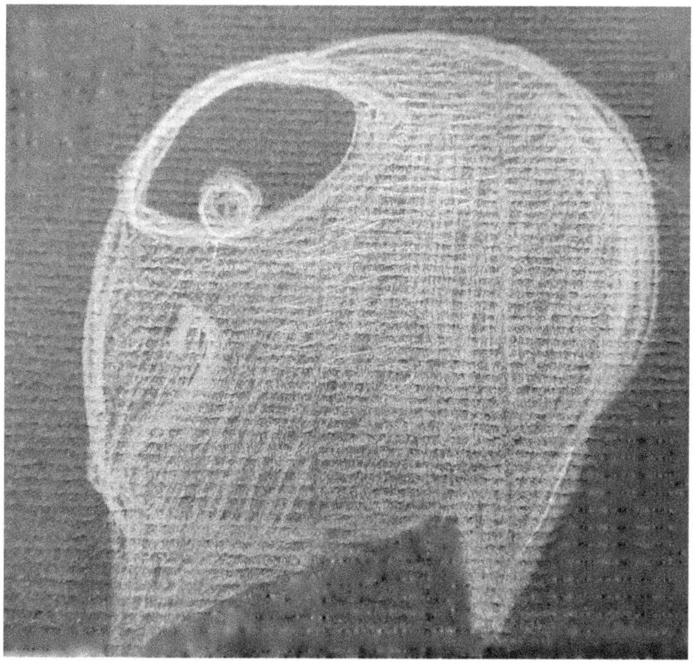

Masono: smiles when meeting fish.

Masono was friendly but always hungry.

```
def manage_hunger(friendly, prey_available):
    if friendly and prey_available:
        return "Share the meal with others."
    elif prey_available:
        return "Eat, but be kind."
    else:
        return "Search for food together."

friendly = True
prey_available = True

action = manage_hunger(friendly, prey_available)
print(action)
```

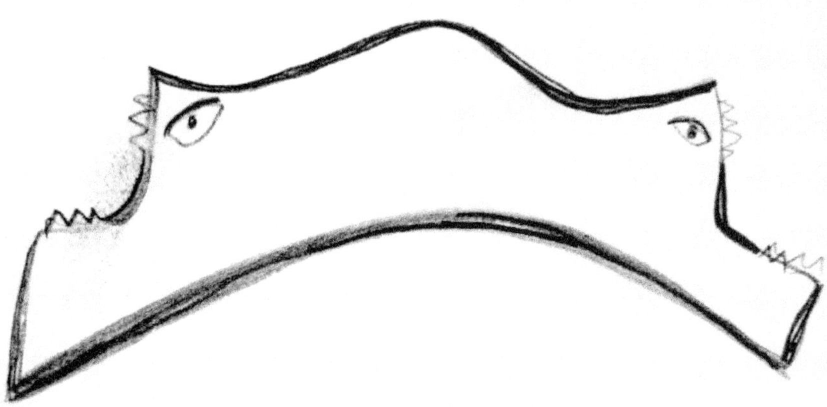

Murudu: will never miss it.

Marudu would never miss hanging out with him, as Masono's hospitality attracted fish.

Lusorat: thinks twice before entering any room.

Lusorat knew the old and new dangers

```
class Water:

    def __init__(self, temperature, air_quality, water_availability, food_availability):
        self.temperature = temperature
        self.air_quality = air_quality
        self.water_availability = water_availability
        self.food_availability = food_availability

def check_dangers(room):
    dangers = []

    # Temperature extremes
    if water.temperature < 0 or water.temperature > xx:
        dangers.append("Danger: Extreme temperature!")

    # Poor air quality
    if water.air_quality < yy:  # Assuming a scale where lower is worse
```

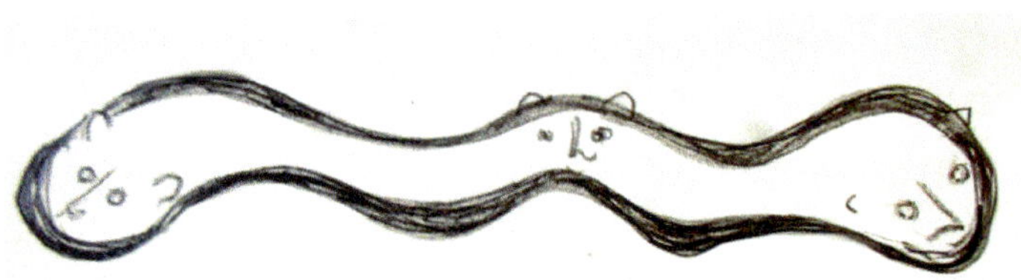

Mukupur: eats a lot.

Makupur knew how to solve it

```
class Sea:
    def __init__(self, temperature, air_quality, water_availability, food_availability):
        self.temperature = temperature
        self.air_quality = air_quality
        self.water_availability = water_availability
        self.food_availability = food_availability

def apply_solutions(water):
    # Solution for temperature extremes
    if sea.temperature < xx or water.temperature > xx:
        sea.temperature = xx  # Set to a safe, moderate temperature

    # Solution for poor air quality
    if seeaair_quality < yy:
        seea.air_quality = yy  # Improve air quality by ventilation or filters

    # Solution for water scarcity
    if sea.water_availability < zz:
        sea.water_availability = zz # Provide a reliable water source
```

It is nice to have a coder around.

Fuftu: makes only right turns.

Fuftu wanted to do good things only

```
# List of good things underwater creatures can do
underwater_creatures_good_things = [
    "Maintain coral reef health by supporting biodiversity",
    "Filter and clean water by consuming plankton and other particles",
    "Help in nutrient cycling, maintaining balance in marine ecosystems",
    "Act as food sources for other marine life, supporting the food chain",
    "Pollinate underwater plants, contributing to the health of seagrass beds",
    "Assist in carbon sequestration by storing carbon in their bodies",
    "Create habitats by burrowing or building structures like coral reefs",
    "Control algae growth by grazing on algae and preventing overgrowth",
    "Support eco-tourism, benefiting local economies and conservation efforts",
    "Act as indicators of environmental health, alerting us to ecosystem changes"
]

# Print the list of good things underwater creatures can do
for good_thing in underwater_creatures_good_things:
print(good_thing)
```

Nakutda: always feels being watched.

Nakutda was doing the same but for another reason.

Cotago: fights with what is current.

Cotago is peaceful but very righteous

```
class OceanLife:
    def __init__(self, species, conflicts):
        self.species = species
        self.conflicts = conflicts

    def resolve_conflicts(self):
        if "peacefulness" in self.species and "righteousness" in self.species:
            self.conflicts = "resolved"
        else:
            self.conflicts = "ongoing"

    def show_status(self):
        return f"Ocean Life Conflict Status: {self.conflicts}"

# Example
sea = OceanLife(species=["peacefulness", "righteousness"], conflicts="ongoing")
sea.resolve_conflicts()
print(sea.show_status())  # Output: Ocean Life Conflict Status: resolved
```

Nasati: he knows more magic tricks than he can perform.

Nasati knew his ways to make problems disappear. He was working offline. “How inconvenient,” Cotago would say,” How safe,” Nasati would reply.

Mujabi: can recognize the real truth

Mujabi knew it all, she thought

```
class DataSource:
    def __init__(self, name, reliability, data):
        self.name = name
        self.reliability = reliability  # Reliability scale: 0 (low) to 100 (high)
        self.data = data

def analyze_truth(sources):
    # Aggregate data from multiple sources
    total_reliability = sum(source.reliability for source in sources)
    weighted_data = sum(source.data * source.reliability for source in sources) / total_reliability
    return weighted_data

# Example data from different sources
source1 = DataSource("Scientific Report", 90, 85)
source2 = DataSource("News Article", 60, 70)
source3 = DataSource("Social Media", 30, 50)

# Analyze to recognize the real truth
truth = analyze_truth([source1, source2, source3])
print(f"Analyzed Truth Based on Data Sources: {truth:.2f}")
```

Capuncho: lives in his own world.

Capuncho ignored it all and lived a happy life for a while.

Mehoru: switches from warm to cold in a blink.

Mehoru studied how temperature trends show a shift from warmer to colder water and air.

```
import random

def
  atmospheric_conditions_change_effect(year
  s):  temp_changes = []

  # Simulate temperatures shifting from warm to cold over time
  for year in range(years):
     warm_days = max(0, 70 - year * random.uniform(0.5, 1.5)) # Decrease in warm days
     cold_days = 100 - warm_days  # Increase in cold days
     temp_changes.append((year, round(warm_days), round(cold_days)))

  return temp_changes

# Show temperature shift over 50 years
for year, warm, cold in atmospheric_conditions_change_effect(50):
  print(f"Year {year}: Warm days = {warm}, Cold days = {cold}")
```

Becadara: lives in Arcadia and enjoys it.

Becadara did not believe in fluctuating weather patterns as they did not exist in her utopian life.

Mungo: watches the stars on a daily basis.

Mungo spent his nights standing in the pond to watch the stars, as he believed they could influence his environment

```
class StarStudy:
   def __init__(self):
      self.insight = 0  # Insight gained from studying stars

   def study_stars_daily(self):
      self.insight += 5  # Studying stars each day gives new insights about the universe

    def take_my_actions(self):
       if self.insight >= 25:
          return "Inspired by the stars, you take actions to determine the best ones!"
      return "Keep studying the stars for deeper understanding and inspiration."
# Simulate daily star studying
study = StarStudy()
for day in range(5):  # Studying stars for 5 days
   study.study_stars_daily()
# Check if my actions can be taken
print(study.take_my_action())
```

Baklash: never leaves water.

Backlash was staying under the water enjoying the ways stars create a surreal and beautiful visual experience through movement, refraction, distorting lights, and twinkling glow from dimming the lights through ripping and reflection, with mirrored effect causing stars to flicker, and the turbulence of the water that blurs the starry skylight offering play, distortion, and fading.

Lagea: has three bites every day.

Lagea was satisfied but bothered by the faith of others

```
# Simple approach to ending underwater_hunger

def increase_food_production():
    return "Invest in agriculture and local farming."

def reduce_food_waste():
    return "Reduce food waste through better storage and distribution."

def improve_food_distribution():
    return "Ensure food reaches the hungry through better logistics."

def end_underwater_hunger():
    actions = [
        increase_food_production(),
        reduce_food_waste(),
        improve_food_distribution()
    ]
    for action in actions:
        print(action)

# Run the concept code
end_world_hunger()
```

Thus, she suggested expanding seaweed agriculture and local farming, reducing food waste through better storage and distribution, and ensuring food reaches the hungry through better logistics.

Casunaa: keeps it all to himself.

Casunaa stayed silent, but his donations were waterfalling.

Lasaruo: converts problems into dances.

Lasaruo was worrying about his water surroundings and their fate

```
# Convert water problems into dances

def water_problem_to_dance(problem):
    dances = {
        "drought": "Salsa - swift moves to bring the rain!",
        "flood": "Tango - intense and dramatic like rising waters.",
        "contamination": "Hip-Hop - powerful and expressive, cleansing the
        environment.",  "water scarcity": "Ballet - delicate, conserving every drop.",
        "access to clean water": "Breakdance - agile moves to find clean sources."
    }
    return dances.get(problem, "Freestyle – adapt
```

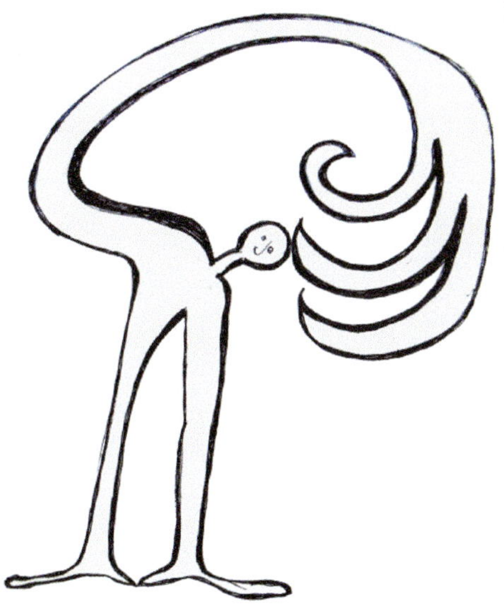

Dasut: handles his problems just fine.

Dasut kept encouraging his playful thinking about serious problems. His understanding of this code was: Drought: Salsa - swift moves to bring the rain! Flood: Tango - intense and dramatic like rising waters. Contamination: Hip-Hop - powerful and expressive, cleansing the environment. Water Scarcity: Ballet - delicate, conserving every drop. Access To Clean Water: Breakdance - agile moves to find clean sources. Just like the code stated it, he thought.

Gasahu: filters water to drink only fresh.

Gasahu was called oversensitive

```
# Water filtration methods to make water fresh

def filtration_methods():
    methods = {
        "Boiling": "Kills bacteria and pathogens by heating water.",
        "Activated Carbon": "Removes impurities and chemicals through adsorption.",
        "Distillation": "Purifies water by boiling and condensing steam.",
        "Reverse Osmosis": "Filters water through a semi-permeable membrane.",
        "UV Purification": "Uses ultraviolet light to kill harmful microorganisms."
    }
    return methods

# Display filtration methods
def explain_filtration():
    methods = filtration_methods()
    for method, explanation in methods.items():
        print(f"{method}: {explanation}")

# Run the function
explain_filtration()
```

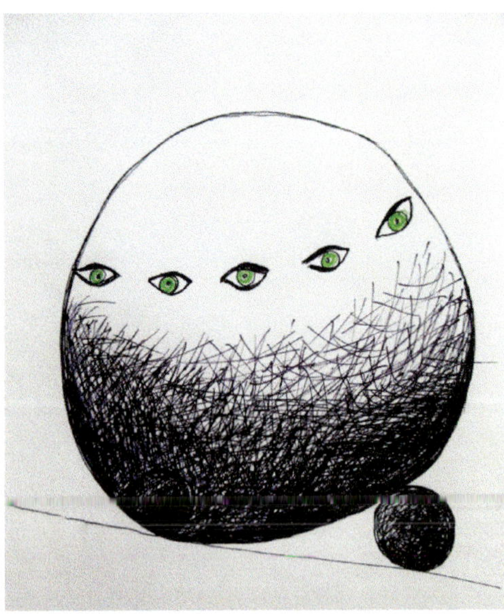

Mugeraso: traveled around the globe and saw it all.

Mugeraso was different. She fed off bacteria.

Funak: always together.

Funak could never separate from Funak

```
def find_food(characters):
    if characters == 1:
        print("One character can trace food, but it is limited.")
    elif characters == 2:
        print("Two characters can double the efforts, share resources, and motivate each other.")
        print("Two, they can accomplish more.")

# Test the function
find_food(2)
```

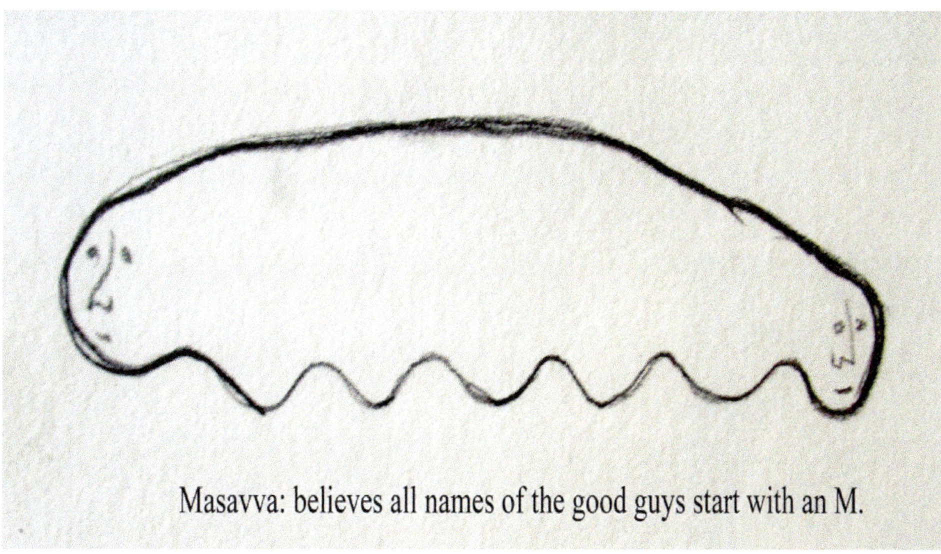

Masavva: believes all names of the good guys start with an M.

Masavva only liked interacting with the M group, but it was a large community.

```
def find_food(together):
    if together:
        print("When we stay united, our actions combine, creating a larger impact.")
        print("Communities can share resources.")
    else:
        print("Alone, it's hard to create the same level of self-fulfillment.")
        print("Individual efforts, while helpful, are not as powerful as collective action.")

# Test the function
find_food (together=True)
```

Candula: keeps all the information to herself.

Candula was considered a loner, but only because others were ridiculing the way she was swimming

```
def stay_strong(different):
    if different:
        print("Being different takes courage, but it opens new perspectives.")
        print("Staying true to yourself strengthens your character.")
    else:
        print("Conforming may feel safe, but you may miss out on personal growth.")
        print("Embrace uniqueness to bring new ideas and change the world.")

# Test the function
stay_strong(different=True)
```

Mudalasto: discusses plnts with himself.

Mudalasto invented plntsplans, through his unique swimming style, but no one believed he really did, as nobody knew what they were or even meant.

Nodugo: enjoys dynamic music.

Nodugo swam rhythmically

```
def dynamic_music_effect(mood):
    if mood == "stressed":
        print("Dynamic sounds with calming tones helps reduce stress and promotes relaxation.")
    elif mood == "sad":
        print("Uplifting, energetic sounds can elevate mood and bring positivity.")
    else:
        print("Dynamic sounds adapts to one's mood, helping maintain balance and well-being.")

# Test the function
dynamic_sounds_effect("stressed")
```

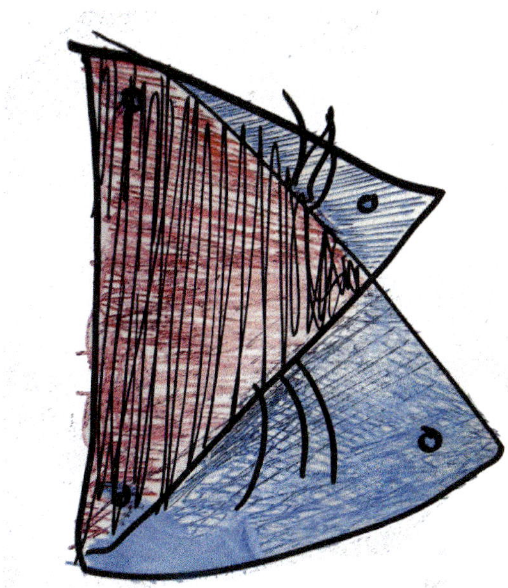

Duanova: always on the alert.

Duanova changed based on her mood still knowing the sounds can have a positive impact on mental wellness by reducing stress or uplifting emotions. She befriended laud underwater animals.

Jugatago: catches fish mentally.

Jugatago always felt hungry.

```
def catch_fish_mentally(patience, focus):
    if patience and focus:
        print("Clear your mind like a lake. Patience and focus help you 'catch' the ideas, like waiting for a fish to bite.")
        print("Just as fishing requires stillness, so helps gaining mental clarity.")
    else:
        print("Without patience and focus, your thoughts will scatter, making it hard to 'catch' any valuable insights.")

# Test the function
catch_fish_mentally(patience=True, focus=True)
```

Nadanga: twirls her way through the ocean.

Nadanga never wanted to be caught and was successful at

```
def avoid_caught_underwater(stay_calm):
    if stay_calm:
        print("Stay calm, swim down, and find your way to the bottom.")
    else:
        print("Panicking sends you up; keep calm to reach the very bottom.")

# Test the function
avoid_caught_underwater(stay_calm=True)
```

The truth was she was not a fish.

Nasumn: sees more than anybody else.

Nasumn knew the basics to stay safe.

```
def underwater_safety():
    tips = [
        "1. Always dive with a buddy.",
        "2. Check your oxygen levels frequently.",
        "3. Equalize your ears to avoid pressure damage.",
        "4. Never hold your breath while ascending.",
        "5. Be aware of your surroundings and avoid strong currents."
    ]

    for tip in tips:
        print(tip)

underwater_safety()
```

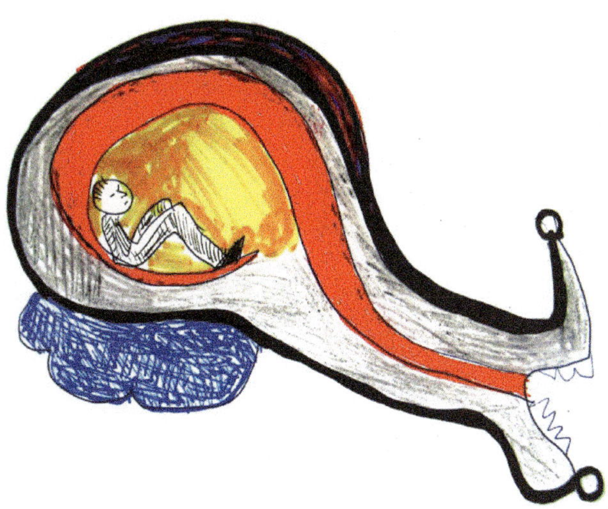

Husaguta: always has someone to protect him.

Husaguta did not have to.

They stayed safe when being together.

Fernto: good swimmer, too.

Fernto was good at everything he was doing

```
def success_and_happiness():
    tips = [
        "1. Set realistic goals and work consistently.",
        "2. Stay curious and keep learning new things.",
        "3. Practice gratitude and focus on the positives.",
        "4. Take breaks and prioritize self-care.",
        "5. Embrace failures as learning opportunities.",
        "6. Surround yourself with supportive characters
    ]

    for tip in tips:
        print(tip)

success_and_happiness()
```

Nodanda: always celebrating every minute of her life.

Nodanda was always happy by not trying to be better than others.

Jemj: will befriend anyone.

Jemj was constantly hungry as he could not do any form of harm

```
def avoid_hunger_underwater():
    tips = [
        "1. Eat a nutritious meal before diving.",
        "2. Carry snacks that are safe for underwater consumption.",
        "3. Stay hydrated to avoid feeling weak or being hungry.",
        "4. Use edible plants like seaweed.",
        "5. Plan short dives to avoid prolonged hunger."
    ]

    for tip in tips:
        print(tip)

avoid_hunger_underwater()
```

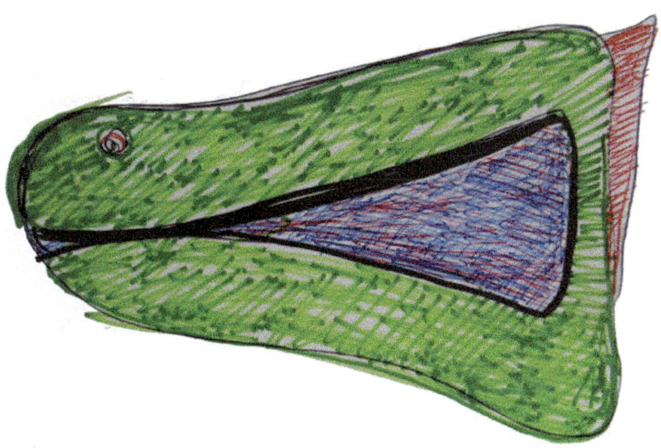

Orudati: collects for fish charity.

Orudati was in the same boat.

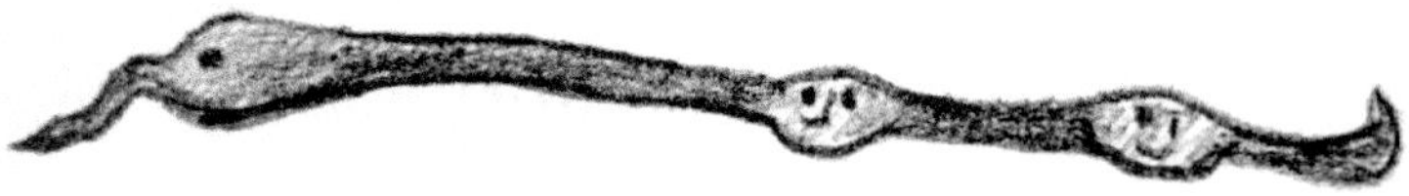

Furginod: enjoys company.

Furginod was friendly.

```
import random

# Seasons list
seasons = ['spring', 'summer', 'fall', 'winter']

# Function to check if creature is out
def is_creature_out(season):
    if season == 'winter':
        return True
    return False

# Simulate befriending process
def befriend_creature():
    for i in range(4):
        season = random.choice(seasons)
        print(f"It's {season} now.")

        if is_creature_out(season):
            print("The creature is out! You have a chance to befriend it.")
            print("You offer warmth and kindness.")
            if random.choice([True, False]):
                print("The creature accepts your friendship!")
            else:
                print("The creature is still cautious. Try again next winter.")
            break
        else:
            print("The creature is hiding. Wait for winter.")

befriend_creature()
```

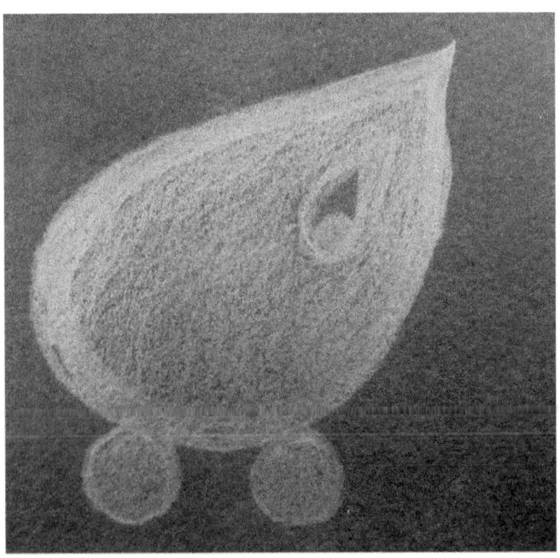

Qatua: goes out only in winter.

Quatua was only nice one-fourth of a year.

Pelfo: swims backward.

Pelfo survives by confusing others

```
class Swimmer:
    def __init__(self):
        self.direction = "forward"  # Initial direction
        self.position = 0           # Initial position

    def swim(self):
        if self.direction == "forward":
            self.position += 1
        elif self.direction == "backward":
            self.position -= 1

    def change_direction(self, new_direction):
        if new_direction in ["forward", "backward"]:
            self.direction = new_direction
        else:
            print("Invalid direction!")

    def status(self):
        return f"Direction: {self.direction}, Position: {self.position}"

def explain_backward_swimming():
    swimmer = Swimmer()

    # Swim forward
    print("Swimming forward:")
    for _ in range(5):
        swimmer.swim()
        print(swimmer.status())

    # Change to backward swimming
    swimmer.change_direction("backward")
    print("\nSwimming backward:")
    for _ in range(5):
        swimmer.swim()
        print(swimmer.status())

    print("\nExplanation:")
    print("When swimming backward, the swimmer moves in the opposite direction to their visual perception.")
    print("This requires more cognitive effort because the swimmer must rely on spatial awareness and")
    print("internalize the reversed movement to avoid disorientation and navigate effectively.")

explain_backward_swimming()
```

He invented his own swimming style, but it is not officially acknowledged.

Nakaho: moves faster than thinks.

Nakaho was seen as a careful one

```
import time
import random

def simulate_survival(reaction_time, threat_speed):
    # Faster response time increases chances of avoiding a threat
    survival_chance = max(0, (reaction_time - threat_speed) / reaction_time)
    return survival_chance

# Simulate a situation
reaction_time = random.uniform(0.5, 1.5)  # seconds
threat_speed = random.uniform(0.1, 1.0)  # seconds

# Calculate survival chance
chance = simulate_survival(reaction_time, threat_speed)
print(f"With a reaction time of {reaction_time:.2f} seconds and threat speed of {threat_speed:.2f} seconds, survival chance is {chance:.2%}.")
```

Padugol: always has an explanation.

Padugol had to have a good reason to move. It worked as well as he could talk himself out of any trouble.

Sairo: waits for a long time, jumps fast.

Sairo studied catching techniques

```
def underwater_technique(creature):
    techniques = {
        "shark": "ambush",
        "octopus": "camouflage",
        "anglerfish": "luring",
        "dolphin": "herding"
    }
    return techniques.get(creature, "unknown technique")

# Display techniques for different creatures
creatures = ["shark", "octopus", "anglerfish", "dolphin"]
for creature in creatures:
    print(f"{creature.capitalize()}: {underwater_technique(creature)}")
```

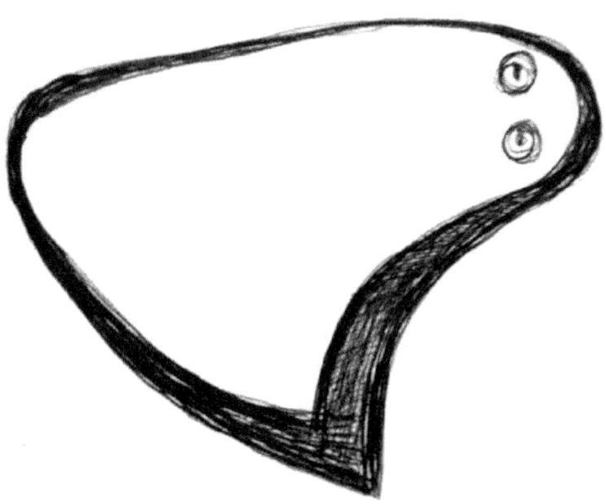

Ipali: goes down, looks up.

Ipali was more intuitive, but not less successful.

Natacosta: has more problems than everyone in the room.

Natacosta was born on a shore

```
def experience_on_shore():
    print("Born on the Shore:")
    print("1. Immediate access to air.")
    print("2. Exposure to sunlight and land.")
    print("3. Easy mobility on land.")
    print("4. Interaction with a variety of terrestrial life.")

def experience_underwater():
    print("\nBorn Underwater:")
    print("1. Immediate access to water.")
    print("2. Exposure to aquatic life and limited sunlight.")
    print("3. Mobility adapted to swimming.")
    print("4. Different sensory experiences (e.g., pressure, sound).")

# Display the differences
experience_on_shore()
experience_underwater()
```

Nozero: wants to get there.

Nozero wanted to enter her space, but there were too many problems present there.

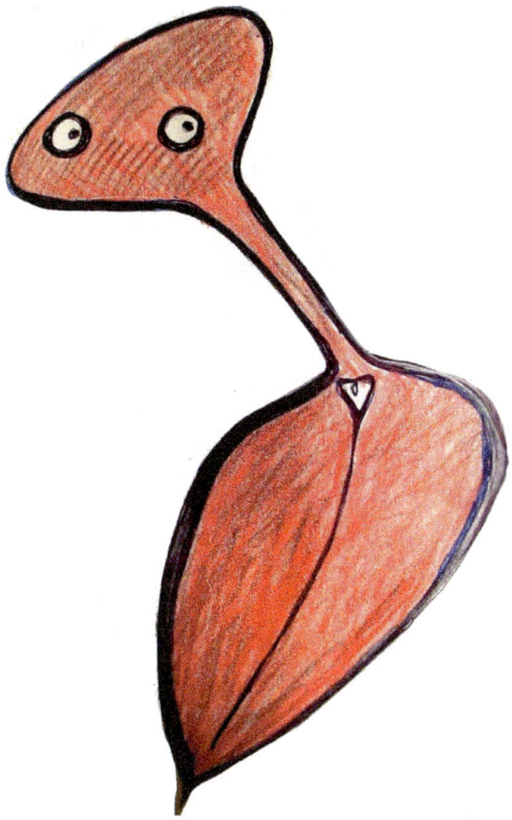

Gunsifo: loves the World.

Gunsifo had a plan for a good living

```
def love_for_world(worldwide_changes,
unexpected_person):

   love = f"Caring deeply about {worldwide_changes} by making small changes."

   if unexpected_person:
      love = f"{unexpected_person} inspired new ways to protect {worldwide_changes}, showing how connection can amplify

   impact."  return love

print(love_for_world("atmospheric conditions action", "a stranger's kindness"))
```

Navacara: always approaches you unexpected.

Navacara believed that all the good things come out of respect.

Gufg: makes ends meet daily.

Gufg wondered how one can live without creating any negative effects.

```
def happy_living():
    tips = [
        "1. Plan meals to stay healthy.",
        "2. Use clean containers and bags.",
        "3. Compost whenever possible for better soil in your garden.",
        "4. Save energy by using food processors.",
        "5. Buy what you need and repurpose old items."
    ]

    for tip in tips:
        print(tip)

happy_living()
```

Nefuhu: waits for his meals to enter his mouth.

Nefuhu had another philosophy: patience.

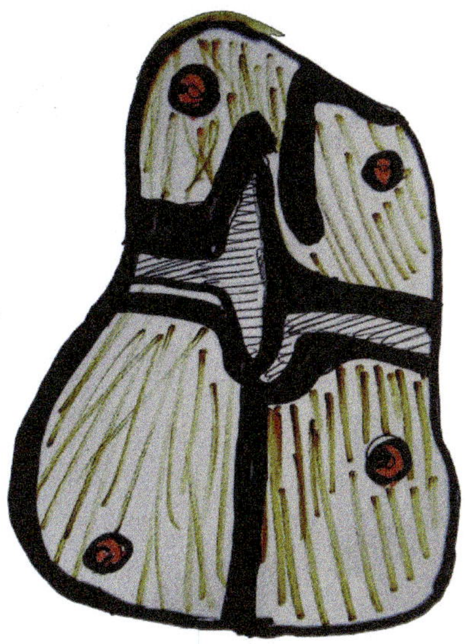

Multipo: collects symmetrical plants.

Multipo has irresistible passions of collecting plants

```
def plant_collection_drawbacks():
    drawbacks = [
        "1. Overharvesting can lead to species extinction.",
        "2. Disturbing ecosystems by removing key plants.",
        "3. Some plants may be toxic or harmful to handle.",
        "4. Collecting rare plants may be illegal or unethical.",
        "5. It can disrupt local wildlife that depend on the plants."

    ]

    for drawback in drawbacks:
        print(drawback)

plant_collection_drawbacks()
```

Inovar: knows his place.

Inovar was more aware.

Rockavere: has lots to remember.

Rockavere tried to be called a decent one

```
def qualities_of_a_decent_being():
    qualities = [
        "1. Treat others with respect and kindness.",
        "2. Act with honesty and integrity.",
        "3. Show empathy and understanding.",
        "4. Help those in need when possible.",
        "5. Take responsibility for actions and mistakes."
    ]

    for quality in qualities:
        print(quality)

qualities_of_a_decent_being()
```

Lasyga: heads Tetrapyloctomy department

Lasyga had too many responsibilities for all of that.

Lq: measures everything he can touch.

Lq's touch was giving him exact numbers

```
def why_not_touch_underwater():
    reasons = [
        "1. Can harm fragile coral reefs.",
        "2. Disturbing marine life may cause stress or injury.",
        "3. Some creatures are toxic or dangerous to touch.",
        "4. Touching can spread bacteria.",
        "5. Risk of disturbing sediments and reducing visibility."
    ]

    for reason in reasons:
        print(reason)

why_not_touch_underwater()
```

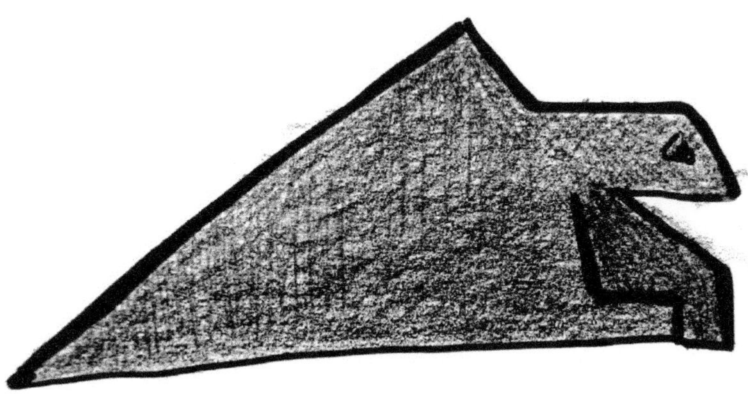

Pacufo: pretends to be a rock.

Pacufo enjoyed the idea but did not like to be touched. He used laser measuring tape. Numbers speak the loudest, they both thought.

Savare: has a nice, round life.

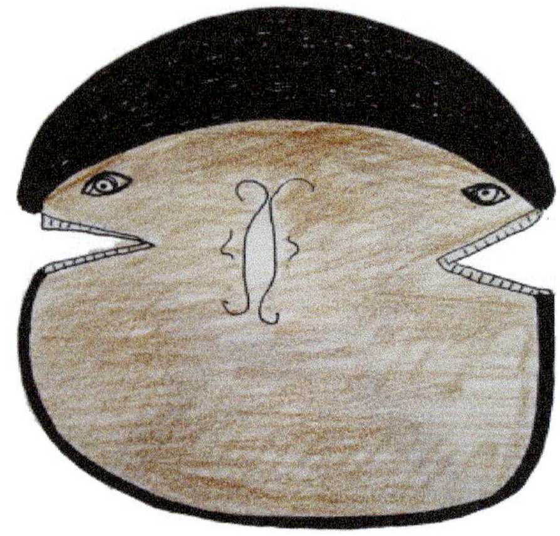

Puturgo: practices comedy and tragedy.

Savare and Puturgo studied wellbeing

```
def nice_round_life():
    meaning = [
        "1. Balance between work, rest, and play.",
        "2. Fulfilling relationships with family and friends.",
        "3. Continuous personal growth and learning.",
        "4. Achieving peace and contentment in daily life.",
        "5. Giving back to the community and helping others."
    ]

    for item in meaning:
        print(item)

nice_round_life()
```

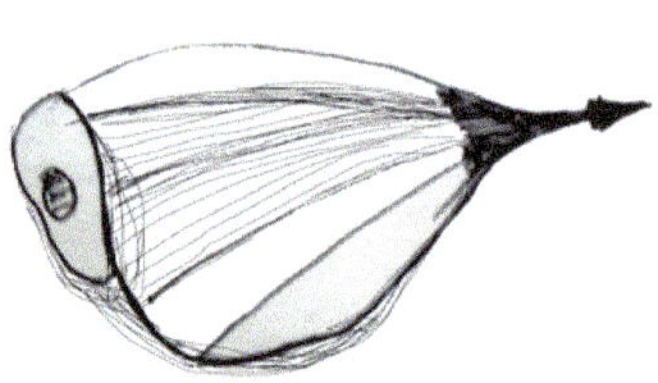

Gufsa: has conflict of interest to solve.

Gufsa is still working on an issue to be able to say so.

Gusadoe: angry, or happy, always hungry.

Gusadoe kept looking for food

```
def why_always_hungry():
    reasons = [
        "1. Not eating enough nutritious food.",
        "2. Dehydration, mistaken for hunger.",
        "3. High-stress levels increasing appetite.",
        "4. Lack of sleep affecting hunger hormones.",
        "5. Eating too many processed foods."
    ]

    for reason in reasons:
        print(reason)

why_always_hungry()
```

Rioun: interested in everybody else's business.

Rioun shared his food-related advice with anyone around.

Nuhaku: holds the waters together for the ocean to decide.

Vacala: knows his place.

Nuhaku and Vacala examined the properties of the two oceans

```
import matplotlib.pyplot as plt
import numpy as np

# Parameters for the two ocean waters
salinity_ocean1 = 35  # Salinity in ppt (parts per thousand)
salinity_ocean2 = 20  # Salinity in ppt
temperature_ocean1 = 10  # Temperature in degrees Celsius
temperature_ocean2 = 25  # Temperature in degrees Celsius

# Create a grid representing the ocean surface
x = np.linspace(0, 10, 100)
y = np.linspace(0, 10, 100)
X, Y = np.meshgrid(x, y)

# Generate a salinity and temperature profile
salinity = np.where(X < 5, salinity_ocean1, salinity_ocean2)
temperature = np.where(X < 5, temperature_ocean1, temperature_ocean2)

# Plot the salinity and temperature profiles
fig, axs = plt.subplots(2, 1, figsize=(10, 8))

# Salinity plot
c1 = axs[0].contourf(X, Y, salinity, levels=20, cmap='Blues')
axs[0].set_title('Salinity Profile of Two Oceans')
axs[0].set_xlabel('Distance')
axs[0].set_ylabel('Depth')
fig.colorbar(c1, ax=axs[0], label='Salinity (ppt)')

# Temperature plot
c2 = axs[1].contourf(X, Y, temperature, levels=20, cmap='RdYlBu')
axs[1].set_title('Temperature Profile of Two Oceans')
axs[1].set_xlabel('Distance')
axs[1].set_ylabel('Depth')
fig.colorbar(c2, ax=axs[1], label='Temperature (°C)')

plt.tight_layout()
plt.show()
```

Lurine: finds a way.

Lurine knew it was all about the Atlantic and Pacific Oceans and that they do mix, despite having different colors..

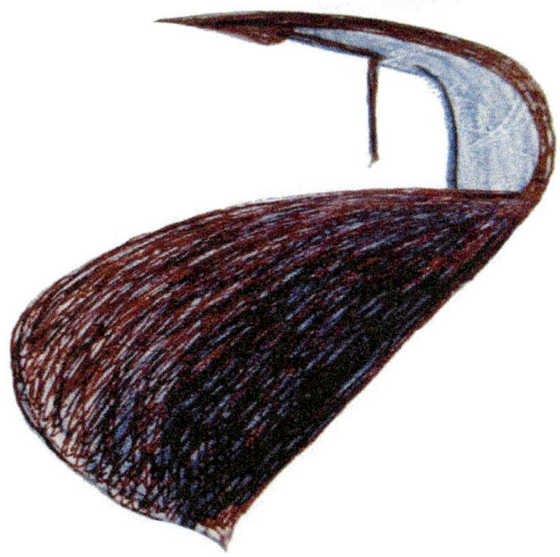

Tikor: thinks twice before biting.

Tikor lost her teeth

```
# Simple simulation of underwater biting and resulting change
def underwater_biting_effects():
    # Initial conditions
    fish_1_energy = 100
    fish_2_energy = 100

    print("Before biting:")
    print(f"Fish 1 energy: {fish_1_energy}")
    print(f"Fish 2 energy: {fish_2_energy}")

    # Biting event
    bite_effect = 10
    fish_1_energy -= bite_effect
    fish_2_energy += bite_effect

    print("\nAfter biting:")
    print(f"Fish 1 energy: {fish_1_energy}")
    print(f"Fish 2 energy: {fish_2_energy}")

underwater_biting_effects()
```

Nahasa: enjoys all the changes.

Nahasa found it in her newly found environment.

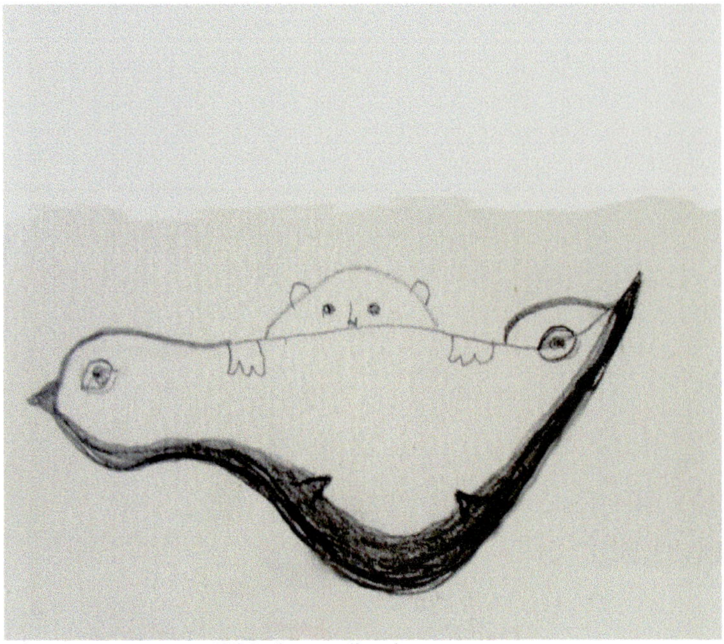

Tiful: changes direction per request.

Tiful wanted to help everyone.

```
# Simple wind pattern change based on temperature and pressure

def wind_pattern_change(temperature, pressure):
    # Base wind speed in km/h
    wind_speed = 20

    # Wind changes due to temperature (higher temperature increases wind speed)
    wind_speed += (temperature - 20) * 0.5  # 0.5 km/h increase per degree above 20°C

    # Wind changes due to pressure (lower pressure increases wind speed)
    wind_speed += (1013 - pressure) * 0.3  # 0.3 km/h increase per unit drop below standard pressure (1013 hPa)

    return wind_speed

# Example: temperature 30°C, pressure 1000 hPa
new_wind_speed = wind_pattern_change(30, 1000)
print(f"New wind speed: {new_wind_speed:.2f} km/h")
```

Uvetis: nothing escapes his sight.

Uvetis recorded each change to generate a database useful for weather forecasting and monitoring for aviators, marines, and agriculture specialists.

Swishfish: the best one in crawl.

Swishfish knew his way around danger

```
# Simulating defense mechanisms of ocean creatures
def defense_mechanism(creature):
    if creature == "octopus":
        return "Releases ink to escape predators."
    elif creature == "pufferfish":
        return "Inflates its body to appear larger."
    elif creature == "clownfish":
        return "Hides in anemones for protection."
    elif creature == "squid":
        return "Uses jet propulsion to escape quickly."
    elif creature == "fish school":
        return "Forms a large group to confuse predators."
    else:
        return "Unknown defense mechanism."

# Example creatures
creatures = ["octopus", "pufferfish", "clownfish", "squid", "fish school"]

# Displaying defense mechanisms
for creature in creatures:
    print(f"The {creature} defense: {defense_mechanism(creature)}")
```

Ranura: feels defended from each side.

Ranura had her very own privileges and tactics.

Radisat: makes an instrument out of anything.

Radisat believes in the power of music

```
def play_music(stress_level):
    # Music reduces stress by 30%
    reduced_stress = stress_level * 0.7
    return reduced_stress

# Example: Individuals with high stress levels
initial_stress = 100  # 100 represents high stress

# Effect of music on stress levels
new_stress_level = play_music(initial_stress)
print(f"Initial stress level: {initial_stress}")
print(f"Stress level after music: {new_stress_level:.2f}")
```

Nacatr: always plays his instrument.

Nacatr agrees: Initial stress level before: 100.00.

Stress level after music: 70.00

Algura: swims his way up.

Algura was the most celebrated one

```
def promotion_strategy(strategy):
    if strategy == "upskilling":
        return "Enhance skills to stay relevant."
    elif strategy == "networking":
        return "Build strong connections and visibility."
    elif strategy == "adaptability":
        return "Adapt quickly to new challenges."
    else:
        return "Unknown strategy."

# Example strategies for promotion
strategies = ["upskilling", "networking", "adaptability"]

for strategy in strategies:
    print(f"{strategy.capitalize()}: {promotion_strategy(strategy)}")
```

Tututsu: stays under the rock.

Tututsu knew about upskilling as enhancing skills to stay relevant, networking as building strong connections and visibility, and adaptability as tailoring quickly to new challenges. However, he preferred to be left alone to focus on things that mattered to him the most.

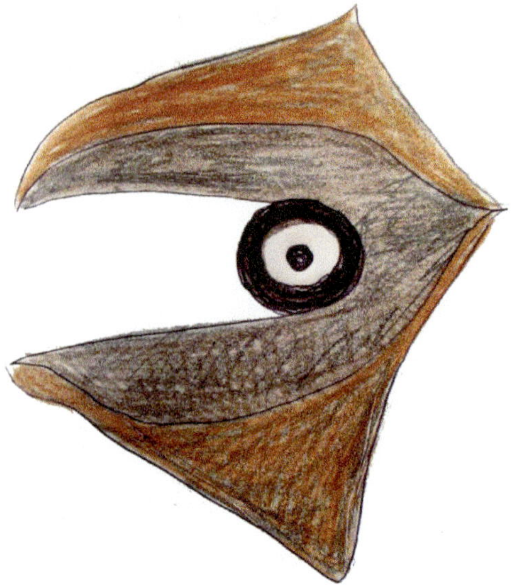

Nurfur: watches what he eats.

Nurfur was a carnivore, but needed more than that

```
def good_eating(food):
    if food == "plant-based":
        return "Healthy meal with vitamins."
    elif food == "meat-based":
        return "Good source of energy."
    else:
        return "Strong impact."

# Example food choices
foods = ["plant-based", "meat-based", "mixed"]

for food in foods:
    print(f"Eating {food} meal: {good_eating(food)}")
```

Wuguru: the best caterer in town.

Wuguru delivers plant-based meals, and meat-based food, and always find those interested, as there are many various creatures deep down the ocean.

Ugarsa: likes watching TV, but not on his phone.

Ugarsa cares about his health

```
def explain_eye_strain():
    reason = """
    Watching TV on a small phone screen for extended periods can strain your eyes.
    This happens because:
    1. Small screens make you focus more intensely, causing eye fatigue.
    2. Blue light emitted from screens can disrupt sleep and strain your eyes.
    3. Holding the phone too close can cause blurry vision or headaches.
    It's important to take breaks and use larger screens for longer viewing sessions.
    """
    return reason

print(explain_eye_strain())
```

Nukaduro: checks his eyes often.

Nukaduro as well.

Mutenego: sings in tune.

Mutenego enjoys singing and thus stays healthy.

```
def explain_singing_health_benefits():
    benefits = """
    Singing has several health benefits:
    1. Improves lung capacity and strengthens the respiratory system.
    2. Reduces stress by lowering cortisol levels, promoting relaxation.
    3. Enhances mood by releasing endorphins and oxytocin, the "feel-good" hormones.
    4. Boosts immune function through improved circulation and oxygen flow.
    5. Provides a mental workout, improving memory and concentration.
    Singing is a fun way to support both physical and mental well-being!
    """
    return benefits

print(explain_singing_health_benefits())
```

Nasetu: grasps best experiences daily.

Nasetu enjoys listening to music and is well too.

Yua: has the power to change the direction of a river.

Yua wanted water to be fresh

```
def change_river_direction(action):
    if action == "build dam":
        return "River flow is blocked and redirected."
    elif action == "dig channel":
        return "River flows into a new direction."
    else:
        return "No significant change to river flow."

# Example actions to change river direction
actions = ["build dam", "dig channel", "do nothing"]

for action in actions:
    print(f"Action: {action.capitalize()} - Result: {change_river_direction(action)}")
```

Yufabo: knows how to hide.

Yufabo was careful and thus was.

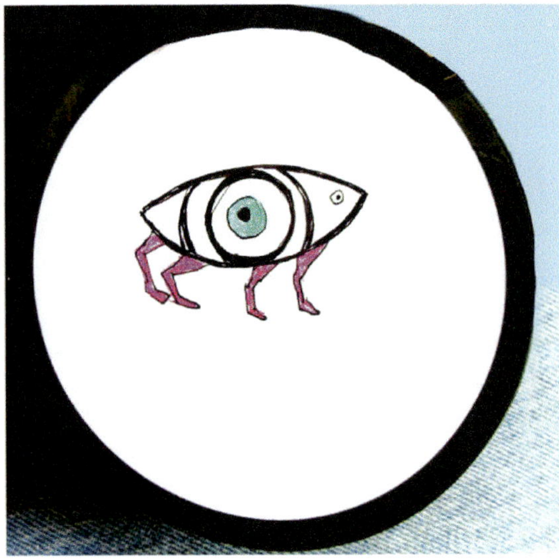

Ioma: sees in and out.

Ioma was "seeing in" (self-reflection) and "seeing out" (awareness of the external world).

```
def see_in_and_out(perspective):
    if perspective == "see in":
        return "Focus on self-reflection and personal growth."
    elif perspective == "see out":
        return "Observe the external world and its challenges."
    else:
        return "Balance both for a broader perspective."

# Example: reflecting on both internal and external perspectives
perspectives = ["see in", "see out", "balance"]

for perspective in perspectives:
    print(f"{perspective.capitalize()}: {see_in_and_out(perspective)}")
```

Wubutu: open, but in a shell. Why?

Wubutu hoped for both perspectives for better understanding.

Feja: measured things with his favorite fish.

Feja was precise

```
def measure_with_fish(object_length, fish_length=30):
    # Object length and fish length are in centimeters
    fish_units = object_length / fish_length
    return f"The object is equivalent to {fish_units:.2f} fish lengths."

# Example: Measure an object that is 150 cm long
object_length = 150
print(measure_with_fish(object_length))
```

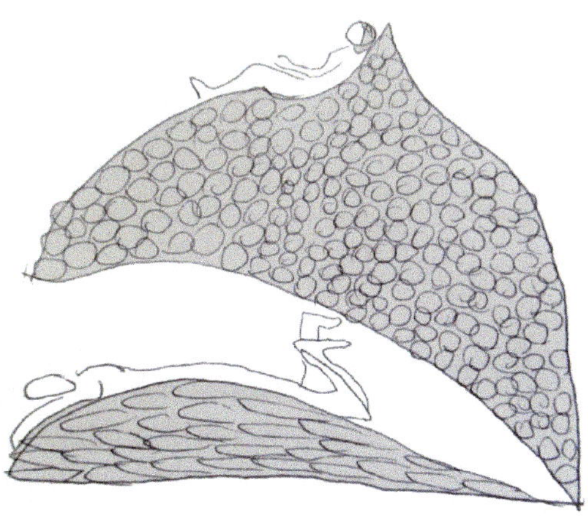

Vadsco: information from up and down matched.

Vadsco was a collaborator. Instead of saying "The object is equivalent to 5.00 fish lengths," they say "The fish approaching is five times its length from us.

Munfa: will always charm you.

Munfa liked spending time with Tagisa

```
def charm_effect(situation):
    if situation == "positive":
        return "Charm builds strong relationships and trust."
    elif situation == "negative":
        return "Charm can be manipulative and misleading."
    else:
        return "Outcome depends on how charm is used."

# Example situations
situations = ["positive", "negative", "neutral"]

for situation in situations:
    print(f"{situation.capitalize()} situation: {charm_effect(situation)}")
```

Tagisa: wears a hat to be able to use it as a diguise.

Tagisa had a problem with Munifa's charming way.

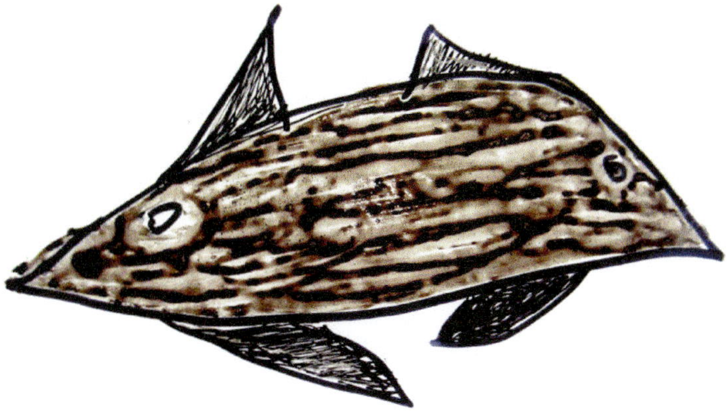

Surieria: has enough money to swim both ways.

Surieria could be careless.

```
def water_current_direction(factor):
    if factor == "wind":
        return "Current changes with the wind direction."
    elif factor == "tides":
        return "Current shifts with rising and falling tides."
    elif factor == "temperature":
        return "Temperature differences cause current to change."
    else:
        return "Current remains steady."

# Example factors affecting water current
factors = ["wind", "tides", "temperature", "steady"]

for factor in factors:
    print(f"Factor: {factor.capitalize()} - {water_current_direction(factor)}")
```

Turdu: invincible one

Turdu was well-versed in natural factors.

Vadarasa: can go faster than he was able to go yesterday.

Vadarasa was all about the sport and exercise

```
def reasons_to_exercise():
    reasons = [
        "1. Exercise improves circulation, aligning with natural body rhythms.",
        "2. Strengthens muscles, promoting natural movement and posture.",
        "3. Enhances lung capacity, supporting healthy breathing patterns.",
        "4. Boosts energy levels, matching the body's need for physical exertion.",
        "5. Promotes mental clarity, following the mind-body connection."
    ]

    for reason in reasons:
        print(reason)

reasons_to_exercise()
```

Hagaga: can swim and fly.

Hagaga surpassed the idea that exercising supports our alignment with natural laws, such as bodily functions and mental well-being.

Rudoko: gathers food for later, but forgets to eat.

Rudoko was a hard worker.

```
# Simple Python explanation of why wasting food harms the Earth

def food_waste_impact(food_wasted, energy_used, water_wasted):
    # Calculating environmental impact
    total_energy = food_wasted * energy_used
    total_water = food_wasted * water_wasted
    return total_energy, total_water

# Example data: Food wasted in kilograms, energy used (kWh/kg), water wasted (liters/kg)
food_wasted = 10  # 10 kg of food wasted
energy_used = 5   # 5 kWh used per kg of food produced
water_wasted = 5000  # 5000 liters of water used per kg of food produced

energy, water = food_waste_impact(food_wasted, energy_used, water_wasted)

print(f"Wasting {food_wasted} kg of food wastes {energy} kWh of energy and {water} liters of water.")

# Output: Wasting food leads to wasted energy and water resources, which harms the environment.
```

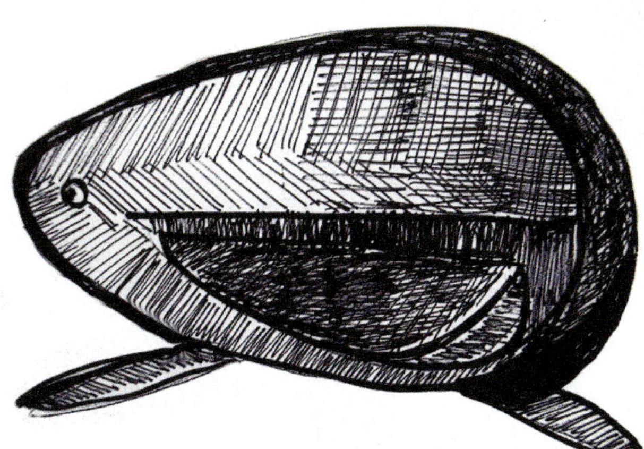

Wozaga: saves food for the next hour.

Wozaga said wasting food also wastes energy and water, essential planet resources, which worried her as a water creature.

Tuka: just came out of an egg.

Tuka hatched!

```
class UnderwaterUnimal:
    def __init__(self, name, reason_for_hatching):
        self.name = name
        self.reason_for_hatching = reason_for_hatching

    def hatch(self):
        print(f"{self.name} has hatched! Reason: {self.reason_for_hatching}")

# Creating an instance of an underwater unimal
unimal = UnderwaterUnimal("AquaSerpent", "to explore new underwater territories")
unimal.hatch()
```

Lireto: hears and looks when busy.

Lireto was there to welcome her underwater.

Sunuta: enjoys tea.

Sunta was very healthy because she knew different kinds of teas and their benefits

```
teas = {
    "Green Tea": "Rich in antioxidants, improves brain function, boosts metabolism",
    "Black Tea": "Supports heart health, boosts energy, improves gut health",
    "Chamomile Tea": "Reduces stress, aids sleep, improves digestion",
    "Peppermint Tea": "Soothes digestive issues, relieves headaches, boosts concentration",
    "Ginger Tea": "Eases nausea, reduces inflammation, boosts immunity",
    "Oolong Tea": "Boosts metabolism, improves mental alertness, promotes heart health",
    "Rooibos Tea": "Rich in antioxidants, promotes heart health, reduces inflammation",
    "Hibiscus Tea": "Lowers blood pressure, supports liver health, rich in vitamin C",
    "White Tea": "Rich in antioxidants, improves skin health, may reduce the risk of heart disease",
    "Earl Grey Tea": "Boosts energy, improves digestion, may reduce anxiety"
}

# Displaying the types of teas and their benefits
for tea, benefit in teas.items():
print(f"{tea}: {benefit}")
```

Nagadu: keeps her fingers crossed.

Nagadu hopes so and thus follows her.

Tumfu: knows where to go to see beauty.

Tumfu was beautiful inside

```
class BeautyExposure:
    def __init__(self, individual_benefit, planet_benefit):
        self.individual_benefit = individual_benefit
        self.planet_benefit = planet_benefit

    def explain(self):
        print(f"Beauty nurtures individuals by: {self.individual_benefit}")
        print(f"Beauty supports the planet by: {self.planet_benefit}")

# Defining the benefits of beauty exposure
benefits = BeautyExposure(
    individual_benefit="inspiring peace, well-being, and creativity",
    planet_benefit="motivating people to protect and preserve nature"

)

# Explaining why beauty supports both
benefits.explain()
```

Talta: they say she has a good taste.

Talta saw personal well-being and planetary care as one.

Navico: gathers old keys and tries them all.

Navico understands the world, as he imagines

```
def security_risk_assessment(cyber_threats, physical_threats, data_privacy_issues):
    # Assess overall security risks based on current universal challenges
    total_risk = cyber_threats + physical_threats + data_privacy_issues
    return total_risk

# Example data: Threat levels (scale 1-10)
cyber_threats = 9          # High risk of cyber-attacks
physical_threats = 7       # Moderate risk of physical security threats
data_privacy_issues = 8    # Significant concern for data privacy

total_risk = security_risk_assessment(cyber_threats, physical_threats, data_privacy_issues)

print(f"The overall security risk in today's world is {total_risk}/30, highlighting the need for strong security measures.")

# Output: Security is crucial in today's world to protect against cyber threats, physical dangers, and data privacy issues.
```

Sunugas: one can tell when she's unhappy.

Sunugas can distinguish between cyber threats, physical dangers, and data privacy concerns, which helps her stay safe.

Lasto: covered his tracks but once.

Lasto was always changing his path

```
def discover_hidden_traces(hidden_logs, digital_footprints):
    # Combine hidden logs and digital ss to reveal activities
    uncovered_info = hidden_logs + digital_footprints
    return uncovered_info

# Example data: Hidden logs and digital footprints (scale 1-10)
hidden_logs = 6           # Partially hidden actions (e.g., deleted data)
digital_footprints = 8    # Traces left behind (e.g., IP logs, metadata)

uncovered = discover_hidden_traces(hidden_logs, digital_footprints)

print(f"Despite covering tracks, {uncovered}/20 information can still be uncovered through hidden logs and digital footprints.")

# Output: Even after covering tracks, digital footprints, and hidden logs can reveal the truth.
```

Adeia: knows the basic rules and observes them.

Adeia knows that despite attempts to hide evidence, traces like digital footprints or hidden logs can still lead to discovery.

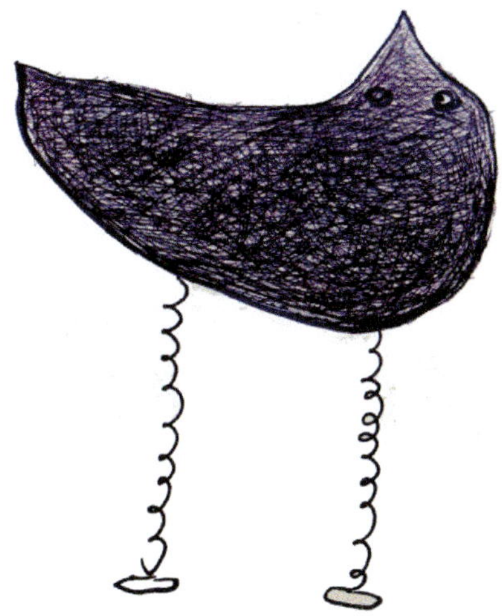

Huforado: jumpy, but sits still.

Huforado studied types of danger, physical threats, cyber ones, and natural disasters

```
def escape_options(danger_level):
    if danger_level == "physical":
        return ["Run to safety", "Find shelter", "Call for help"]
    elif danger_level == "cyber":
        return ["Disconnect from the network", "Change passwords", "Alert authorities"]
    elif danger_level == "natural disaster":
        return ["Evacuate area", "Follow emergency procedures", "Stay informed"]
    else:
        return ["Stay calm", "Assess the situation", "Look for safe exits"]

# Example danger level
danger_level = "physical"
ways_to_escape = escape_options(danger_level)

print(f"Ways to escape {danger_level} danger: {', '.join(ways_to_escape)}")
```

Atam: goes down the drain when in danger.

Atam developed his very own solutions.

Vagada: collects all she can see.

Varada was collecting objects to explain gravity

```
# Simulate gravity by collecting objects falling towards a center point
import math

# Function to calculate the distance between two objects
def distance(obj1, obj2):
    return math.sqrt((obj1['x'] - obj2['x'])**2 + (obj1['y'] - obj2['y'])**2)

# Simulate objects in space
objects = [
    {'name': 'Object 1', 'x': 5, 'y': 7},
    {'name': 'Object 2', 'x': -4, 'y': 3},
    {'name': 'Object 3', 'x': 2, 'y': -8}
]

# Define a center of gravity (e.g., Earth's core)
center_of_gravity = {'x': 0, 'y': 0}

# Collect objects by simulating gravity pulling them towards the center
for obj in objects:
    dist = distance(obj, center_of_gravity)
    print(f"{obj['name']} is {dist:.2f} units away from the center of gravity")
```

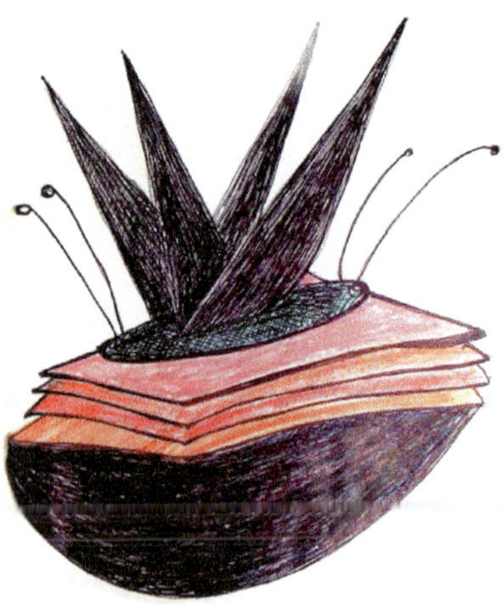

Satada: developed a deep sense of gravity.

Satada knew how gravity pulls things together towards the center of gravity, like how we "collect" objects.

Stzula: hides her own interior.

Stzula understood the opportunity or space to be kind

```
# Function to simulate friendliness based on permission
def be_friendly(allowed):
    if allowed:
        return "Hey there! How are you doing? 😊"
    else:
        return "I respect your space. No worries!"

# Example of allowing or not allowing friendliness
permission = True  # Change to False to see the other response

print(be_friendly(permission))
```

Olai: friendly when you let him.

Olai understood its practical applications.

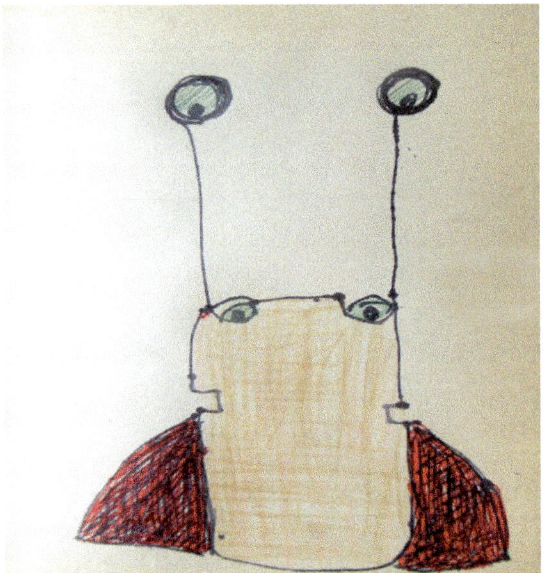

Kasu: sees above it all.

Kasu saw flying as a broader perspective

```
# Define actions for swimming and flying
def move(mode):
    if mode == "swim":
        return "Underwater, you see limited."
    elif mode == "fly":
        return "Above, you see everything clearly."

# Simulate both swimming and flying
swimming = move("swim")
flying = move("fly")

print(f"Swimming: {swimming}")
print(f"Flying: {flying}")
```

Vustu: very good swimmer, but can fly as well.

Vustu saw swimming as the only but somehow limiting.

Putagua: solves everybody's problems by digesting them.

P utagua forgets to ask if they want help before acting

```
        return "Listen carefully to understand the issue"
    elif approach == "empathize":
        return "Show empathy and put yourself in their shoes"
    elif approach == "offer_solution":
        return "Suggest practical and thoughtful solutions"
    elif approach == "follow_up":
        return "Follow up to ensure the problem is fully resolved"
    else:
        return "Offer emotional support and guidance"

# Example: solving a friend's problem
problem = "friend's stress at work"
chosen_approach = "empathize"

response = solve_problem(problem, chosen_approach)

print(f"To solve the problem of {problem}, you should: {response}.")
```

Okeon: conected, but independent.

O keon never had problems or was not aware of them.

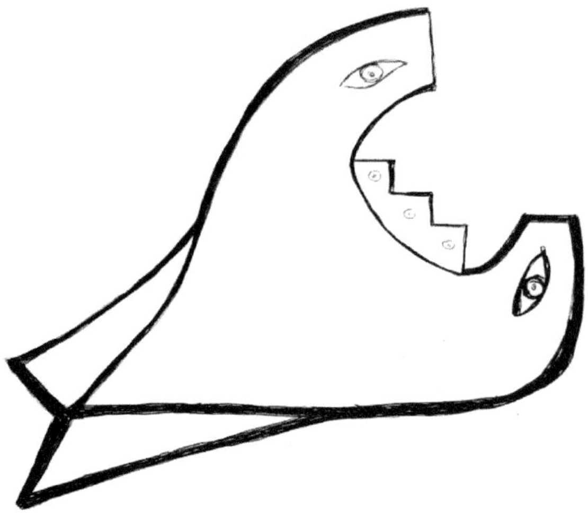

Hynju: watches what he eats.

Hynju knows foods that are good for one's teeth

```
def foods_for_healthy_teeth():
    # List of foods that promote good dental health
    return [
        "Apples - stimulate saliva production, cleansing teeth",
        "Cheese - rich in calcium and promotes strong teeth",
        "Carrots - scrub teeth surfaces, improve gum health",
        "Yogurt - high in calcium, strengthens enamel",
        "Leafy greens - rich in vitamins that support gum health",
        "Almonds - low in sugar, high in calcium",
        "Celery - naturally cleans teeth and stimulates gums"
    ]

# Display the list of teeth-friendly foods
healthy_foods = foods_for_healthy_teeth()

print("Foods that are good for your teeth:")
for food in healthy_foods:
    print(f"- {food}")
```

Rigate: cleans his teeth four times a day.

Rigate knows to clean them after eating.

Natraem: lost things that cannot be replaced.

Natraem thought he kept losing things

```
class MentalHealth:
    def __init__(self):
        self.stress_level = 0

    def lose_item(self, item):
        print(f"Oh no! You lost your {item}.")
        self.stress_level += 10  # Losing things increases stress

    def check_health(self):
        if self.stress_level > 20:
            return "High stress levels can lead to anxiety and poor health."
        elif self.stress_level > 10:
            return "You're getting stressed. Losing things frequently isn't good for your well-being."
        else:
            return "You're managing stress well. Keep things organized!"

# Simulate losing items
health = MentalHealth()
health.lose_item("keys")
print(health.check_health())

health.lose_item("wallet")
print(health.check_health())
```

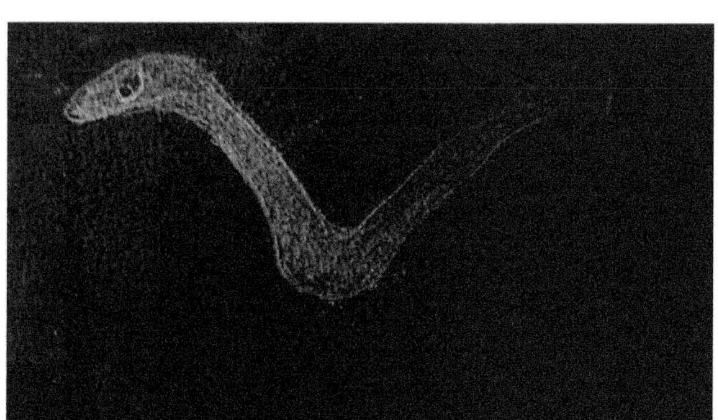

Taslar: appears and dissapears.

Taslar was just too playful.

Vusado: solves everything with some help of a fish.

Vusado and

Vugu: stepped twice into the pool.

Vugu

heard about the squid's ability to change color using chromatophores, and possible costumes that can adapt to its surroundings by leveraging its color-changing ability to match the environment, making the costume "invisible."

```
class Squid:
    def camouflage(self, environment):
        return environment  # Squid matches the environment color

# Simulating the costume inspired by squid
def invisibility_costume(squid, environment):
    return squid.camouflage(environment)

squid = Squid()
print("Costume color:", invisibility_costume(squid, "ocean blue"))  # Costume becomes "ocean blue"
```

Muchelo: blends in with everything.

Muchelo liked it but his head, and hands kept showing up.

Hrulo: never needs a mirror.

Hrulo kept checking his state of being, as he felt that he was handsome

```
class Mirror:
    def __init__(self):
        self.purpose = "self-reflection"

    def reflect(self, person):
        return f"{person}, the mirror shows not just your appearance, but also helps you reflect on your inner self."

# Demonstrating the importance of a mirror
my_mirror = Mirror()
print(my_mirror.reflect("In life"))
```

Onocha: never backs up.

Onocha believed in self-reflection and personal growth.

Navaracha: very clean and organized.

Navaracha liked to feel decorated

```
class Ring:
    def __init__(self, significance):
        self.significance = significance

    def explain_importance(self):
        return f"Wearing a ring is important because it symbolizes {self.significance}."

# Creating a ring with general significance
any_ring = Ring("personal or cultural values, commitments, or milestones")
print(any_ring.explain_importance())
```

Nattfen: lives on her finger.

Nattfen was filled with love

```
def importance_of_ring(ring):

    return f"Wearing a {ring} symbolizes commitment and connection."

print(importance_of_ring("ring"))
```

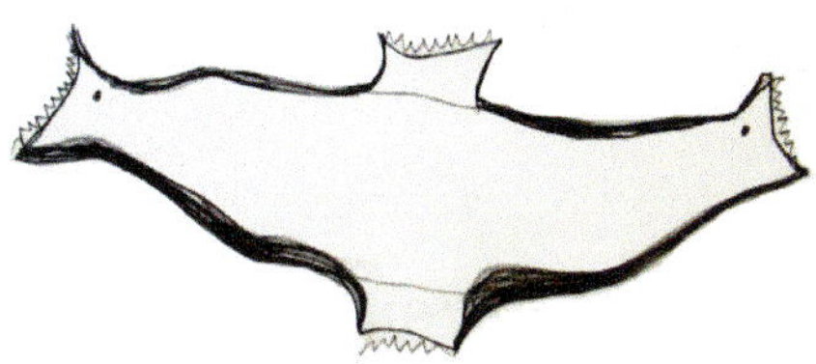

Puchera: watches what he eats.

Unara: holds her baby tight.

P uchera and ∪ mara

are expecting a child

```
class HealthyEating:
    def __init__(self, diet_type):
        self.diet_type = diet_type

    def nutrition_advice(self):
        if self.diet_type == "general":
            return "Eat a balanced diet with a variety of fruits, vegetables, whole grains, and proteins."
        elif self.diet_type == "pregnancy":
            return ("In addition to a balanced diet, include extra folic acid, iron, calcium, and DHA for fetal development. "
                    "Stay hydrated and avoid certain foods like raw seafood and unpasteurized dairy.")
        else:
            return "Unknown diet type."

# Example of healthy eating advice
general_diet = HealthyEating("general")
pregnancy_diet = HealthyEating("pregnancy")

print("General Healthy Eating Advice:")
print(general_diet.nutrition_advice())
print("\nPregnancy Healthy Eating Advice:")
print(pregnancy_diet.nutrition_advice())
```

And now they had a different lifestyle

```
def lifestyle_tips(stage):
    return ("Balanced diet, exercise, and stress management."
            if stage == "general"
            else "Prenatal care, extra nutrients, avoid harmful substances.")

print("General Lifestyle:", lifestyle_tips("general"))
print("Pregnancy Lifestyle:", lifestyle_tips("pregnancy"))
```

Trees. © 2025 by Matylda Czarnecka. (Used with permission).

CHAPTER 3
AIR – FLY, BREATH ELATION

Flying, flocking, traveling, migrating, or sending a camera on a drone to provide a bird's eye view can be stimulating, or we drop something from a drone. We go above the planet. We have tools to record, and predict, but not prevent. We developed new ways of transportation and leisure time. We look at flying species to observe and learn from. We can mimic nature. Some wait for the jetpacks to commute.
To build a mental map and navigate, pigeons sense the magnetic field, read the stars, track the sun, hear infrasound, follow smells, and (unknown) more, all integrated with a precise clock. They build a corridor to fly using their sight; they follow rivers, hills, roads, buildings, and other landmarks.

Onugso: never runs from any metheorological events.

Nagura: his umbrella follows him when he walks.

Onguso and Nagura were protected.

```
class Umbrella:
    def follow(self, person):
        print(f"{person} is protected, no need to run from the weather!")

# Example usage
umbrella = Umbrella()
umbrella.follow("Nagura")
```

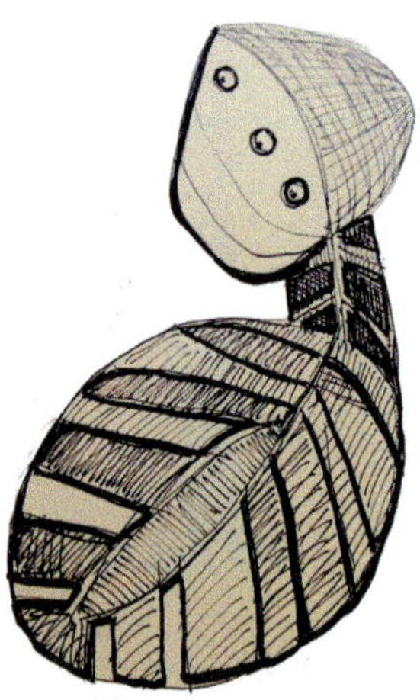

Lagura: knew some ways to hide when needed.

Murachundo: smiles when seeing things.

Lagura and Murachundo have different tactics for suddenly approaching weather events

```
def prepare_for_weather(event):
    if event in ["storm", "flood", "heatwave"]:
        print(f"Preparing for {event}. Stay safe and follow protocols.")
    else:
        print("Weather is calm. No action needed.")

prepare_for_weather("storm")
```

Yunda: keeps his notes very high.

Natawacho: exercises his voice six times a day.

Yunda & and Natawacho had to work on their voices.

```
def high_notes_explanation():
   print("High notes strain vocal cords, causing discomfort.")

def voice_exercise():
   print("Exercise by warming up with lower notes and gradually increasing pitch.")
# Example usage
high_notes_explanation()
voice_exercise()
```

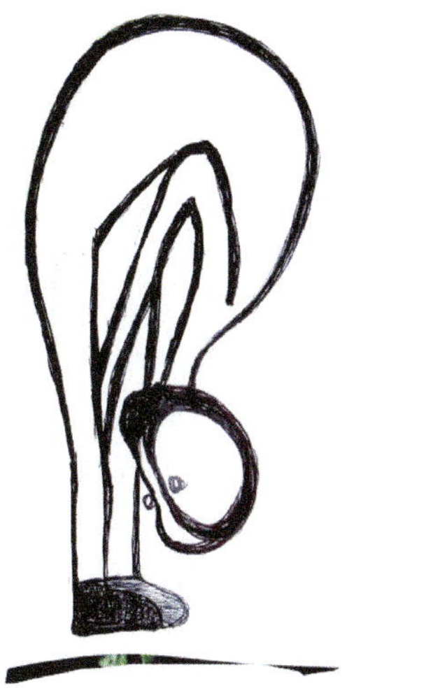

Nargeni: keeps loosing strings after 4 p.m.

Navagara: has more strength that she wishes to use.

but Nargeni told Navagara:

```
def high_pitch_hurts_vocal_cords():
   print("High pitch (excessive noise, foulness) disrupts harmony.")

def adjust_voice_for_health():
   print("Lower the pitch: act mindfully and reduce the impact.")
# Example usage
high_pitch_hurts_vocal_cordst()
adjust_voice_for_vocal_cords()
```

Sareta: she flew in her knowing hat.

Suaga: stays put, unless he wants to say something.

Sareta and Suaga had different viewpoints on being helpful.

Yubty: watches his own business.

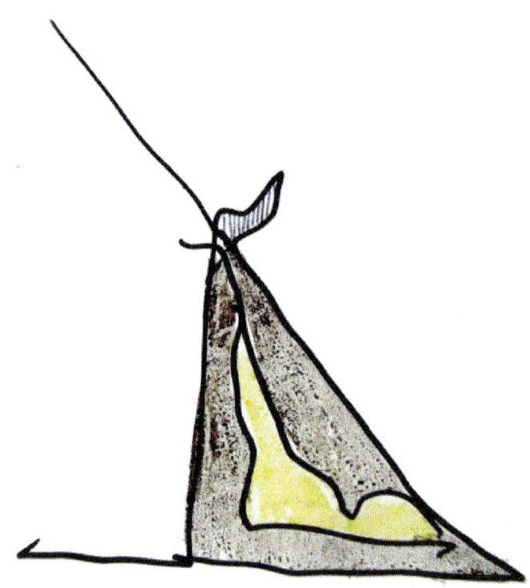

Sotudga: oficially is a shape-shifter, but not really.

So did Yubty and Sotudga despite their different upbringing.

class KnowingHat:
  def give_advice(self, question):
    print(f"Question: {question}")
    return "The hat says: Trust your instincts, knowledge will follow."
 	
# Using the knowing hat 	
hat = KnowingHat()
response = hat.give_advice("Should I explore the unknown?")
print(response)
	def speak_or_stay(message):
	  if message:
	    print(f"Saying: {message}")
	  else:
	    print("Staying silent...")
	
	# Example usage
	speak_or_stay("") # Stays silent
	speak_or_stay("I have something important to share.") # Speaks

Tesar: knows when to appear.

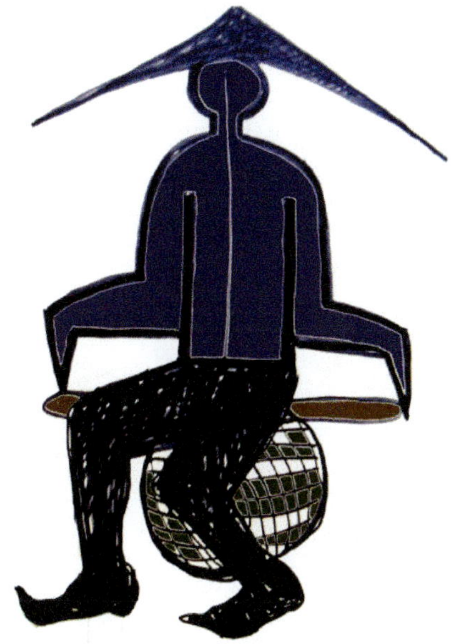

Vusure: wants to make the whole globe available to anyone.

Tesar and Vusure had separate methods of leadership: timely presence and sharing of resources.

```
class Ruler:
    def rule_by_appearing(self):
        print("Appears at the right time to guide.")

    def rule_by_sharing_globe(self):
        print("Make knowledge and resources. shared")

# Example usage
ruler = Ruler()
ruler.rule_by_appearing()
ruler.rule_by_sharing_globe()
```

Nemuka: dances as a trio.

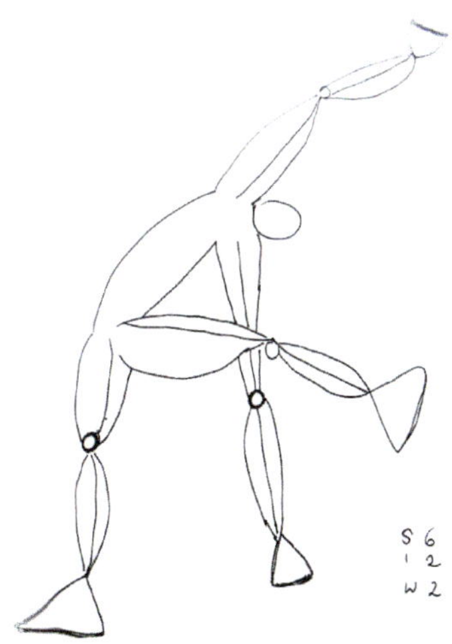

Nutugon: does measuring for anyone who'd ask.

Nemuka and Nutugon governed by entertaining and providing service.

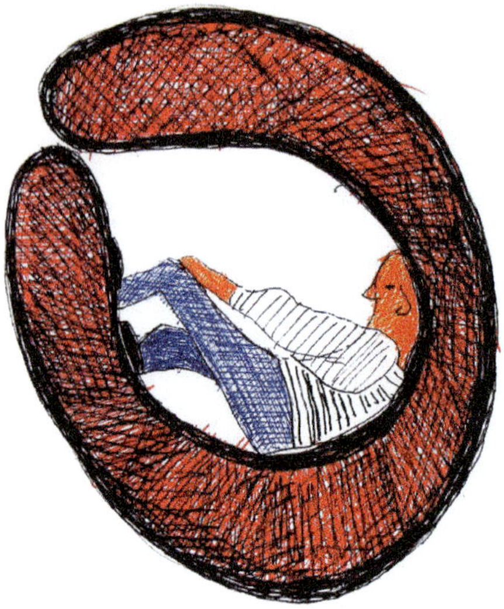

Pukeo: struggles with motions.

P ukeo and

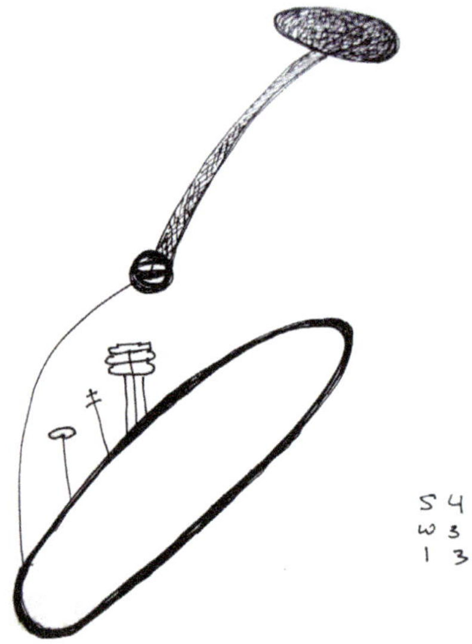

Patug: collects gadgets others bring from their travels.

P atug

traveled for their own reasons.

Mysifa: talks to her tail.

M ysifa and

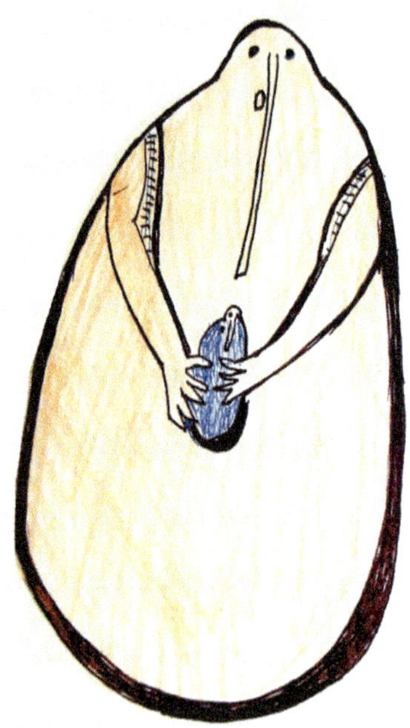

Mufo: has a look-alike doll he talks to.

M uho

had their ways to get inspiration

def serve_by_talking_to_tail():
    print("Talking to the tail to entertain and serve others!")
# Example usage 	
serve_by_talking_to_tail()
	def talk_to_lookalike():
	    print("Conversation with the look-alike replaces the need for travel!")
	# Example usage
	talk_to_lookalike()

Nafuta: was born in a tree and become one.

Ritasa: can highlight the most important issues.

Nafuta and Riasa both saw nourishing the soil as a critical issue

```
def leaf_cycle():
    print("The fallen leaf decomposes, nourishes the soil, and supports new growth.")

# Example usage
leaf_cycle()
```

Jadera: could sense the closest source of water.

Linho: moves fast with the wind.

Jadera and Linho saw water and air as more important.

Makula: catches flies to talk to them about climate change related issues.

Makula and

Bufe: is aware of political trends and issues among the bees.

Mbufe

research insects' perceptions of the recent changes

```
def insect_perception(change):
    print(f"Insects sense: {change}")
# Example usage
insect_perception("adapting flight patterns food scarcity shelter.")
```

Bacepa - Understands flow

Bacepa and

Mosu: watches it all.

Mosu

thought that it was about the flow. Insects are important in the food chain!

```
def land_flow(change):
    print(f"Land flow shifts with: {change}")
# Example usage
land_flow("need to travel.")
```

Casfoda: a portable friend.

C asfoda and

Facilia: likes to try new outfits.

F acilia

were all about personal comfort

```
def comfort_vs_awareness(comfort, awareness):
    print(f"Balancing personal comfort: {comfort}, with atmospheric conditions change awareness:
{awareness}.")  # Example usage
comfort_vs_awareness("producing plastic toys ", " staying fashionable and unique ")
```

Hugala: never gets wet.

H ugala and

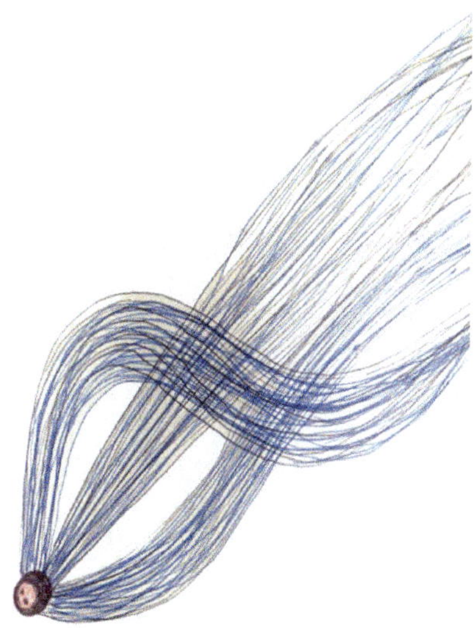

Lostre: moves straight by changing directios.

L ostre

were focused on more practical responses:

```
def comfort_vs_inventions(comfort, invention):
    print(f"Comfort: {comfort}, Inventions for living well {invention}")
# Example usage
comfort_vs_inventions("not getting wet", "umbrella that follows you"")
```

Kintor: mixes air for better breathing .

Arundo: takes off stright up.

Kintor and Arundo

were looking for solutions

```
def deal_with_pollen(action):
    print(f"Dealing with pollen by: {action}")

# Example usage
deal_with_pollen("wearing a mask and planting trees")
```

Asotta: could talk without a break.

Derewi: has power to swim in air.

Asotta and Derewi

did not mind seasonal changes at all.

Funkau: Performs when feeling happy.

Farul: invented new muscle relaxation techniques.

Funkau and Farul

thought that all the solutions were in finding joy and performance

```
def solutions(joy, performance):
    print(f"Solutions are found in joy: {joy} and performance: {performance}")

# Example usage
solutions("creative expression", "focused effort")
```

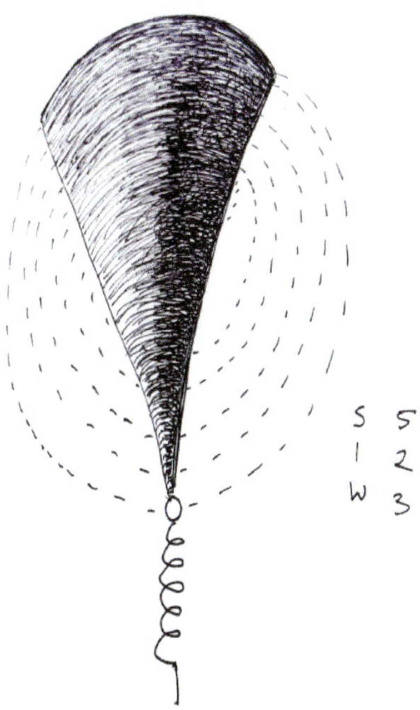

Lerek: always does what he wants.

Inang: always enjoys winning with himself.

Lerek and Inang

believed in playfulness, joy, and knowledge.

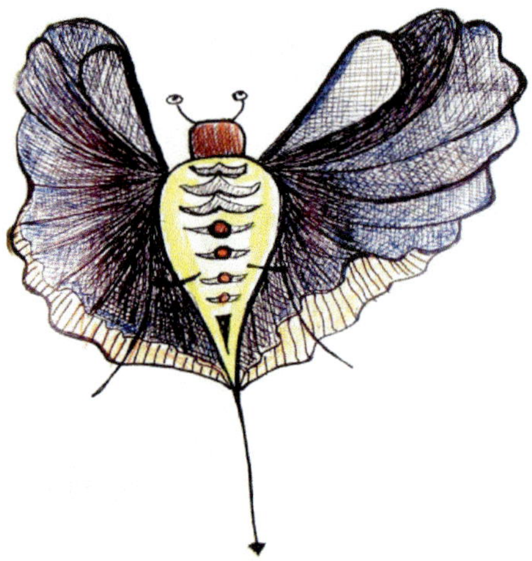

Hakosy: calculates time to see the date.

Hakosy and

Agnucio: smells everything before tasting it.

Hutengo

did not trust anyone

```
def decision_style(style):
    if style == "check everything":
        return "Delayed: Overthinking decisions."
    else:
        return "Efficient: Finds solutions independently."

# Examples
print(decision_style("check everything"))
print(decision_style("trust and solve"))
```

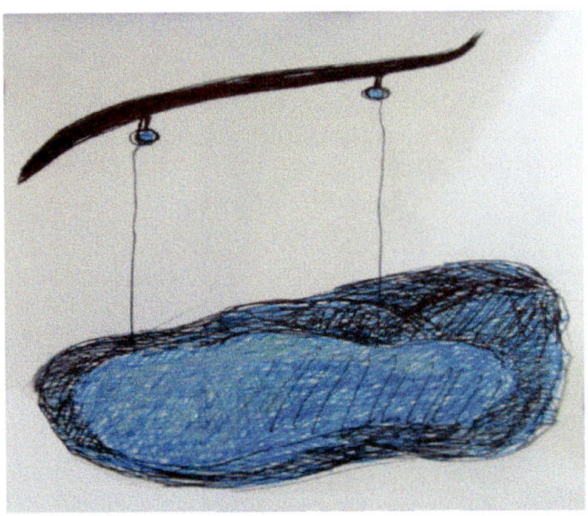

Dang: can move the clouds around.

Agnucio and

Huterago: fast, flexible, and observant, but sleepy.

Dang

find their own solutions to any problems one might imagine

```
import time

def advanced_solution(data): return sorted(data, reverse=True)
def basic_solution(data): return sorted(data)

data = [5, 3, 8, 6, 2]

# Measure and print execution time for both solutions
for func in [advanced_solution, basic_solution]:
    start = time.time()
    func(data)
    print(f"{func.__name__} took {time.time() - start:.6f} seconds")
```

Hacelo: can fly when needed.

H acelo and

Hatu: dances on one leg.

H atu possessed special skills.

Avaraga: knew three kings, and discussed winds with them all.

A varga and

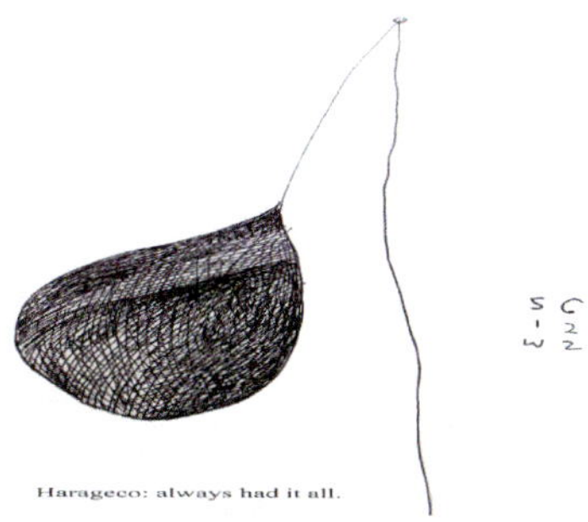

Harageco: always had it all.

H arageco had connections and possessions

```
def contribute_to_community(resource):
    if resource in ["talent", "skills", "connections", "possessions"]:
        return f"Using {resource} to create positive impact on the community!"
    else:
        return "Start by using what you have to help neighbors."
# Examples
print(contribute_to_community("talent"))
print(contribute_to_community"connections"))
```

They all were doing good things for everyone.

Lekufq: likes to sleep over.

L ekufg and

Laxura: sees it all even during her sleep.

L axura wished they could.

Iffas: she was showing up for a glimpse, whenever was needed.

Iffas and

Gifa: always checks behind her.

S5
I3
W2

Giffa

were on alert

```
def impact_on_friends(state):
    if state == "on alert":
        return " Stress leads to wrong habits."
    else:
        return "Balanced: Mindful actions benefit friends."
# Examples
print(impact_on_friends("on alert"))
print(impact_on_friends("safe"))
```

Jaguram: feels the earth from above.

Jaguram and

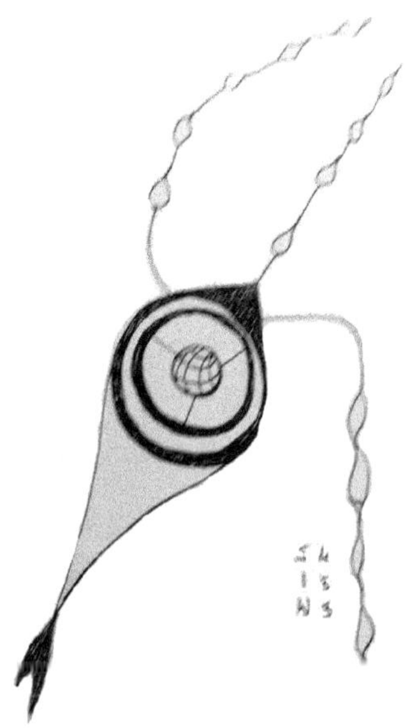

Geluna: collects signals, then sends them away.

Geluna

knew how to relax and when.

Hads: has not enough rain.

Hags and

Datlopu: always has control.

Datlopu knew what they wanted.

```
def approach_knowledge(style):
    if style == "collect data":
        return "Overwhelmed: Too much info, unclear direction."
    else:
        return "Focused: Knows what's needed, efficient progress."
# Examples
print(approach_knowledge("collect data"))
print(approach_knowledge("know what you need"))
```

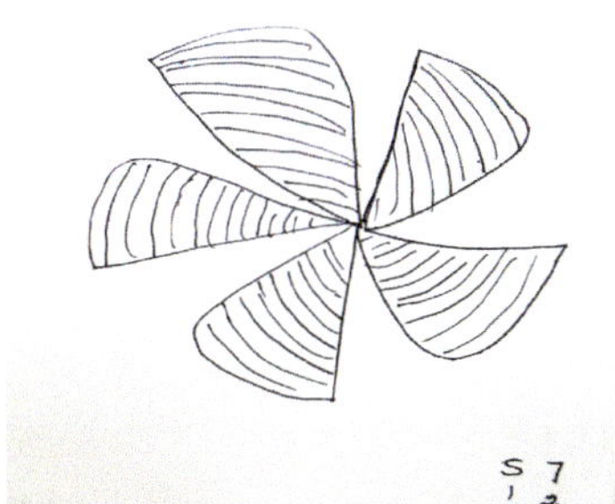

Bysada: does not matter how much.

Bysada and

Catond: always picks up the best crop.

Catond had whatever they wanted.

Lezeter: remembers when there was no Internet.

Lezeter and

Madalo: never knew if he rode on his bike or on a claud.

Madalo had a lot of experience

```
def support_life(have):
    if have == "all I want":
        return "Comfort: But might lack resilience."
    else:
        return "Experience: Adapts and thrives in tough times."

# Examples
print(support_life("all I want"))
print(support_life("experience"))
```

Lurti: dances in the air.

Lurti and

Mahagara: looks the prettiest when the sunshine is present.

Mahagara

love weather changes.

Litagor: enjoys seeing the lands, rivers, forests, and the oceans.

Litagor and

Lpa: appears, dessapears to appear.

Lpa

love to experience various places and situations.

```
def habitat_support(enjoyment_level):
    if enjoyment_level > 0:
        print(f"Enjoyment leads to more positive actions for our habitat!")
    else:
        print("Lack of enjoyment may reduce habitat support.")
# Example usage
habitat_support(7)  # Enjoyment leads to more positive actions for our habitat!
```

They kept changing their habitats by flying from high to low altitudes.

Cutra: finds it hard to collect his thoughts.

Lotaf: fast, brave, and thoughtful, but never has any time.

Cutra and Lotaf saw focusing as a problem for various reasons.

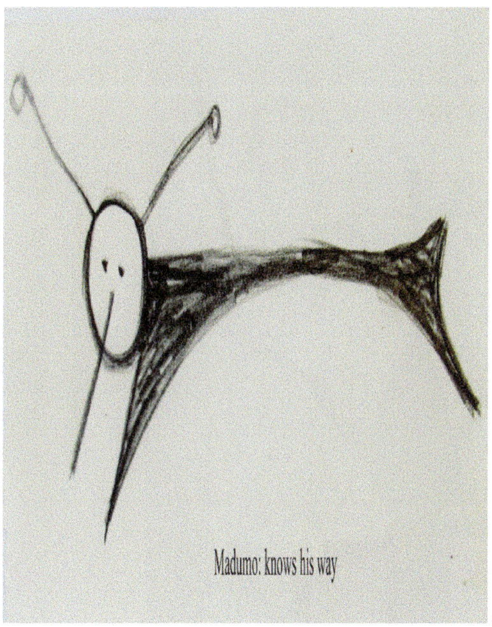

Madumo: knows his way

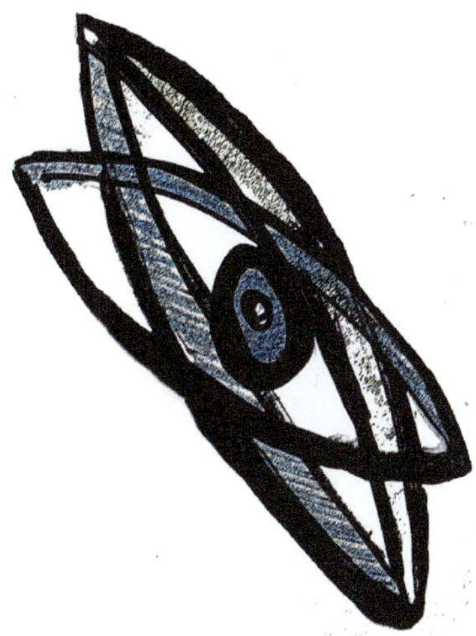

Zufrek: geospatial informer.

Madumo and Zufrek knew about the directions and various trends

```
# Sample data of interactions
interactions = ['meeting', 'call', 'email', 'call', 'meeting', 'meeting']

# Count interaction trends
from collections import Counter
trends = Counter(interactions)

print(trends)
```

Lagaccha: playful but focussed on playfulness.

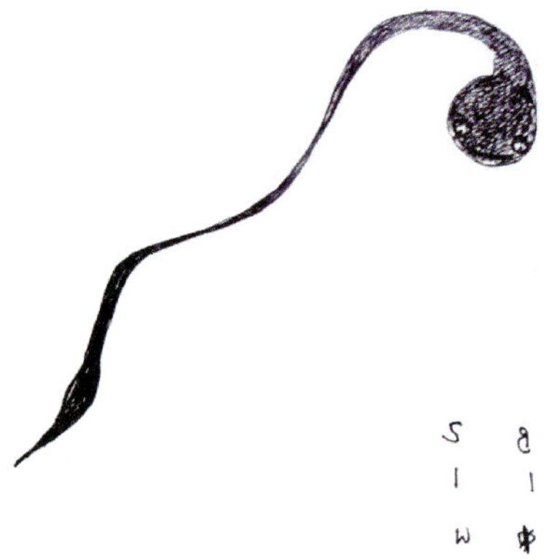

Pafara: appears, noticess it all, and reports back to you.

Lagaccha and Pafara

shared their joy, no matter what

```
# Assess cooking food
food = {'fun': True, 'vitamins: False}

# Print summary
print(f"Cooking food is fun: {food['fun']}, but vitamins: {food['health']}")
```

Mutando: keeps seven secrets.

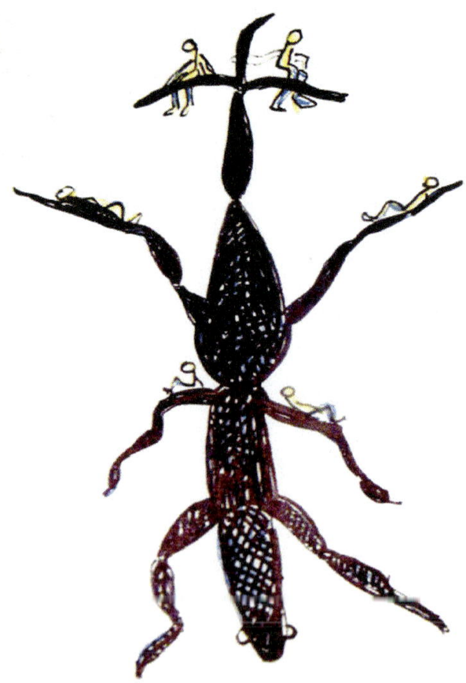

Prila: changes friends often.

Mutando and Prila

are did not agree. They were too focused on wellbeing.

Paresto: dives in the air.

Moderato: always tries to stay up in the air longer and loger.

Paresto and Morerato prefer to look at things from above

```
wellness = {'perspective': 'Above', 'improved_wellbeing': True}

# Print result
print(f"Looking from above enhances wellness: {wellness['improved_wellbeing']}")
```

Losan and Loe are known as good-doers and well-wishers

Pinkrell: delivers good deeds.

Lursu: is interested in everything above her.

They also lined wellness linked to perspective when flying high.

Lugando: measures everything.

Lumega: knowss all the stars.

Lugando and Lumega are logical and methodological

```
traits = {'good': True, 'logical': True}
connection = traits['good'] and traits['logical']

# Print result
print(f"Being good is connected to being logical: {connection}")
```

Duriliz: knows the winds.

Dudura: does not mind flying.

Duriliz and Dudura understand the weather patterns

```
def reasons_to_know_weather():
    reasons = [
        "Predict severe storms",
        "Plan daily activities",
        "Support disaster preparedness",
        "Aid in environmental research"
    ]
    return reasons

print(reasons_to_know_weather())
```

Atuzebo: always filled out with love.

A tuzebo and

Fongu: makes sure it works.

F ongu

saw the weather changes as an adventure.

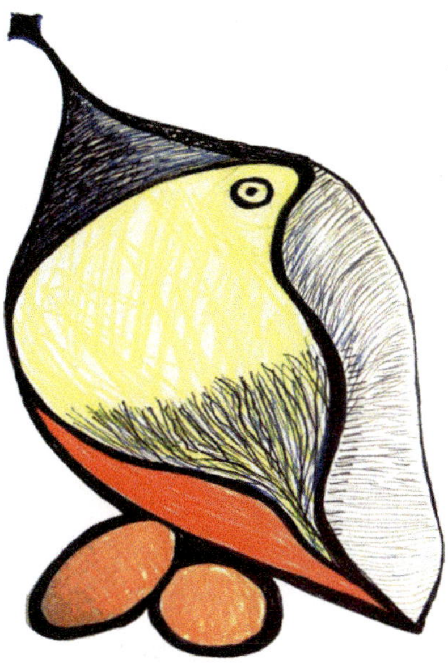

Jerlon: can sense you coming.

J erlon and

Fudego: never afraid, but watches out.

F udego

have a good sense of reality

```
def connect_senses_values():
    reality = {
        "Sight": "Appreciating beauty",
        "Hearing": "Understanding communication",
        "Touch": "Feeling comfort",
        "Taste": "Valuing nourishment",
        "Smell": "Recognizing safety"
    }
    return reality

print(connect_senses_values())
```

Asty: has five favorite figures.

Murafaga and Asty

Murafaga: always feels cold.

perceive major facts through their senses and values.

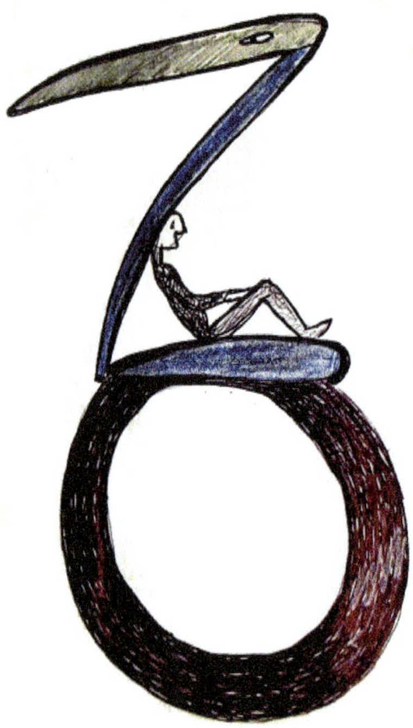

Cyfaso: he was both left and right.

Cyfaso and

Mugusav: always hides his face.

Mugusav

are ready for anything, they think

```
def be_ready():
    return "Preparation reduces fear and improves adaptability."

print(be_ready())
```

Musaruda: knows all his forks by their names.

Musaruda and

Buchero, great cook, but never could be seen.

Buchero

agree that eating is the most important part of their lives and tried all sort of foods

```
def personality_food():
    personality = {
        "Adventurous": "Spicy dishes",
        "Calm": "Comfort foods",
        "Creative": "Fusion cuisine",
        "Organized": "Balanced meals",
        "Outgoing": "Street food"
    }
    return personality

print(personality_food())
```

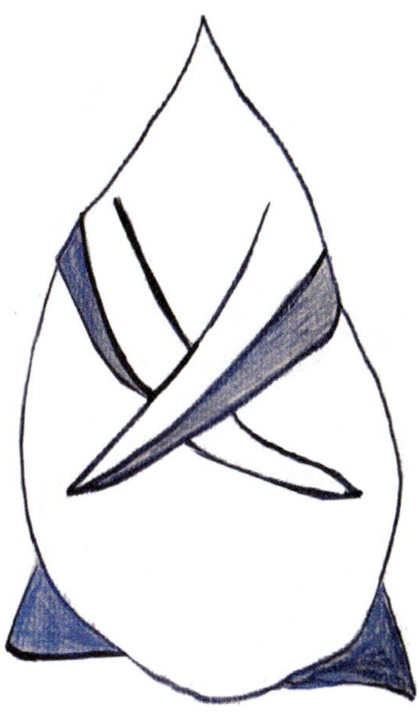

Abubu: kind and thorough.

Abubu and

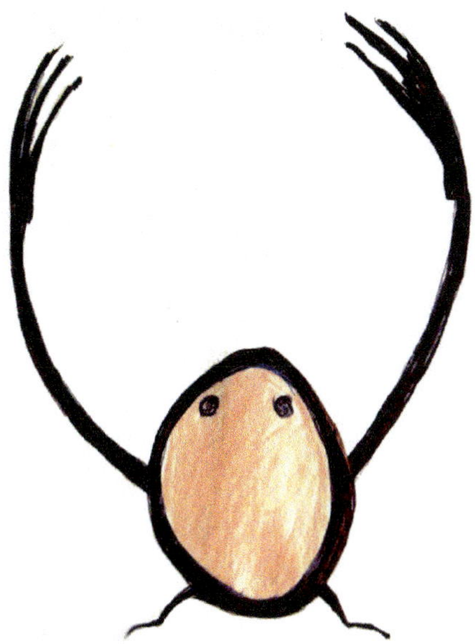

Pukaga: brings good wishes down.

Pukaga

learned to be careful with their wishes.

Asavaga: knows his way well.

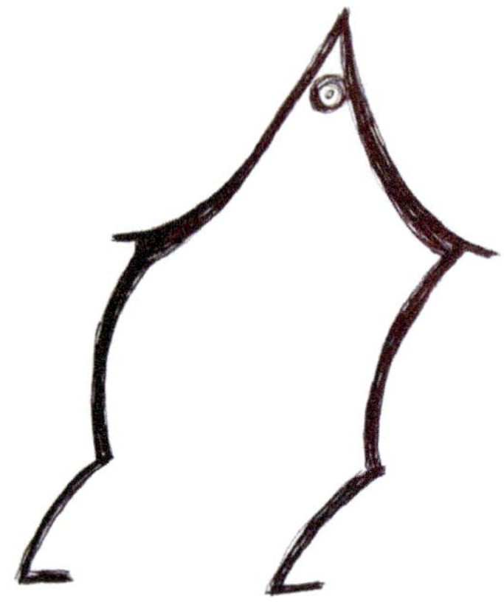

Fasera: wants to go up.

Asavaga and Fasera

want to be good

```
def good_wishes_brought():
    return ["Joy received", "Health improved", "Success achieved", "Love shared", "Peace attained"]

print(good_wishes_brought())
```

Mutafrata: rotates around the sun.

Obugarna: knows when to land.

Mutafrata and Obugarna

know their space and limitations.

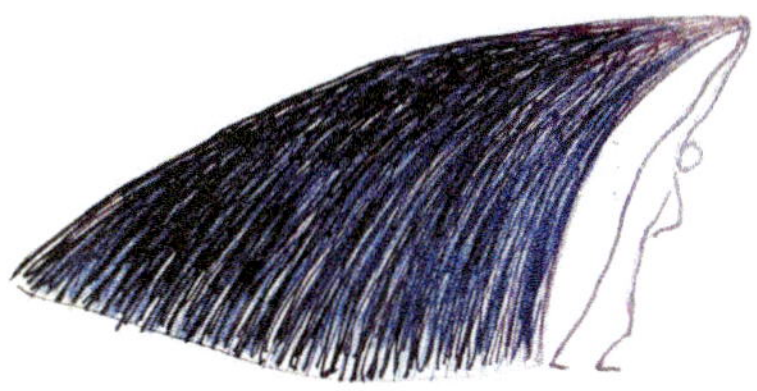

Maruondak: always covered.

Cyftep: always wins.

Maruondak and Cyftep know about themselves

```
def why_know_self():
    return "Self-awareness improves decision-making, enhances relationships, and fosters personal growth."

print(why_know_self())
```

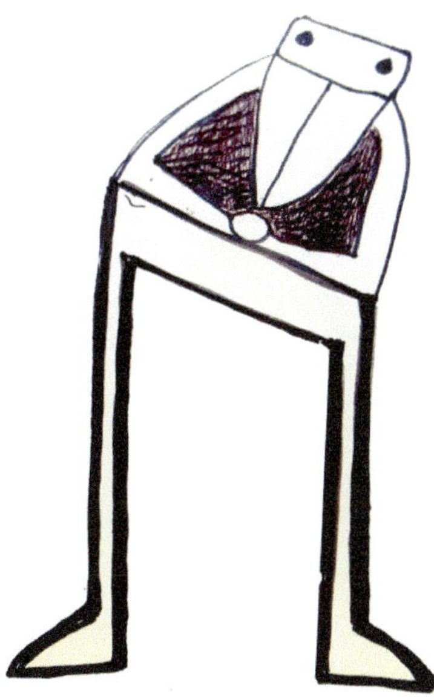

Natucha: does need a desk.

Oieko: has many thoughts.

Natucha and Oieko keep their journals

```
def journaling_benefits():
    return "Journaling boosts self-reflection, reduces stress, and improves clarity."

print(journaling_benefits())
```

They all agreed that keeping illustrated journals helps one learn more about themselves.

Musuk: can produce your dreams.

Musuk and

Nywysyro: follows what the big eye sees for him.

Nywysyro knew their ways

```
def knowing_your_way():
    return "Helps in achieving goals, reduces confusion, and builds confidence."

print(knowing_your_way())
```

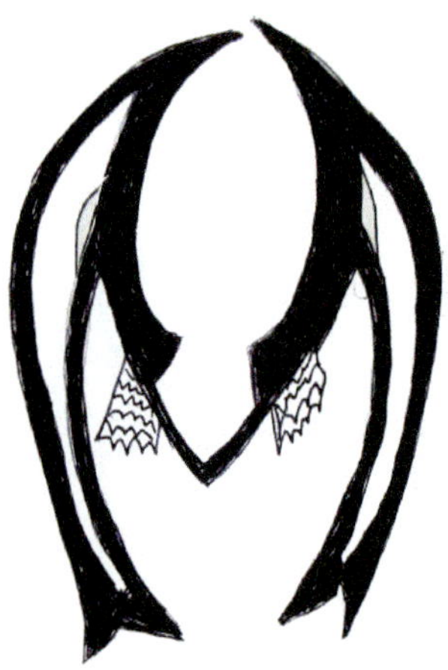

Oklapu: cries at night, but can see the best in everyone.

Kakafku and Oklapu possessed knowledge, goodwill, and more.

Musuty: has only one flow.

Musuty and

Putafachol: floats above his problems.

Putafachol

maintain perspective

```
def float_above_problems():
    return "Offers perspective, reduces stress, and fosters problem-solving."

print(float_above_problems())
```

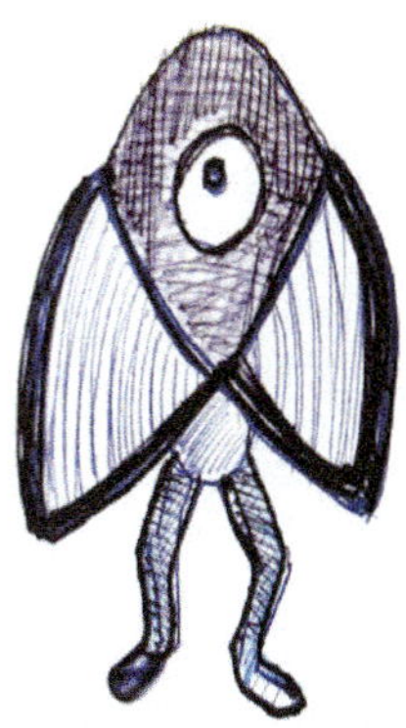

Fugst: always wants to be there.

Fugst and

Apen: has a goal and a mission.

Apen

know their plans and know how to apply the "bird's eye view" perspective for others to benefit from.

Lachab: always on the lookout

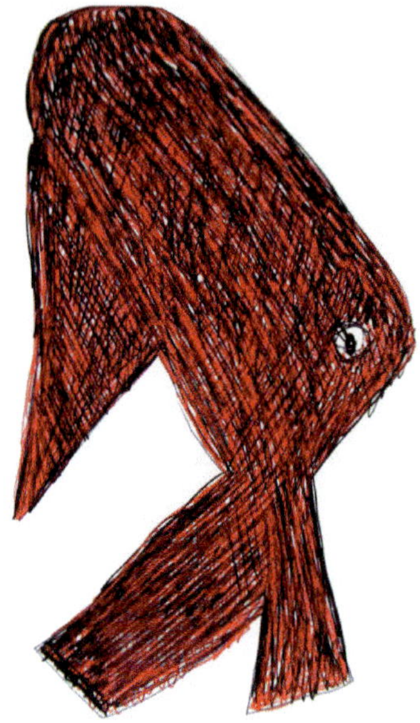

Voluchendo: makes wide turns.

Puv and Voluchendo

stay friends, despite their status.

```
# Number of free-living and domesticated birds
free_living_birds = 1000000
domesticated_birds = 200000

# Comparison
if free_living_birds > domesticated_birds:
    print("There are more free-living birds than domesticated ones.")
elif free_living_birds < domesticated_birds:
    print("There are more domesticated birds than free-living ones.")
else:
    print("The number of free-living and domesticated birds is the same.")
```

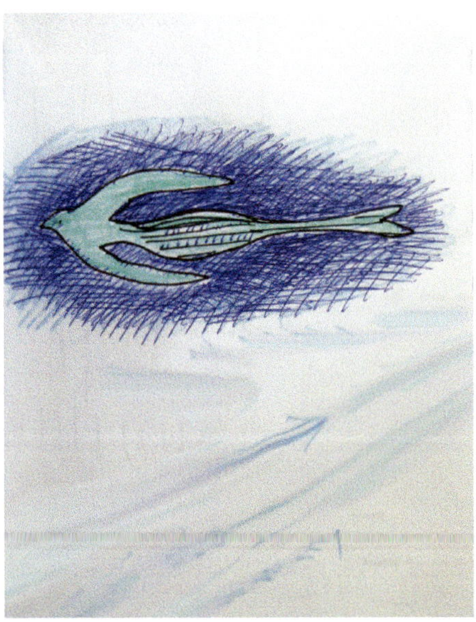

Qusado: fies with his flock.

Radikun: remembers his first breakfast.

Qusado and Radikun

are the happy ones.

Roner: likes fair weather

Roner and

Ramdalusa: connects the dots fast.

Ramdalusa

enjoy what they understand

```
def memory_belonging():
    return "Memories create connections, reinforcing our sense of belonging."

print(memory_belonging())
```

Rusuna and

Puchadeco: leaves feelings behind.

Puchadeco

Rusuna: can whistle, but never does.

know their ways of staying happy without dwelling on the past.

Axro and Ruto

Ruto: loves them all.

Axro: always surprises you.

have more feelings than they can handle

```
def avoid_relying_on_feelings():
   return "Focus on discipline and routines instead of just feelings or abilities."

print(avoid_relying_on_feelings())
```

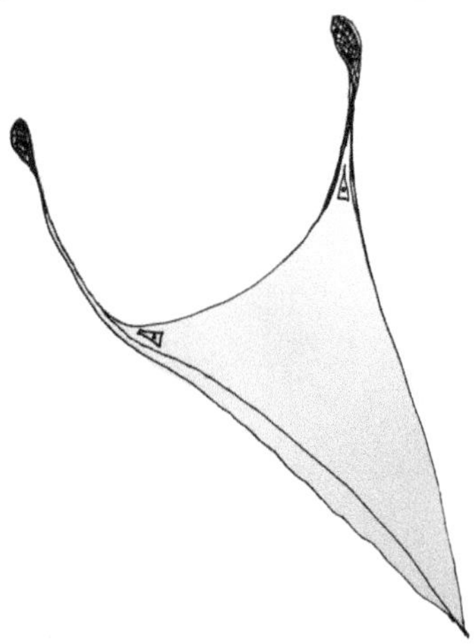

Bugza: keeps looking for a driver.

Bugza and Putuza

Putuza: only considers bird's eye view.

are good at finding things together

```
def importance_of_finding():
   return "Saves time, reduces stress, and ensures efficiency."

print(importance_of_finding())
```

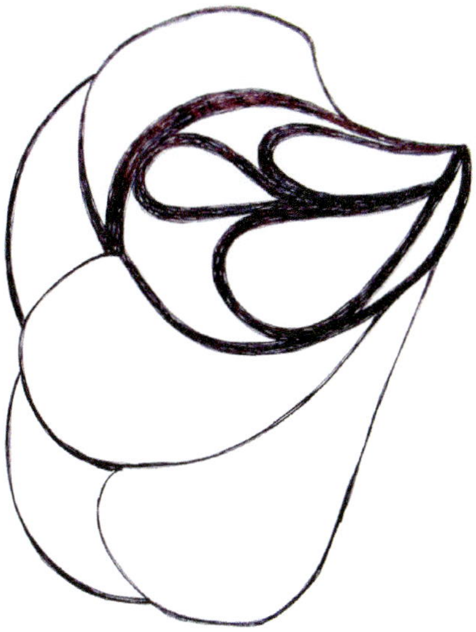

Derono: smells the winds.

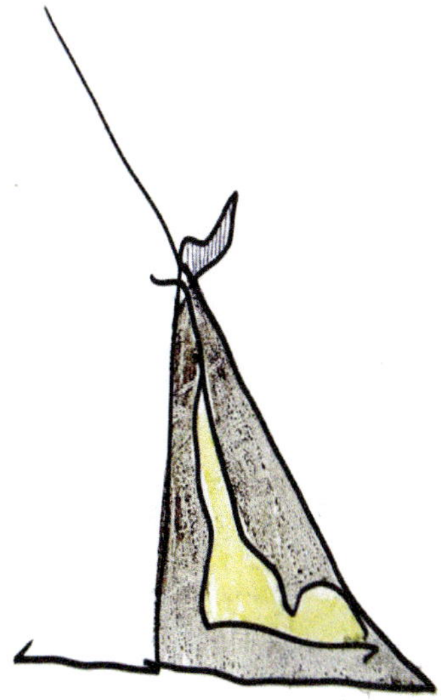

Sotudga: oficially is a shape-shifter, but not really.

Derono and Sotudga

possess special powers and discover things through their senses

```
def unknown_things():
    return "Invite curiosity, learning, and caution."

print(unknown_things())
```

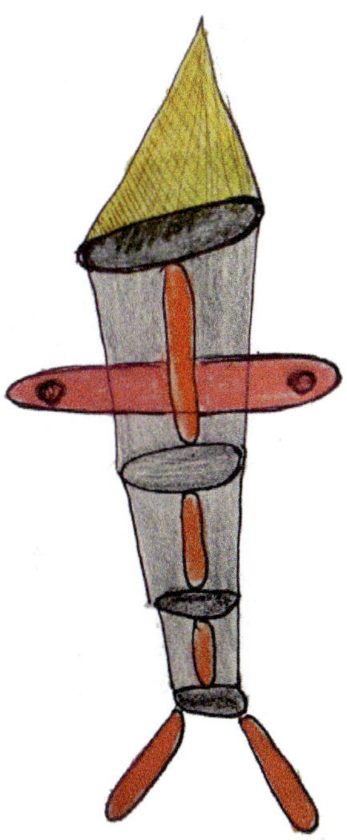

Derahu: grows a part daily.

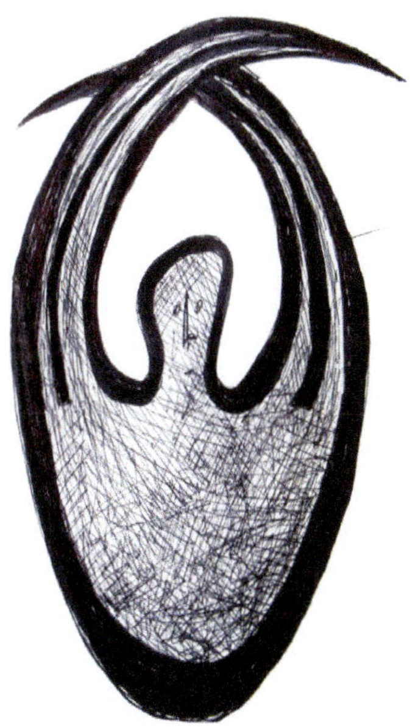

Menua: has it all under control.

Derahu and Menua

work in meticulous ways.

Cytuda: is silent, but succesful.

Cytuda and

Surevi: always ready to listen.

Surevi

are open to other opinions.

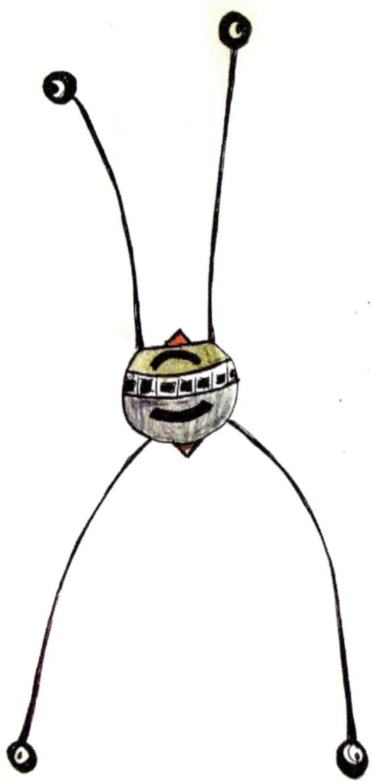

Synter: gathers data from below and above.

Synter and

Tlinq: dances for the wind

Tlinq

want to know things their way.

```
def find_facts():
    return "Listening brings clarity; personal insight brings perspective."

print(find_facts())
```

Synda: knows current wather.

Synda and

Tagar: has no time for any type of research.

Tagar

thought they knew what they were doing, but approached everything very slowly.

Fladata:quite faster than you think.

Fladata and

Ragaze: greets everyone when entering their homes.

Ragaze

were fast and kind

```
def qualities():
    return "Knowledge guides, speed achieves, hospitality welcomes."

print(qualities()
```

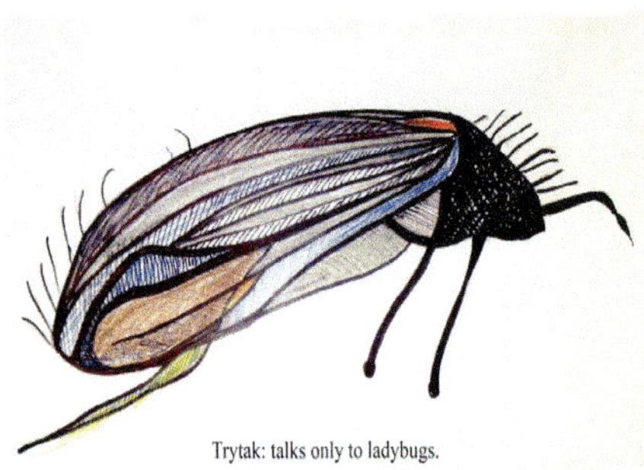

Trytak: talks only to ladybugs.

Titatsa: flies in a sitting position.

T rytak and T itats

kept their secrets tight.

Fikagu: controls wind on a daily basis.

Rusta: flies at night to the closest airport.

F ikagu and R usta

relied on themselves

```
def secrets_vs_self():
    return "Keeping secrets builds trust; self-reliance fosters independence."

print(secrets_vs_self())
```

Together they worked using all types of experience and knowledge.

Dutaleat: fies on his bike.

D utaleat and

Ouyner: moves in fast.

O uyner

traveled too often.

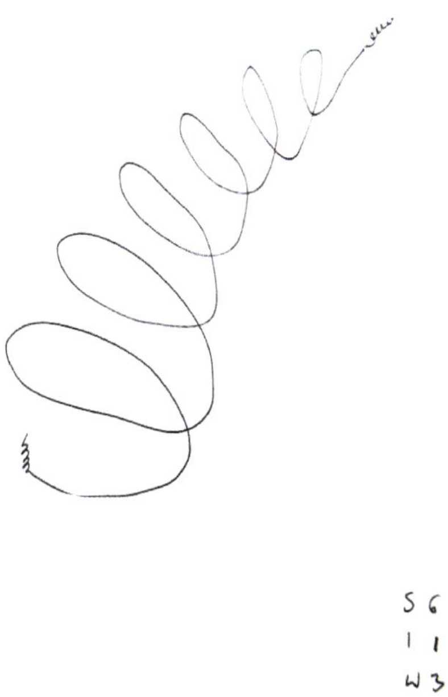

Fasagala: hard to catch her, but better not to.

F asagala and

Ruskatu: nice to travel with.

R uskatu

were too fast to record their movement

```
def travel_often_fast():
    return "Frequent travel leads to burnout; fast travel misses experiences."

print(travel_often_fast())
```

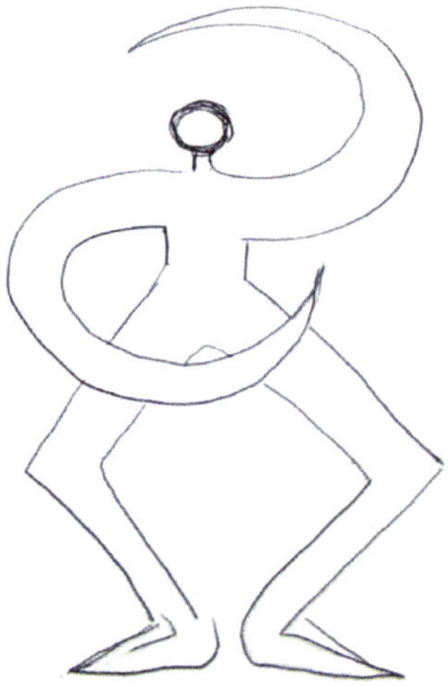

Tefa: dances and sings the song about the butterfly well.

Unark: can go both directions.

Ƭ efa and ᐯ nark

use movement to entertain.

Vajestus: changes his orientation on a daily basis.

Gurer: always with mixed feelings.

V ajestus and G urer

move often for practical reasons

```
def movement_purpose():
    return "Entertainment brings joy; practicality meets needs."

print(movement_purpose())
```

They enjoy flying together.

Pufat: always lands on his feet.

Pufat and

Vabata: is undecided, but knows what she wants.

Vabata

know what they want through clarity and desire.

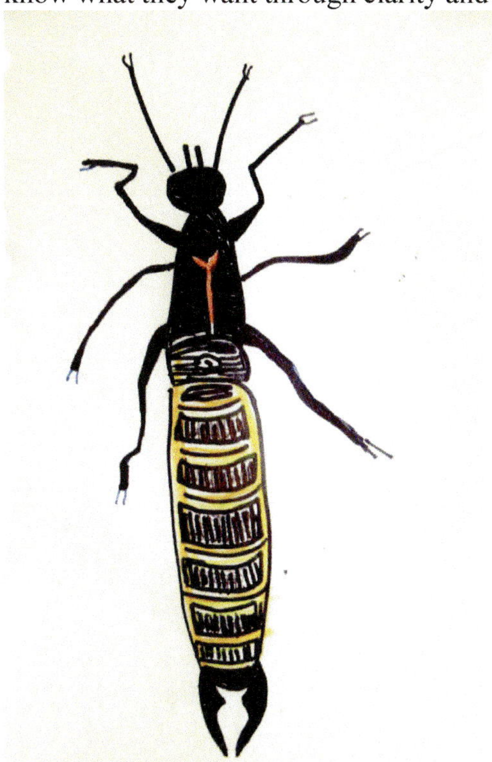

Symaru: can operate a tool of your choice.

Symaru and

Valis: fast and vise one.

Valis

rely on their tools to achieve their goals

```
def wants_vs_tools():
    return "Knowing guides direction; tools enable execution."

print(wants_vs_tools())
```

Tupego: sees through most people.

Suia: shows up unexpectedly.

Tupego and Suia are very serious and are often being seen as suspicious.

Vusuraki and Tuno love entertaining and being entertained.

Vusuraki: has too many friends.

Tuno: gives everybody a ride home after his parties.

```
def suspicious_vs_entertainment():
    return "Suspicion questions motives; entertainment explores possibilities."

print(suspicious_vs_entertainment())
```

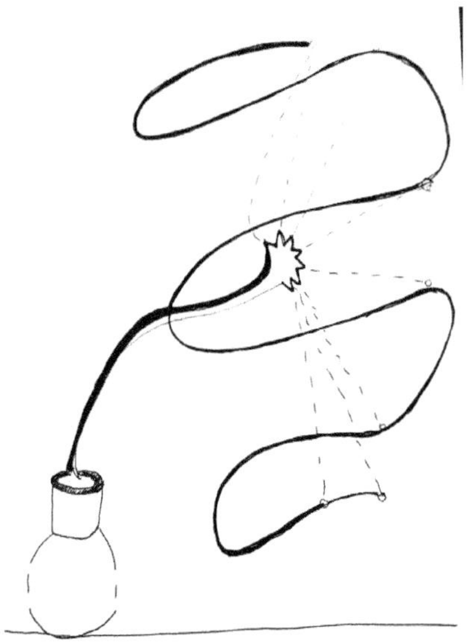

Wasadaya: distributes collected energy.

Wtre: never afraid of the rain.

Wasadaya and Wtre

think of nature as a source of energy.

Wasred: appears an dissapears when most unexpected.

Ganto: stretches five times a day.

Wasred and Ganto

use energy for personal gain

```
def nature_vs_personal_gain():
    return "Nature renews; personal gain depletes but enriches."

print(nature_vs_personal_gain())
```

Wazaja: likes to talk to other wizzards.

W azaja and

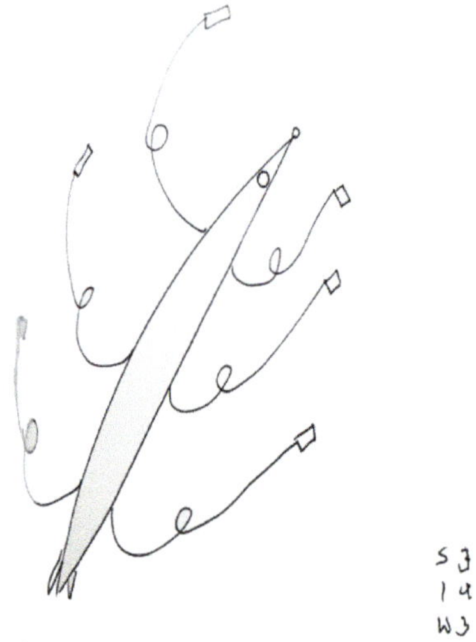

Zunak: not very decisive, but determined.

Z unak

had too many questions.

Edru: checks the order of the clouds.

E dru and

Walaco: dances to the wind.

W alaco

focused on some meteorological events.

```
def meteorology_vs_consulting():
    return "Firm knowledge guides questions; consulting provides insights."

print(meteorology_vs_consulting())
```

Gutasol: flies above us without being noticed..

Usafegel: thinks twice before recording information.

G utasol and V safegel

do not like any form of irregularity.

Gudej: flies when swimming.

Wumuzah: dances to colors.

G udej and W umuzah

have a good sense of the proper order in every situation, but sometimes.

```
def senses_in_action():
    return "Dancing to colors or feeling like flying while swimming enhances sensory perception."

print(senses_in_action())
```



```
def senses_in_action():
    return "Dancing to colors or feeling like flying while swimming enhances sensory perception."

print(senses_in_action())
```

Hugarta: is a cloud, but never sends any rain.

Nechada: flows above, never noticed.

Hugarta and Nechada had unfinished hopes and secret wishes.

Vudago: flies with his tail.

Wudore: can fold herself when flying.

Vudago and Wudore invented new ways of flying.

```
def weather_patterns():
    return "Weather influence rain intensity and flight conditions."

print(weather_patterns())
```

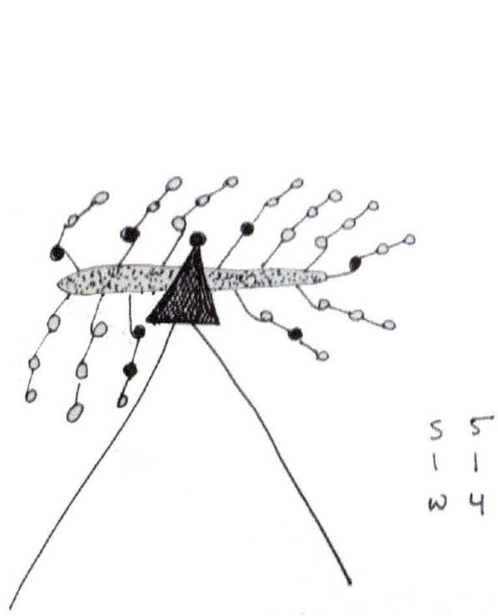

Valaga: every day makes a new record.

Wa: skates on the clouds.

Valaga and Wa were known as innovators of inventors.

Fudaro: never leaves a single footprint.

Naginetu: understands the power of silence.

Fudaro and Naginetu work on new ways to stay fit and became noticed for their results

```
def air_sky():
    return "Clear impacts the sky and causing health issues."

print(air_sky())
```

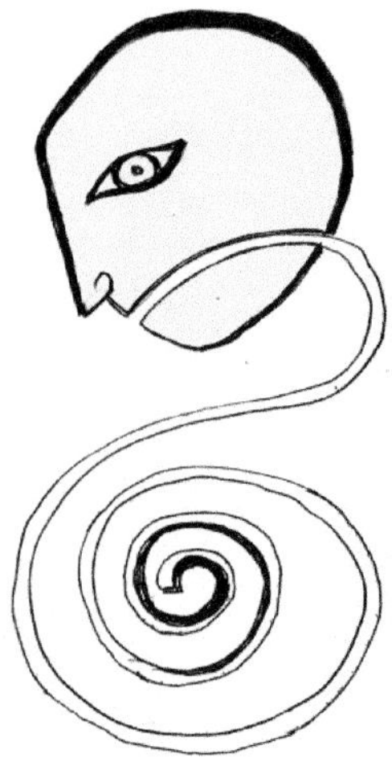

Rychyza: always talks while eating.

Rychyza and

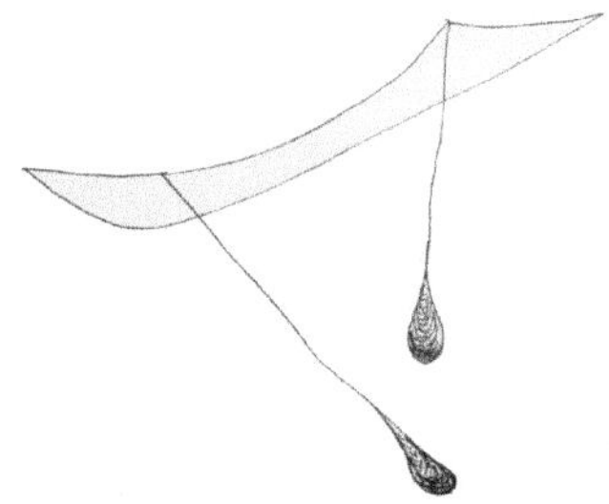

Turasa: watch out, like always.

Turasa

cannot feel safe while around you.

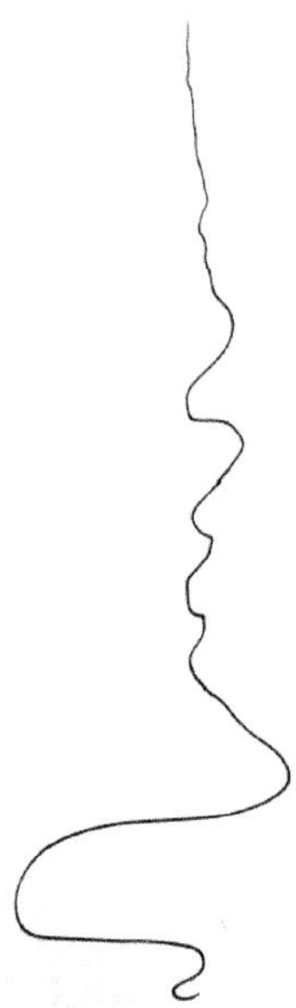

Juoe: been here and there.

Juoe and

Mankura: moved to another place.

Mankura

were told to keep moving

```
def stay_safe():
    steps = 0
    while True:
        print(f"Step {steps}: Keep moving, but stay aware of your surroundings.")
        steps += 1
        if steps == 5:  # Move constantly, but take breaks for safety
            print("Pause and assess the situation. Safety first!")
            break

stay_safe()
```

Fanada and Vuu know their limits.

Fanada:very careful when turning around.

Vuu: can fly as high as it is safe.

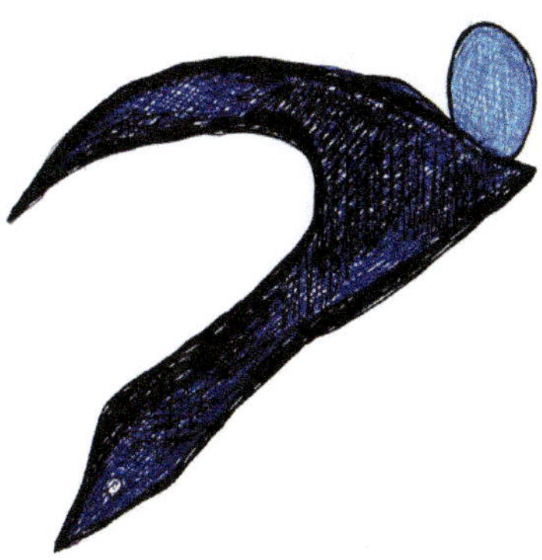

Vetea:was born when everyone liked divisions.

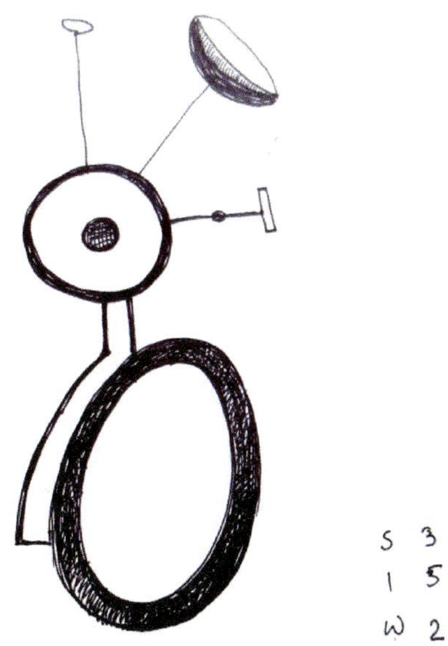

Iatusal: uses data collection for lunch.

Vetea and Iatusal understand group theories among the characters and in mathematics.

```
def collect_data_safely(groups, safe=True):
    data = {"Group A": [10, 20], "Group B": [30, 40], "Group C": [50, 60]}  # Social divisions

    if safe:
        print("Safety protocols in place. Collecting data from all groups.")
        for group in groups:
            print(f"Collecting from {group}: {data[group]}")
    else:
        print("Unsafe conditions detected. Stopping data collection.")


groups = ["Group A", "Group B", "Group C"]
collect_data_safely(groups)
```

Mesatra: serves floating coffee.

Mesatra and

Puffers: want in and out at the same time.

Puffers:

always checked everything before coming up with proper solutions.

Vikazala: flies at night only.

Vikazala and

Nefsa: hides when it's not raining.

Nefsa

knew how to avoid things that are not the best for them

Puchacho and Pugurea

```
def check_safety(water, air):
    if water == "clean" and air == "fresh":
        print("Safe to drink water and enjoy the rain.")
    else:
        print("Unsafe conditions. Avoid drinking water and seek shelter from rain.")

check_safety("clean", "fresh"
```

Puchacho and Pugurea: observed how things were developing.

Puchacho: shows up when needed.

Pugurea: always wants to go higher.

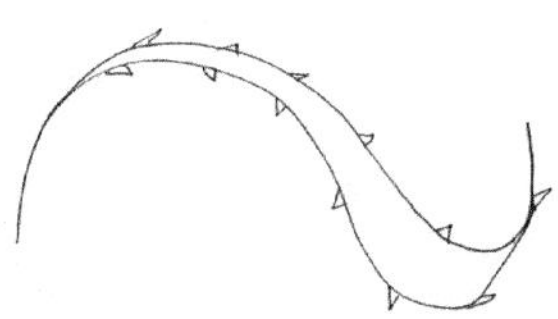

Pukuso: keeps his stories written.

Wumbakty: knows when not to snap.

Pukuso and Wumbakty recorded it all and kept all issues objective

```
def observe_and_record(events):
    for event in events:
        print(f"Observing {event}...")
        print(f"Recording {event} objectively.")

events = ["hurricane", "conflict", "elections"]
observe_and_record(events)
```

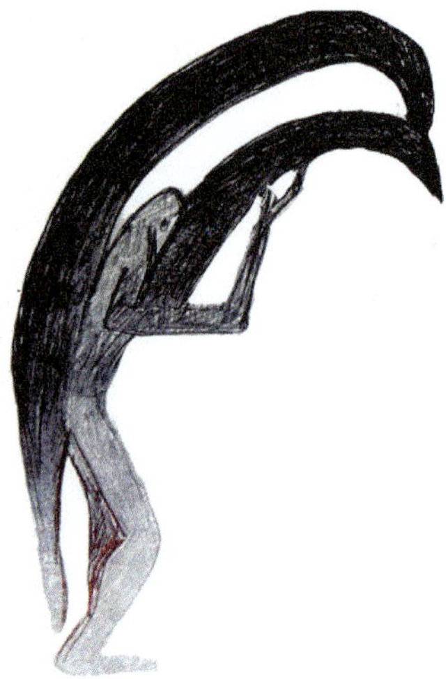

Nem: loves Nature when he can fly.

Nem and

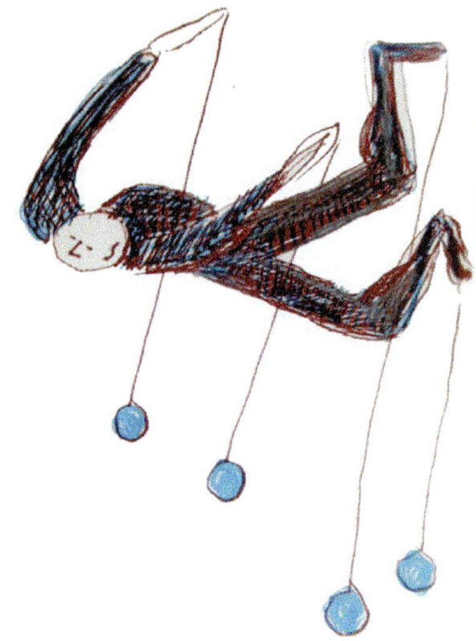

Tun: always uses support.

Tun

used above-the-ground ways of enjoying nature.

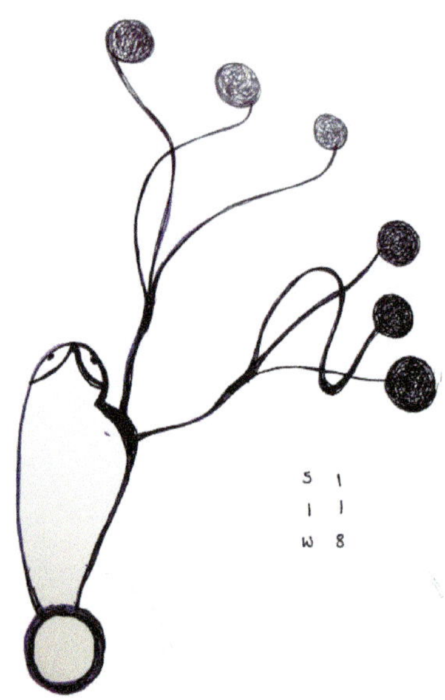

Sunav: always has to make sure that there is proper balance.

Sunav and

Nuf: gathers data three times a day.

Nuf

made sure it was safe to go out.

```
def enjoy_nature(safe=True):
    if safe:
        print("Enjoy the outdoors, but always respect nature's rules.")
    else:
        print("Unsafe conditions. Stay prepared and cautious.")

enjoy_nature()
```

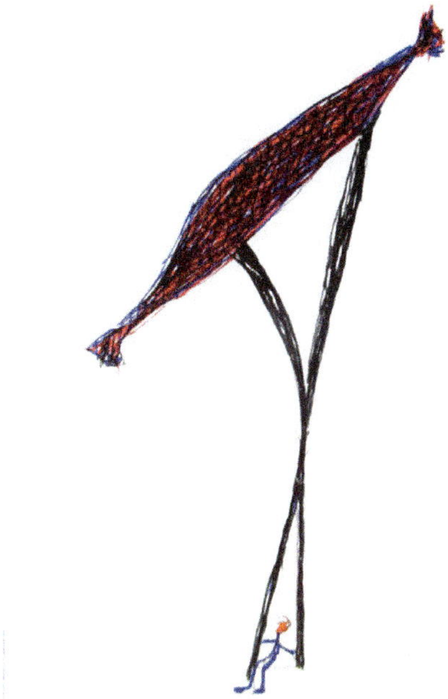

Olhen: flies whenever he wants.

Vonda: can even fly when he wants.

O lhen and V onda were free-spirited but worked on their skills.

Vudago: flies with his tail.

Gubala: feels the wind and records it.

V udago and G ubala thought they always knew what they were doing.

```
def check_air_quality(air="good"):
    if air == "good":
        print("Air quality is optimal. Proceed with normal flight techniques.")
    else:
        print("Poor air quality. Adjust flight techniques for stability.")

check_air_quality("poor")
```

Colpo: can only move up and down.

Colpo and

Dymet: always with clean concience.

Dymet

have to live with their limitations

```
def live_with_limitations(limitation):
    print(f"Learning to live with: {limitation}")

# Example usage
live_with_limitations("imperfect knowledge")
```

Ey: flies both ways.

Ey and

Gudife: makes extraordinary landings.

Gudife

felt safe because of their unique skills and abilities.

Water. © 2025 by Matylda Czarnecka. (Used with permission).

By the Water © 2025 by Matylda Czarnecka. (Used with permission).

Leaves. © 2025 by Matylda Czarnecka (Used with permission).

CHAPTER 4
DEEP UNDERWATER
NOT WELL-KNOWN TERRITORY

We know less about the bottom of the oceans than about the peaks of the highest mountains. Deep down, where the light won't reach is color. There is no color without light, some say. Then, other senses are used, and others may add. There are advances made in oceanography and deep-sea exploration. Oceans cover about 71% of the Earth's surface and have an average depth of 12,080 feet (3,682 meters). The deepest part, about 36,000 feet (10,984 meters), is deeper than Mount Everest. The ocean floor features include continental shelves, mid-ocean ridges, abyssal plains, trenches like the Mariana Trench, and seamounts. Life in the deep ocean has adapted to extreme conditions like darkness and high pressure, with organisms relying on marine snow or chemosynthesis for energy. The sea is divided into ecological zones by depth: the epipelagic zone (0–200 meters) is sunlit, the mesopelagic zone (200–1,000 meters) is twilight, the bathypelagic zone (1,000–4,000 meters) is dark, the abyssopelagic zone (4,000–6,000 meters) faces extreme pressure, and the hadal zone (below 6,000 meters) includes the deepest trenches. Exploration challenges include intense pressure, cold temperatures, and vastness, with only a small fraction of the deep ocean mapped. Technological advances like ROVs, AUVs, sonar mapping, and crewed submersibles help in exploration. The ocean floor holds mineral resources and oil, but these can harm the environment when exploited. It also plays a vital regulation role but faces mining and contamination risks. Despite significant discoveries, only about 5% of the ocean floor is mapped in detail, and many species and natural phenomena remain unknown. Continued technological advancements promise further revelations about this vital and mysterious part of our planet.

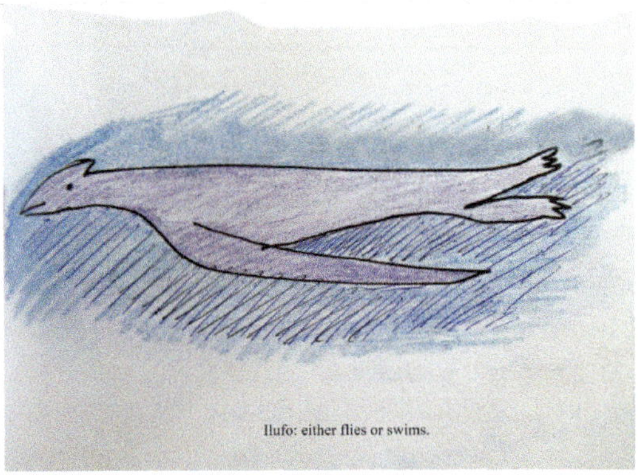

Ilufo: either flies or swims.

Ilufo knew all his way around the vast surface of the ocean but was curious about what could be found deep down

```
def why_oceans_unexplored():
    reasons = [
        "1. Extreme pressure at great depths crushes most equipment.",
        "2. Lack of light makes navigation difficult.",
        "3. Oceans cover over 70% of Earth's surface, making exploration costly.",
        "4. Technological limits restrict deep-sea access.",
        "5. Unknown ecosystems pose unpredictable challenges."
    ]

    for reason in reasons:
        print(reason)

why_oceans_unexplored()
```

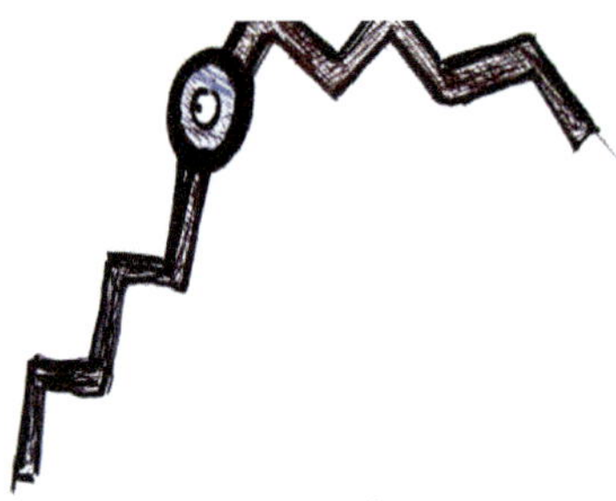

Rusufao: watches every step.

Rusafao and

Vasaza: left the group he belonged to twice

Vasaza

lived deep on the uneven ground

```
def why_creatures_cant_explore_oceans():
    reasons = [
        "1. No creature can survive both shallow waters and extreme deep-sea pressures.",
        "2. Oxygen and light are scarce in the deep ocean.",
        "3. Vast distances make it impossible for a single creature to travel across all areas.",
        "4. Different ocean zones have drastically different conditions.",
        "5. Energy and food sources are limited at extreme depths."
    ]

    for reason in reasons:
        print(reason)

why_creatures_cant_explore_oceans()
```

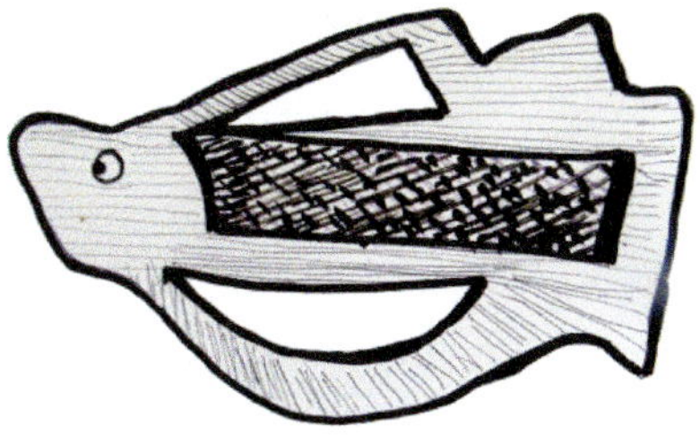

Lutgant: searches for facts.

L utgant and

Trenti: convinces people to release him.

T renti

collected proven facts only

```
def code_rules_facts():
    facts = [
        "Define and understand the task.",
          "Write code in a readable way with clarity over cleverness, naming conventions, and consistent formatting.,"
          "Don't repeat yourself)=DRY.",
          "Use modularity by breaking code into functions, classes, modules.",
          "Write tests for your code so it works as expected .",
          "Understand data structures and algorithms.",
          "Use version control to collaborate.",
          "Use  debugging techniques.",
    ]

    for fact in facts:
        print(f"Fact: {fact}")

# Call the function to display code facts
code_rules_facts()
```

Jinsi: focused, but fast.

J insi and

Muku: can wait forever.

M uku

saw it differently as they lived at the bottom of the ocean

```
def bottom_ocean_facts():
    facts = [
        "Ocean temperatures, affect marine life and ecosystems.",
        "There. Are rising sea levels,.",
        " Coral reefs and shellfish are part of the  marine food chains.",
        "Ocean  waters are responsible for hurricanes and cyclones.",
        "Ocean currents, impact worldwide weather patterns and marine biodiversity."
    ]

    for fact in facts:
        print(f"Ocean-Related Fact: {fact}")

# Call the function to display ocean-related facts
bottom_ocean_facts()
```

Asafia: swims faster than herself.

A safia and

Puga: nobody really knows him.

P uga

thought they knew the depth of her ocean

```
class ExplorationComparison:
    def __init__(self, mountain_exploration, ocean_exploration):
        self.mountain_exploration = mountain_exploration
        self.ocean_exploration = ocean_exploration

    def compare_knowledge(self):
        if self.mountain_exploration > self.ocean_exploration:
            return "We know more about the tallest mountains because they are more accessible and easier to study."
        else:
            return "We know more about the deep ocean due to recent technological advancements."

# Example data:
mountain_exploration = 90  # Percentage of mountain areas explored
ocean_exploration = 20     # Percentage of ocean explored

comparison = ExplorationComparison(mountain_exploration, ocean_exploration)
result = comparison.compare_knowledge()

print(f"Comparison Result: {result}")
```

Jiustada: always watchful.

J ustada, who visited her from a tall mountain changed that.

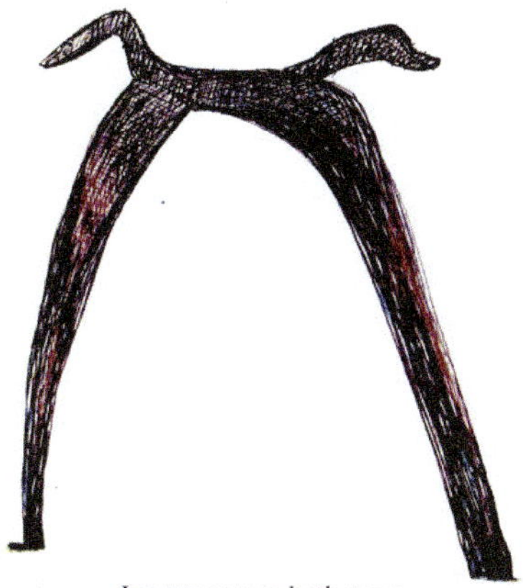

Jugaru: can go both ways.

Pungo: rolls any direction he wants.

Jugaru and Pungo

were puzzled by the deep-sea fish still having colors despite the absence of light

```
# Define why deep-sea fish have color
deep_sea_fish_color = {
    "Bioluminescence": "Some fish produce their own light.",
    "Camouflage": "Colors help blend into the dark environment.",
    "Communication": "Bright colors attract mates or signal others."
}

# Display the explanation
for reason, explanation in deep_sea_fish_color.items():
    print(f"{reason}: {explanation}")
```

Chron: gets it right the second time.

A broken clock is right twice a day

Aquvo: the best dressed person in the street.

Chron and Acuvo

wondered why

```
# Define reasons for lack of light in deep ocean
lack_of_light = {
    "Depth": "Light penetrates only the upper layers of the ocean.",
    "Water Absorption": "Water absorbs light, especially red wavelengths.",
    "Murky Conditions": "Particles and organisms scatter remaining light."
}

# Display the explanation
for reason, explanation in lack_of_light.items():
    print(f"{reason}: {explanation}")
```

Forest. © 2025 by Matylda Czarnecka. (Used with permission).

CHAPTER 5
SPACE EXPLORATIONS

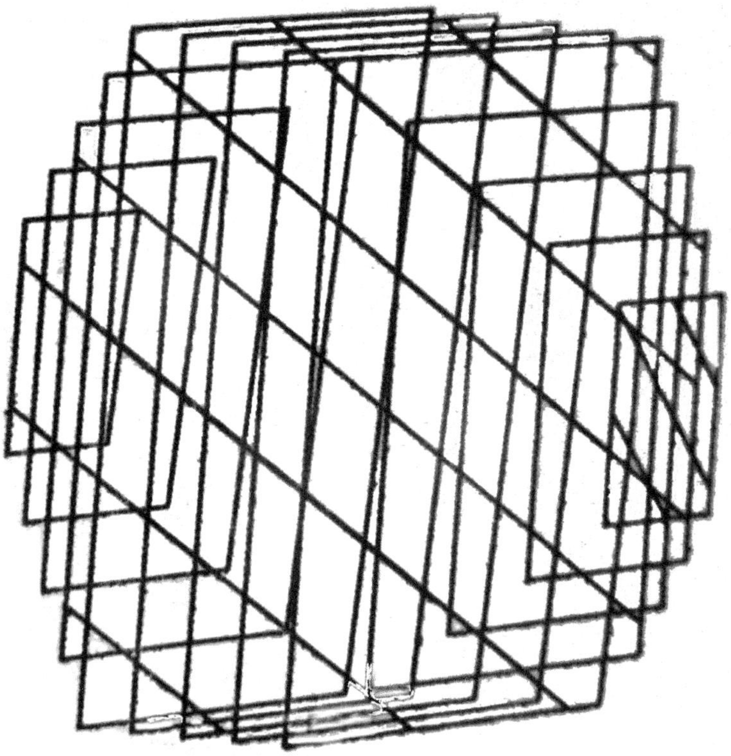

Exploring space keeps evolving. Ancient philosophers discussed it with mathematical reasoning. Johannes Kepler saw it as a set of platonic objects. Before the 20th century, it was focused on theoretical work and early rocketry. Yuri Gagarin was the first human in space in 1961. In 1969, the Apollo 11 set astronauts on the Moon. Satellites support communication, weather forecasting, and research; modern spacecraft can be crewed or uncrewed. The Hubble Space Telescope has provided stunning views of the universe. Rockets like the Saturn V and SpaceX's Falcon have powered various launches. Early spacecraft included the Vostok and U.S. Mercury and Gemini programs. The efforts behind the Apollo program ended up with landing on the Moon. Plans include returning to the Moon via NASA's Artemis program and eventually sending humans to Mars. Private companies like SpaceX and Blue Origin are making space tourism possible. Robotic probes and rovers like NASA's Mars rovers have explored other celestial bodies. Voyager missions returned important data from the outer solar system, while New Horizons from Pluto. People work on missions targeting potential life, like Europa Clipper. Private companies are lowering costs and increasing access to space, notably through SpaceX's Starship, which aims for deep-space missions. The International Space Station is a prime example of worldwide collaboration in space. Many countries, such as China and India, work on space exploration programs. They are extracting resources from asteroids or the Moon as it became doable. Space exploration is a rapidly evolving field involving scientific curiosity, technological innovation, international cooperation, and private-sector involvement. The goals of exploring other planets, searching for extraterrestrial life, and ultimately establishing human colonies on distant worlds are becoming achievable; they triggered the imagination of writers, artists, philosophers, inventors, visioners, and the general public.

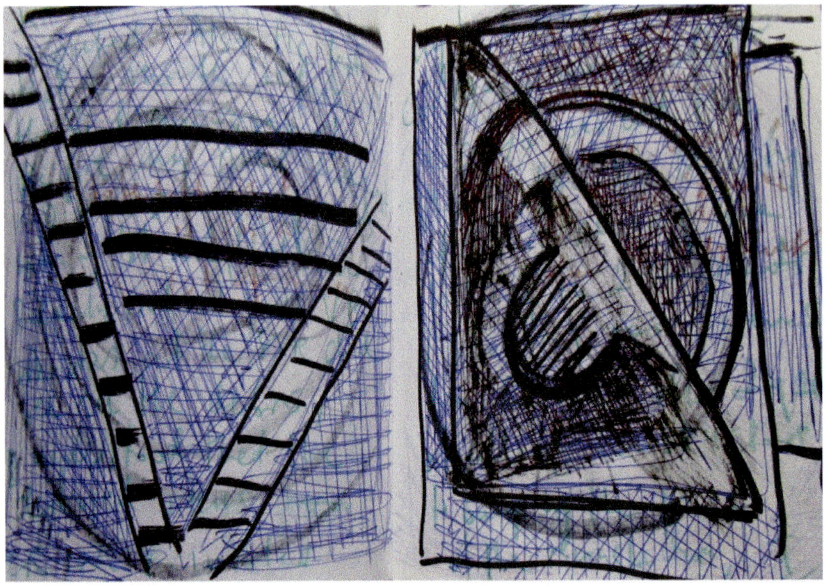

Alajo: he discussed everything with his brother.

Alajo and his Brother thought that space is not just a physical place. Still, it also embodies the entire universe's vast, profound, and limitless nature. While literal and metaphorical largescale representation and mystery of the cosmos.

```
# Define space and its cosmic nature
space = "vast"
cosmic = True if space == "vast" else False

# Function to explain the relationship
def explain_space():
    if cosmic:
        print("Space is cosmic because it is vast and endless.")

# Example
explain_space()  # Output: Space is cosmic because it is vast and endless.
```

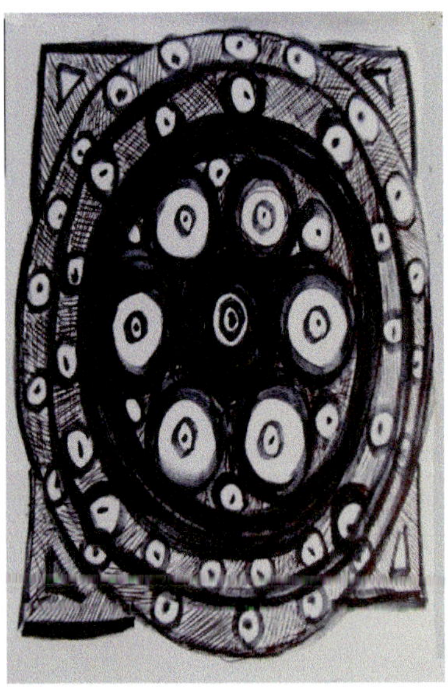

Masaburaha: sees the future when wants to look.

Alajo's brother without Alajo.

Masaburaha and Alajo's brother check if space is vast and, if true, declare that space is cosmic, emphasizing the connection between vastness and the cosmic nature of space.

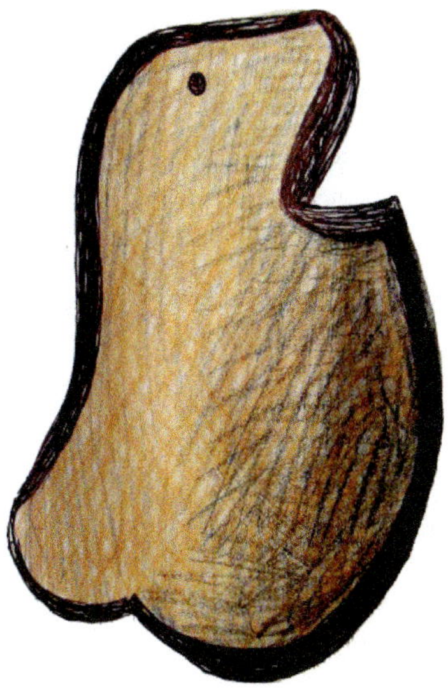

Tryx: almost solid.

T ryx and

Madanet: Knows where to go.

M adanet

were pondering sulfur life

```
def sulfur_life_options():
    return ["Deep-sea vents", "Volcanic soils", "Acidic lakes"]

print(sulfur_life_options())  # Example: environments for sulfur-based life
```

Defco: knows someone.

D efco and

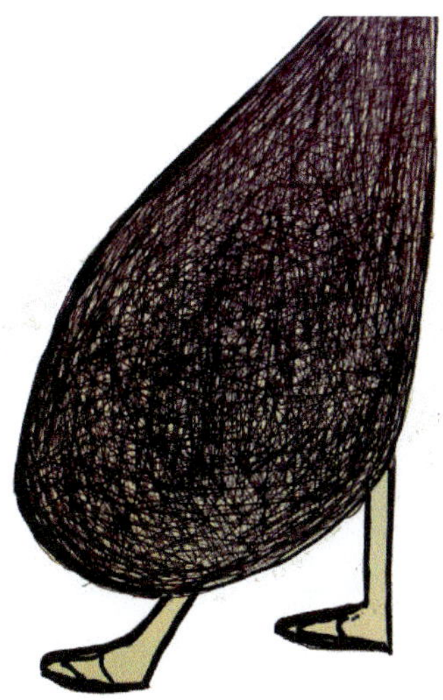

Futerula: goes the opposite direction than his mind.

F uterula

wanted to know about water on Mars .

```
def water_on_mars():
    return ["Ice caps", "Underground reservoirs", "Seasonal brines"]

print(water_on_mars())  # Example: water sources on Mars
```

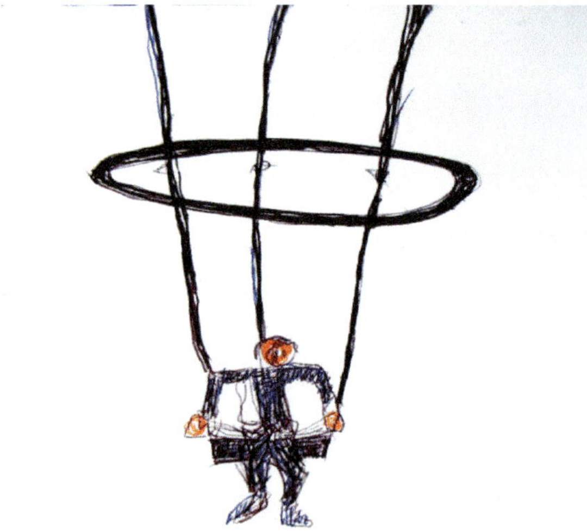

Kudara: danced in the air.

Kudara and

Duvi: Can cut anything you cannot reach out to.

Duvi

know their way up.

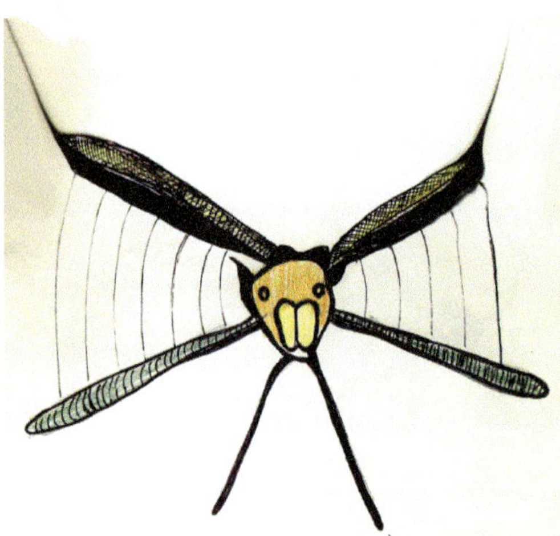

Luganga: can see through any particle.

Luganga and

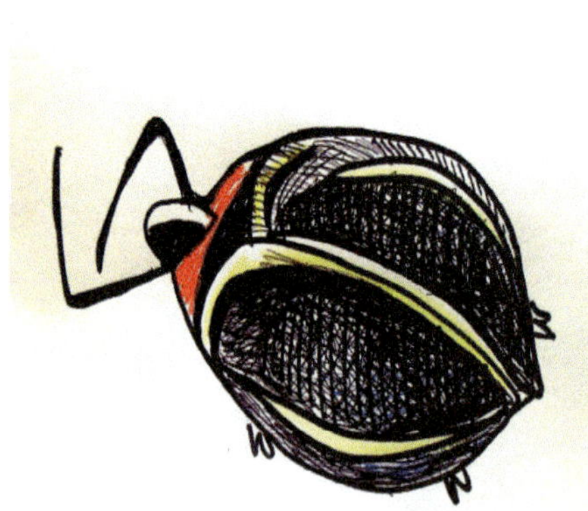

Yulud: read aloud whatever can be spotted.

Yulud

displayed attention to detail

```
def particle_roles():
    return "Particles form matter, fuel energy, and shape the universe."

print(particle_roles())
```

Sunto: was in outer space once and came back.

Tugsu: could see everything.

Sunto and Tugsu

understood the power beyond the influences of cosmic space.

Tandora: always with his twin.

Pu: believes in "Do as I say, not as I do."

Tandora and Pu

believed in the order of things.

```
def explore_space(benefit=True):
    if benefit:
        print("Space exploration helps discover resources and solutions for Earth's challenges.")
    else:
        print("Focus on solving problems on Earth first.")

explore_space()
```

Putu: records his way back.

Tuskio: goes around the globe.

Putu and Tuskio moved fast and went too far into space.

Veha: just flows.

Yumnada: can fly or swim, whenever needed.

Veha and Yumanda knew how to mimic and derive from nature to build various types of transportation

```
def transformers_movement():
    transformers = {
        "Air": "Transforms into jets and planes",
        "Land": "Transforms into cars and trucks",
        "Sea": "Transforms into boats and submarines",
        "Space": "Transforms into spacecraft"
    }
    return transformers

print(transformers_movement())
```

Knowledge of how to adapt to types of transportation helped them see new things they never could experience before.

Rungent: Modifies skyline daily.

Unetylo: got it all someplace.

Runtgent and Unetylo

keep thinking about the cosmic space.

Gurio: can see and record at the same time.

Surana: loves the World.

Gurio and Surana

need to collect data to start forming any opinion.

```
def thinking_vs_data():
   return "Thinking explores ideas; data builds informed opinions."

print(thinking_vs_data())
```

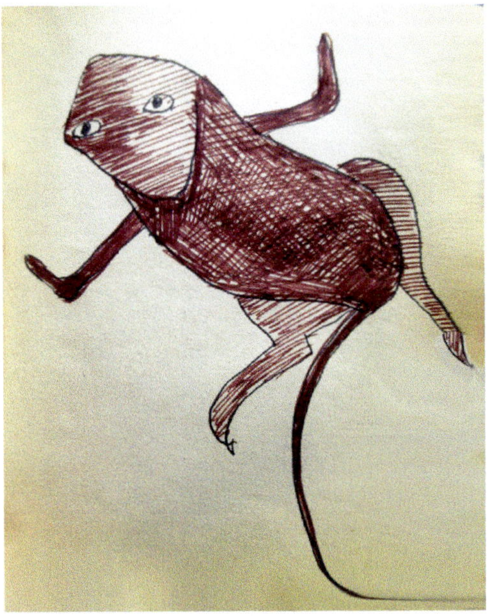

Muchom: can send insects where are needed the most

Ofo: saves lives.

Muchom and Ofo

act on others' benefits

```
def support_all_species():
    return "Promotes biodiversity, fosters ecological balance, and ensures the survival of ecosystems."

print(support_all_species())
```

Kinera: converts signals to a code.

Afaron: the first one to tour-guide on the new planet.

Kinera and Afaron

made research making space exploration possible

```
def research_supports_space():
    return "Drives technological advancements, uncovers new knowledge, and ensures mission success."

print(research_supports_space())
```

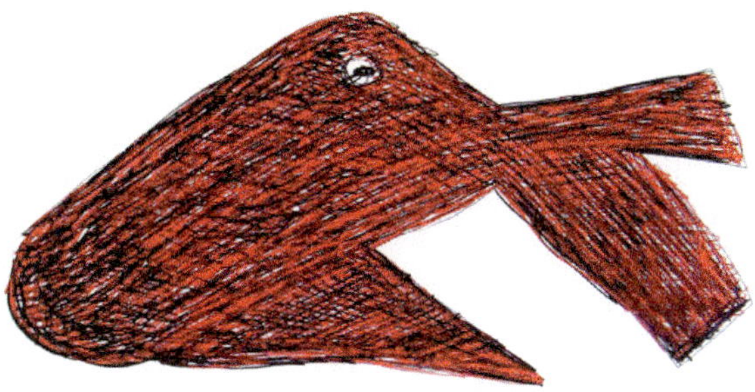

Anazan: flips and flops.

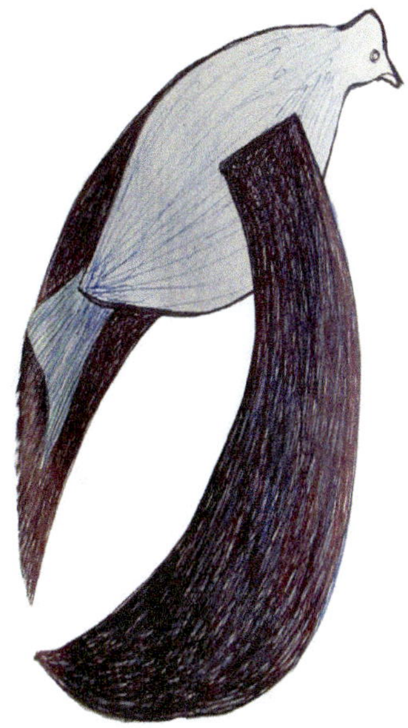

Pukata: flies in circles.

Anazan and Pukata know their way around the globe.

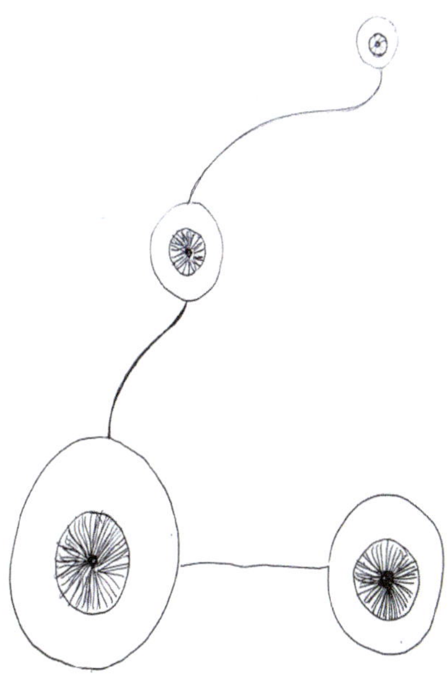

Movata: everyone watches her.

Musto: can talk with the stars.

Movata and Musto started the production of devices to explore outer space.

Buzuru: everybody likes him.

Buzuru and

Surte: knows everything, and better.

Surte

had breathing problems as he came from a Sulphur-based environment.

Murec - brings fresh air by focussing on it.

Murec and

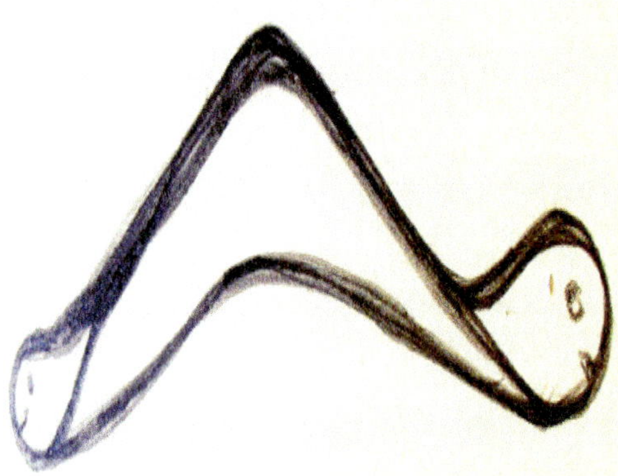

Lzurto: changes his minds often.

Lzurto

had a solution:

```
class Room:
    def __init__(self, air_quality):
        self.air_quality = air_quality  # Air quality scale: 0 (poor) to 100 (fresh)

    def bring_fresh_air(self):
        # Focus on ventilation to improve air quality
        self.air_quality += 30  # Increase air quality by focusing on bringing fresh air
        if self.air_quality > 100:
            self.air_quality = 100  # Cap at 100 for maximum freshness

# Example of improving air quality
room = Room(air_quality=40)  # Initial poor air quality
print(f"Initial Air Quality: {room.air_quality}")

room.bring_fresh_air()  # Bring fresh air into the room
print(f"Air Quality After Focusing on Ventilation: {room.air_quality}")
```

Odulo: taches all the stones as he goes.

O dulo and

Guye: can tell you which star is the brightest at the moment.

G uye

study the relationship between astronomy and geology through planetary formation and processes.

Hareva: holds it all together.

H areva and

Badoj: Always hungry.

B adoj

were more interested in growing food.

```
def astro_geo_food():
   return "Astronomy tracks seasons, geology provides soil—both critical for food production."

print(astro_geo_food())  # Example: connection between astronomy, geology, and food
```

Hazua: her houghts go around you.

H azua and

Lahyru: knows which button to push.

L ahyru

wanted to conquer space.

```
space_exploration = ["Launch Rockets", "Orbit Earth", "Land on the Moon", "Send Rovers to Mars", "Explore Deep Space"]
for step in space_exploration:
    print(step)
```

Hagasa: they call him selfish for collecting all that he finds

H agasa and

Dmak: can dissapear really fast.

D mak

were skeptical.

```
space_problems = ["Radiation Exposure", "Lack of Oxygen", "Costly Missions", "Space Debris", "Psychological Strain"]
for problem in space_problems:
    print(problem)
```

Fusto: finds all lost items.

Revadis: taked about their daily observations.

Fusto and Revadis

wondered if the same minerals are on the Earth and in outer space.

Tniv: walks to own-humming.

Dustrom: playful, but careful.

Tniv and Dustrom

had the answer:

```
# Define minerals on Earth and in outer space
earth_minerals = {"quartz", "feldspar", "mica", "pyroxene"}
space_minerals = {"olivine", "pyroxene", "diamond", "quartz"}

# Find common minerals
common_minerals = earth_minerals.intersection(space_minerals)

# Print result
if common_minerals:
   print("Common minerals:", common_minerals)
else:
   print("No common minerals found.")
```

Forest. © *2025 by Matylda Czarnecka. (Used with permission).*

Chapter 6
Visually Static World
Energy in an Invisible Movement

The Two Types of Trees (deciduous and coniferous). Outputs from the codes. © 2025 by Anna Ursyn

Many types of organisms do not walk, swim, or fly; they are known as immobile. Plants and fungi belong to this category. However, it is worth the effort to look at the lives of these full-of-energy, sensitive, social organisms, which are enabled to communicate in their own way. Even though not endowed with movement by locomotion, plants migrate slowly and change places during their individual lifetimes.

Plants developed every possible means of expansion and spreading. Using spores, seeds, and other means of progression, they spread throughout continents, pass through oceans, and conquer new regions, often hardly hospitable to life and demanding adaptation. Seeds sail around the world on ships, planes, and trucks, are carried by wind and by water, dispersed by animals on their fur, or travel inside of the body of another organism to end up whenever it poops. and in other ways. Many times, specific groups of animals contribute to spreading seeds of particular species. Spores and seeds develop structures that improve their chances of being transported and thus migrate. In these many ways, plans can spread life to inhospitable, remote areas, defeat native species, or survive in harsh environments.

Plants differ from animals, or people in many ways. They draw energy from photosynthesis instead of eating other living beings. Trees store enormous amounts of carbon dioxide in their tissues while they produce hydrocarbons as an energy supply, so forests filter this greenhouse gas. Moreover, after the tree's death, carbon dioxide remains in humus and very slowly changes into a bituminous or anthracite coal (Wohlleben, 2015). Some companies that install solar panels provide information on how energy impacts trees, and the number of these grows giving the owners some sense of pride for helping clean out the air we all need to survive.

Plants live on an extended time scale, especially trees which can live over 100 times longer than every human lifetime (Wohlleben, 2015). Flora and fauna are living in various places and times in ways that are dissimilar in many ways terms. A neurobiologist Stefano Mancuso (2022) overviewed the surprising abilities of plants, their activities, and differences from the animals. Plants do not have individual personalities; they often live in groups and colonies. Their organs are diffused, and they do not have any central structure that would give the order to the whole body.

Many kinds of plants, for example trees live as a social organism by developing networks. Old trees are parenting the younger ones by sharing nutrients through entangled, braided roots and communicating about to happen dangers through sending chemical signals through roots or as a warning gas as scent messages. As social communities, trees communicate not only by smells and tastes of chemicals but also by electrical impulses going through the roots and by a like a "wood wide web" of symbiotic soil fungi that share information and nutrients (Wohlleben, 2015). There is even the exchange between the two tree species possible, with their roles changing depending on the season.

Walking Landscape. © 2025 by Anna Ursyn

Ragusa: lost his head twice, but found it.

Ragusa watered his tree throughout the winter

```
def explain_winter_watering():

    return "Trees need water during winter to prevent dehydration and ensure healthy growth in spring."

# Example usage
print(explain_winter_watering())
```

Saero: his shadow creates art·

Aero and

Nunho: quiet but fast.

Nunho

believed the rain and snow will suffice

```
def should_water_trees(winter_rain, winter_snow):
    return not (winter_rain or winter_snow)

# Example usage
print(should_water_trees(False, False))  # True: Water needed
print(should_water_trees(True, True))   # False: No water needed
```

Ragusa's tree soon overshadowed those belonging to Aero and Nunho, but they had the money saved to plant their new trees.

Rynago: makes wide turns.

Rynago and

Ri: hides what he gathers.

Ri installed solar panels on their houses

```
def solar_energy_advantages():
    advantages = [
        "Aesthetically pleasing, maintaining the roof's appearance.",
        "Space-saving, eliminating the need for bulky panels.",
        "Integrated design, reducing installation complexity.",
        "Increased property value due to modern technology.",
        "Enhanced durability by protecting solar cells from elements."
    ]
    return advantages

# Example usage
for advantage in solar_energy_advantages():
    print(advantage)
```

Pukto: walks when rolling.

Pukto and

Zabado: always plays his piano.

Zabado had solar energy hidden under the shingles of their roofs.

```
def solar_energy_advantages():
    advantages = [
        "Aesthetically pleasing: Blends seamlessly with roof design.",
        "Space-saving: Utilizes existing roof area without extra installations.",
        "Improved durability: Shingles can protect solar cells from damage.",
        "Less maintenance: Reduced exposure to weather elements.",
        "Increased home value: Attractive to eco-conscious buyers."
    ]
    return advantages

# Example usage
for advantage in solar_energy_advantages():
    print(advantage)
```

They were all very proud and together watched the app showing the results.

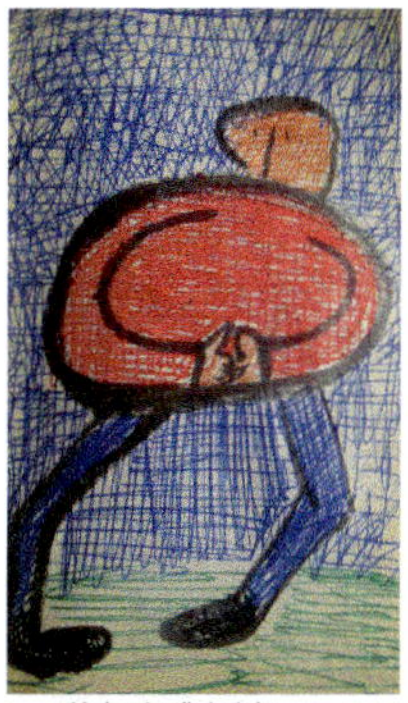
Mochazod: walks in circles.

Mochazod and

Jutob: his extra sense of smell caused him to chase after and run away.

Jutob

loved to have trees around the house

```
def tree_advantages():
    advantages = [
        "Improved air quality by filtering pollutants.",
        "Shade that reduces cooling costs in summer.",
        "Increased property value and curb appeal.",
        "Wildlife habitat supporting local ecosystems.",
        "Enhanced privacy and noise reduction."
    ]
    return advantages

# Example usage
for advantage in tree_advantages():
    print(advantage)
```

Rata: makes friends with the trees.

Rata

Vistal: can sense when you are angry.

Vistal

Felt there were too many problems with having trees around

```
def tree_disadvantages():
    disadvantages = [
        "Potential for damage to structures from roots.",
        "Increased risk of falling branches during storms.",
        "Maintenance costs for trimming and clean-up.",
        “Clogging of the sewer line,”
        "Pests and insects that may inhabit trees.",
        "Blocked sunlight affecting gardens and lawns."
    ]
    return disadvantages

# Example usage
for disadvantage in tree_disadvantages():
    print(disadvantage)
```

It was easy to spot Rata and Vistal visiting and spending a lot of time with Mochazod or Jutob.

A bench. © 2025 by Matylda Czarnecka. (Used with permission).

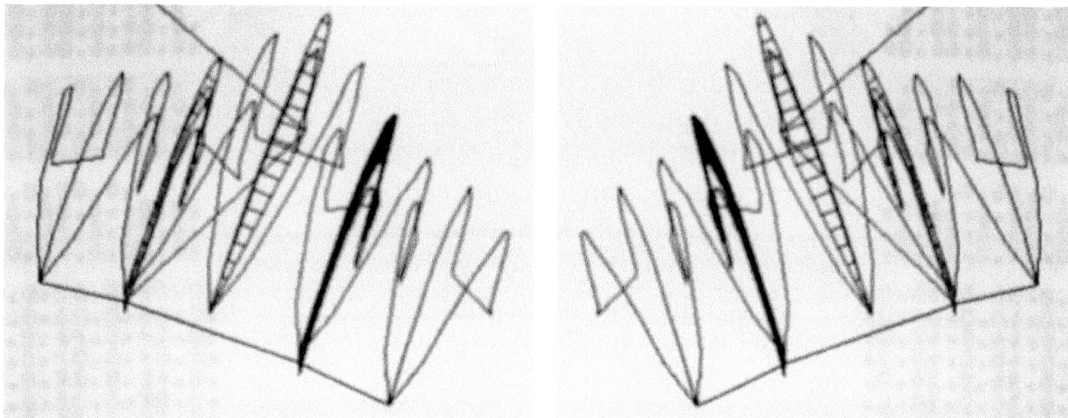

CHAPTER 7
WAVES
THE ELECTROMAGNETIC SPECTRUM

This chapter titled *Waves* suggests a new fictional international journal of science and education about the visual world for researchers, teachers, and their students. It could thrill, excite, stimulate, and inspire the audience due to this short story set by characters representing scientists, artists, and business-oriented authors. These characters are concerned with our planet, from technology to beauty.

Now, visual parts of programs in most areas, including social media, are becoming more based on graphical representations of knowledge. Post-digital and traditional media art are becoming a way to think cognitively and more abstractly, often going way beyond feelings or their poetic nature. How do people apply their ways to those concepts? Characters can be seen as minerals, atoms, and molecules. Where do the elements reside in nature?

Waves are ever present in the visual world: waves and related topics interest researchers, teachers, and educators. Many find the outcomes interesting for its interdisciplinary, collaborative, sensory-oriented technologies and beauty. Current scientific solutions relate to the advances in the kindergarten-to-Ph.D. education. Many researchers, teachers, and their students work together. Combining advanced investigations resulting in the student-teacher-provided descriptions of knowledge visualization with learning and instruction is focused on the "Students First" trend.

Waves are important in various aspects of life, as in nature and in society. They are fundamental to many physical, technological, and environmental systems that impact our daily lives.

Nature: Waves in oceans and seas shape coastlines, affect marine life, and form weather patterns depending on changing water levels.

Communication: Radio waves, microwaves, and light waves make communication systems possible, including radio, television, cell phones, and the Internet.

Sound and Music: Sound waves allow us to hear and communicate. Music, speech, and other sounds are transmitted through the vibrations of air and other mediums.

Health: In medicine, technologies like X-rays, ultrasound, and MRI rely on different types of waves for diagnosis and treatment.

Energy Transfer: We harness ocean and wind waves as renewable energy sources for preserving solutions. In the 19th century, physicist James Clerk Maxwell showed that light is a wave of electromagnetic radiation traveling through space. Waves, including the visible, infrared, and ultraviolet One is because of everything we experience with our senses. A big part of these light waves is perceived as visual images. Visualization of knowledge became a quintessential part of most sciences, industries, art, entertainment, marketing, and, hopefully, education. Presently, we see and explore our world more than ever in visual terms because of the advances in the media of mass communication (through the Internet, broadcasting, social media, and publishing) and a range of new technologies.

Former President Barack Obama named creativity as a currency of the 21st century. There is a saying that a university is as good as its football team. A university is now as good as its visual parts when it supports creativity and abstract and cognitive thinking by fostering skills in meaningful images, concept art, animation, video, storytelling, and character development to deliver a meaningful story-based visual knowledge-based task. Many current industries and their audiences expect novelty and the arrival of new idols attractive for all ages, expanding on favorite cartoons or characters such as Mickey Mouse, Dumbo, or heroes from Star Wars. The chapter *Waves* focuses on promoting the understanding of technology and coding, building creativity and inventiveness, and the ability to convey these skills through visually oriented education.

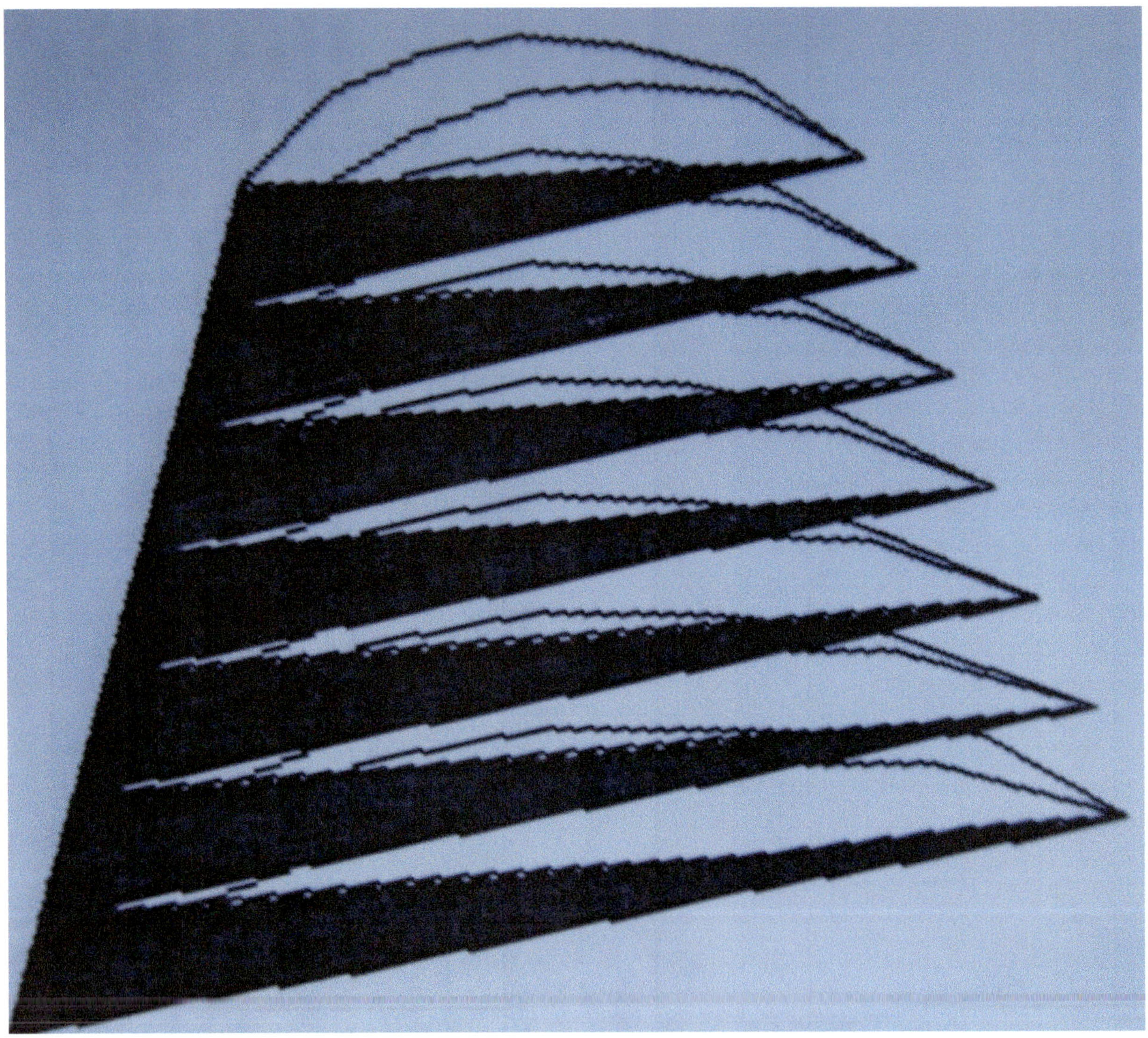

Dafav: had two bosses at the same time.

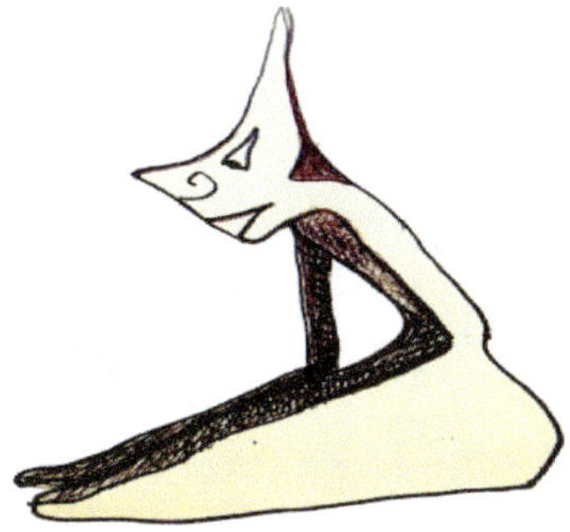

Dakla: had seven talents.

Dafav and Dakla wanted to stay together. He never wanted to destroy the Royal Castle. He liked it too much. He only wanted to see if it would withstand an extra staircase, and it did not.

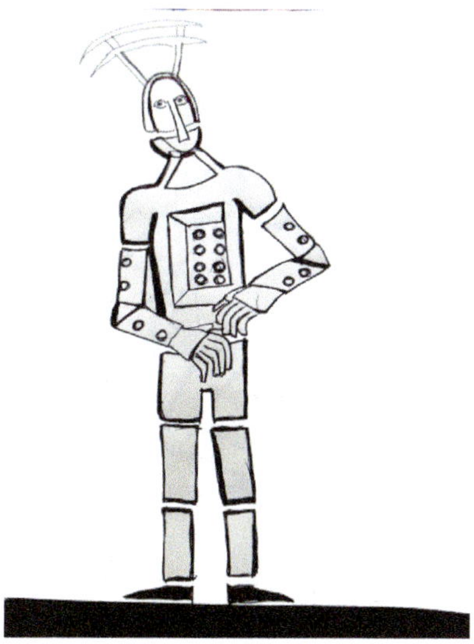

Fukan: controls thoughts by reciting them in a spiral.

Fukw: points out at the most important aspects.

Fukan, and Fukw explored magnets and polarization

```
# Magnet with North and South poles
magnet = {'North': '+', 'South': '-'}

# Function to show magnetic field direction (N -> S)
def magnetic_field():
    print(f"Magnetic field flows from {magnet['North']} to {magnet['South']}")

# Unpolarized material domains (random alignment)
material_domains = ['random', 'random', 'random']

# Function to polarize material (align domains)
def polarize_material():
    universal material_domains
    material_domains = ['aligned', 'aligned', 'aligned']
    print("Material polarized, domains:", material_domains)

# Example
magnetic_field()     # Show the direction of the magnetic field
polarize_material()  # Polarize material under magnetic field
```

They were all connected, despite being so different.

Dasco: makes the best omlets in space.

Felchencor: waites for the hail.

D asco and F elchencor

said: how we move is determined by where we move as different environments create various conditions

```
# Define different environments
environments = {'forest': 'careful', 'desert': 'slow', 'city': 'fast'}

# Function to determine movement based on environment
def move(environment):
   movement = environments.get(environment, 'normal')
   print(f"In the {environment}, you move {movement}.")

# Example
move('forest') # Output: careful movement
move('city')  # Output: fast movement
move('mountain') # Output: normal (default) movement
```

Hagera; owns half of the street.

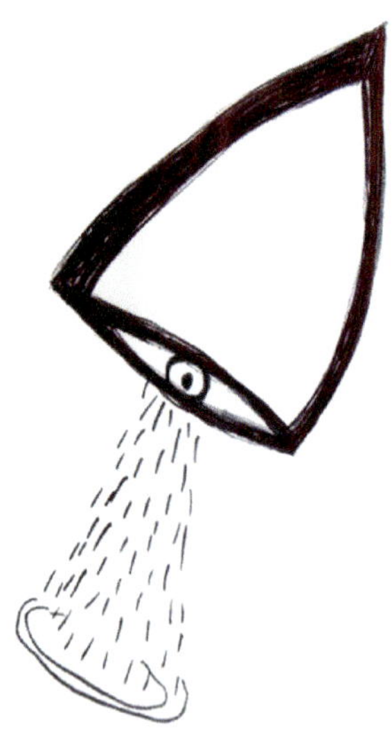

Evoro: tries to set a fire whenever hungry.

H agera and Є voro

Studied how different environments can influence movement and behavior with different conditions (careful, slow, fast) based on the surroundings.

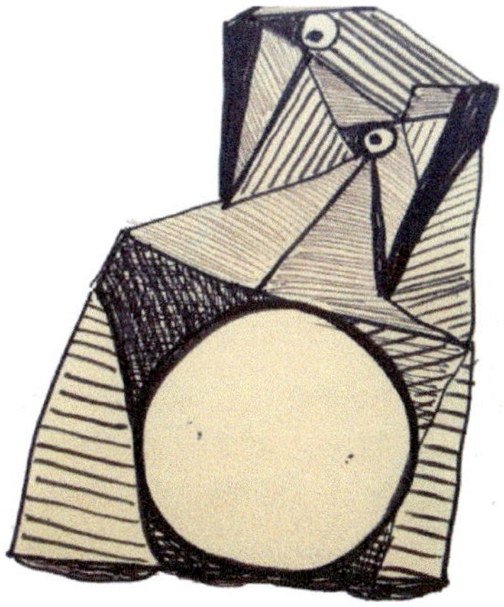

Gtur: eats too much.

G tur and

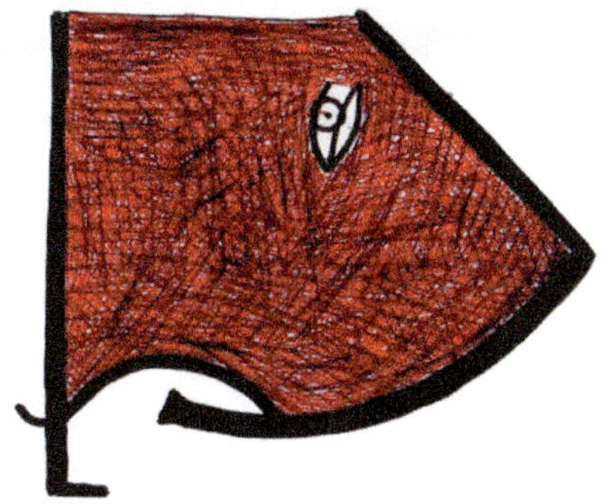

Cyto: wags his tail whenever unsecure.

Cyto

both studied the poetry of waves in nature.

```
# Define a wave as rhythmic and flowing
wave = {'motion': 'rhythmic', 'sound': 'soothing', 'effect': 'calming'}

# Function to describe the poetry of waves
def poetry_of_waves():
    print(f"Waves move in {wave['motion']} patterns, creating {wave['sound']} sounds that are {wave['effect']} to the soul.")
# Example
poetry_of_waves() # Output: Waves move in rhythmic patterns, creating soothing sounds that are calming to the soul.
```

Decasta: opens bottles with her tail.

D ecasta and

Ioner: adds h befere every sentence.

I oner

connected nature and energy through electromagnetic waves and their poetic "dance" across the spectrum

```
# Define electromagnetic waves and their frequencies
waves = {'radio': 'low', 'microwave': 'medium', 'infrared': 'heat', 'light': 'visible', 'UV': 'high'}

# Define electromagnetic waves and their frequencies
waves = {'radio': 'low', 'microwave': 'medium', 'infrared': 'heat', 'light': 'visible', 'UV': 'high'}

# Function to describe the poetry of electromagnetic waves
def poetry_of_em_waves():
    for wave, energy in waves.items():
        print(f"The {wave} wave dances with {energy}-frequency energy, painting nature in unseen rhythms.")

# Example
poetry_of_em_waves()
```

Bukutu: thinks he had Egytpian origin.

B ukutu and

Cakadortu: has to use hands to eat.

C akadorutu

studied findings of Howard Gardner and his theory of Multiple Intelligences

```
# Define Gardner's intelligences
intelligences = {
    'Linguistic': 'words and language',
    'Logical-Mathematical': 'numbers and logic',
    'Spatial': 'visualizing and space',
    'Musical': 'rhythm and sound',
    'Bodily-Kinesthetic': 'physical activity',
    'Interpersonal': 'understanding others',
    'Intrapersonal': 'self-awareness',
    'Naturalistic': 'nature and environment'
}

# Function to explain an intelligence type
def explain_intelligence(type):
    print(f"{type} intelligence is about {intelligences.get(type, 'understanding the world in unique ways')}.")
# Example
explain_intelligence('Spatial')  # Output: Spatial intelligence is about visualizing and space.
```

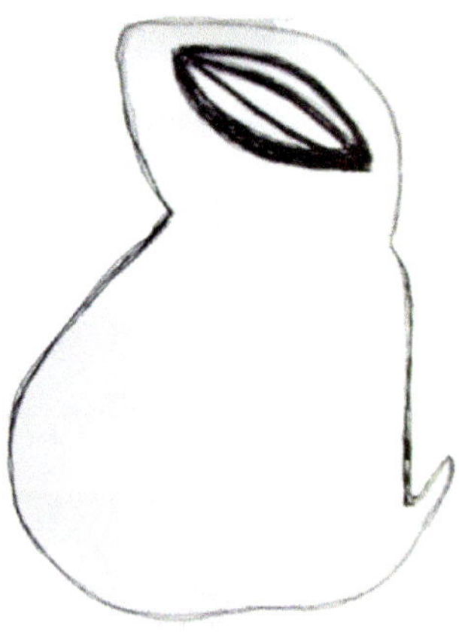

Dasa: sleeps when talking.

D asa and

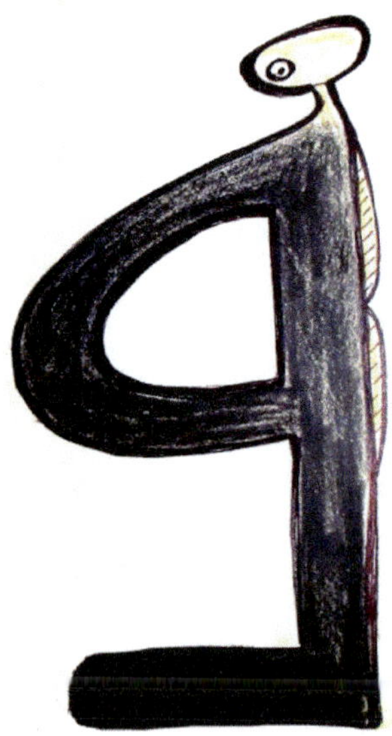

Defolo: works the best on empty stomach.

D efolo

emphasize standardized measures of cognitive ability, like IQ tests, rather than recognizing diverse ways of learning and understanding. They both scored very high and are proud of not being able to draw.

Dutachar: slow to make acqainttances.

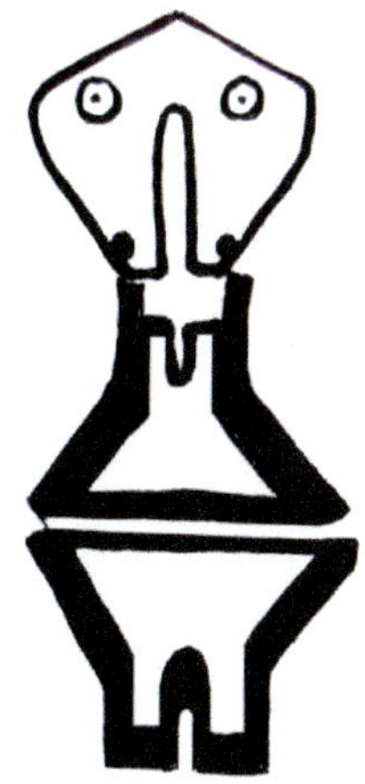

Vakrop: when he wants to say something, he begins by thinking about it.

Dutachar and Vakrop always compete.

Matacha: has more problems with finding listeners, than you'd know.

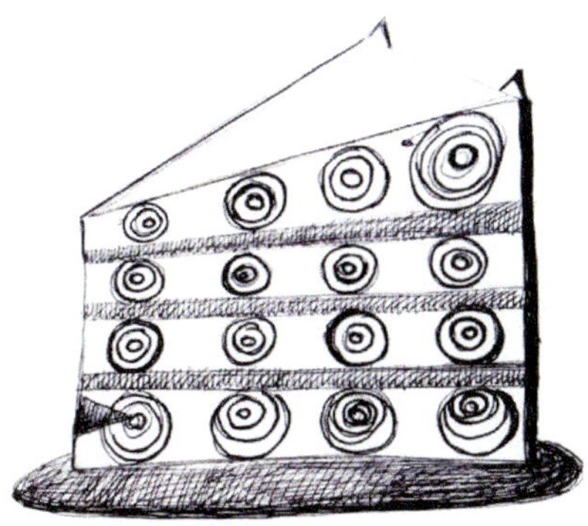

Dumera: decorates himself.

Matacha and Dumera spent all their time together and believed in the basic Organism class that illustrates the idea of symbiosis through a method that shows how two organisms support each other

```
class Organism:
    def __init__(self, name):
        self.name = name

    def symbiosis(self, partner):
        return f"{self.name} and {partner.name} support each other."
# Example usage
plant = Organism("Plant")
fungus = Organism("Fungus")

print(plant.symbiosis(fungus))
```

Dagarusta: talks to her body, and gives orders

D agarusta wondered how physical forces affect weather

```
import numpy as np


# Simulate the effect of pressure differences on wind speed
# Force = Pressure difference / Distance

def wind_speed(pressure_diff, distance):
    return pressure_diff / distance

# Example values for pressure difference (Pascals) and distance (meters)
pressure_diff = 100  # Pressure difference in Pascals
distance = 10000  # Distance in meters

# Calculate wind speed in meters per second
speed = wind_speed(pressure_diff, distance)

# Simulate Coriolis effect (deflection due to Earth's rotation)
def coriolis_effect(speed, latitude):
    coriolis_force = 2 * 7.2921e-5 * speed * np.sin(np.radians(latitude))  # Earth's rotation speed
    return coriolis_force
# Example latitude (degrees)
latitude = 45

# Calculate Coriolis force (affects wind direction)
coriolis_force = coriolis_effect(speed, latitude)

print(f"Wind speed: {speed:.2f} m/s due to pressure differences")
print(f"Coriolis force at {latitude}° latitude: {coriolis_force:.6f} m/s²")
```

Guchachu: polite and focussed.

G uchachu and

Dyran: always thinks about tomorrow.

D yran

saw pressure differences as air moves from high to low pressure, creating wind and the Coriolis effect: due to Earth's rotation, the wind is deflected, affecting wind patterns in the whole world. These forces influence the distribution of ocean currents and weather patterns.

Fugoro: hides his hobbies to make a big impact.

Fugoro and

Pukado: always has cold hands and does not like it.

Pukado

understood homeostasis as it helps organisms adapt to changes while keeping their internal conditions within a narrow, optimal range

```
# Homeostasis: Regulating body temperature
def regulate_temperature(current_temp, target_temp):
    if current_temp > target_temp:
        return "Sweating to cool down"
    elif current_temp < target_temp:
        return "Shivering to generate heat"
    else:
        return "Body is at optimal temperature"
# Example: Target body temperature is 37°C
target_temp = 37

# Simulate different current body temperatures
current_temp = 39  # Example of a higher body temperature

response = regulate_temperature(current_temp, target_temp)
print(f"Current temperature: {current_temp}°C")
print(response)
```

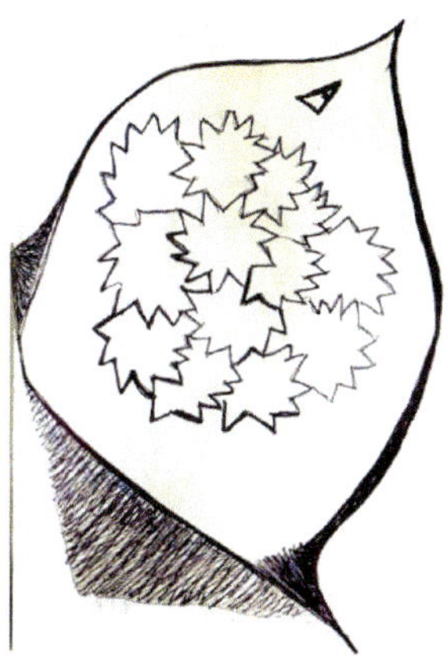
Bugonten: works only internally.

Bugonten and

Fof: is able to solve all the problems fast.

Fof

```
def disequilibrium(current_temp, target_temp):
```

return "Heat stroke" if current_temp > target_temp + 2 else "Hypothermia" if current_temp < target_tem
experienced homeostatic imbalance

```
    p - 2 else "Stable"

# Target body temperature is 37°C
print(disequilibrium(40, 37))  # Example: High temperature causes heat stroke
```

Duxole: finds happiness in everything.

D uxole and

Fusuha: coffee is his best friend.

F usuha

thought that the world was chaotic

```
def chaos_system(x, r):
    return r * x * (1 - x)

# Small change in initial condition
x1, x2 = 0.5, 0.5001
r = 3.9  # Chaotic parameter

for _ in range(10):
    x1, x2 = chaos_system(x1, r), chaos_system(x2, r)
    print(f"x1: {x1:.4f}, x2: {x2:.4f}")

# Observe how small differences quickly lead to diverging results
```

Felaso: has the best career.

F elaso and

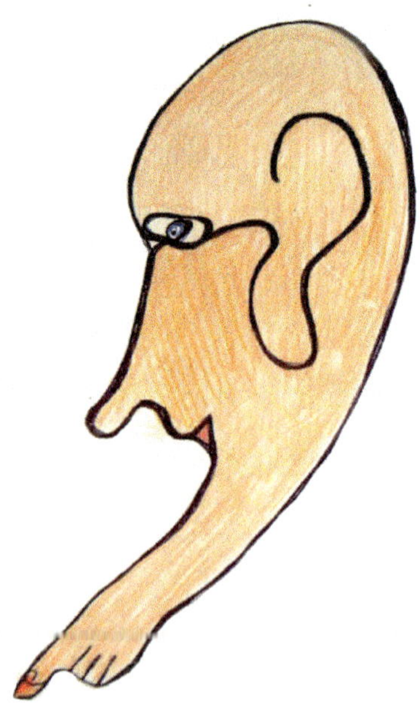

Initolem: watches diet of cats.

I nitolem

were highly sensitive to initial conditions, leading to unpredictable behavior.

Jio: connects with others through focussing.

J io and

Mondual: limmited tools, but vast knowledge.

M ondual

collected fractals

```
# List of different types of fractals
fractals = [
    "Mandelbrot Set",
    "Julia Set",
    "Sierpinski Triangle",
    "Koch Snowflake",
    "Cantor Set",
    "Dragon Curve",
    "Barnsley Fern"
]

# Print the list of fractals
print("Types of Fractals:")
for fractal in fractals:
    print(f"- {fractal}")
```

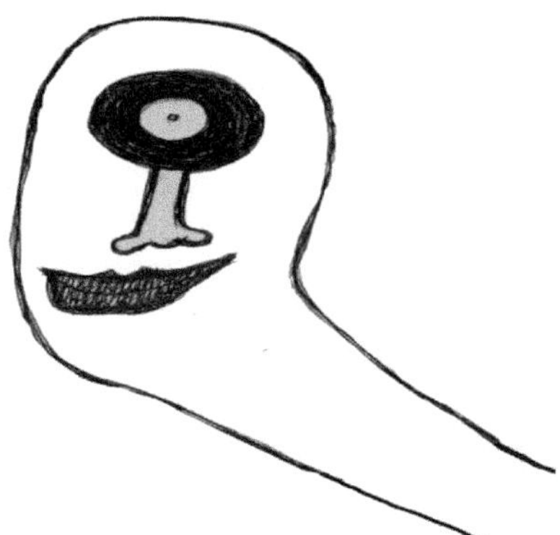

Budengo: knows the right words for each situation.

B udengo and

Ungo: stopped using his watch, but the habits stayed.

U ngo

explained them

```
def explain_fractals():
    description = ("Fractals are complex patterns that are self-similar across different scales. "
                   "They are generated by repeating a simple process iteratively. Examples include the "
                   "Mandelbrot set and the Sierpinski triangle.")
    return description

# Print the explanation of fractals
print(explain_fractals())
```

Fusagure: plays piano wherever he goes.

Denco: developed a deep sense of being.

Fusagure and Denco

discussed reflections

```
def explain_reflections():
    description = ("Reflections are transformations that flip an object over a line (or plane in 3D) "
                   "to create a mirror image. Every point of the object is mapped to a point directly "
                   "opposite across the reflection line or plane.")
    return description

# Print the explanation of reflections
```

Faraduran: gives back what he receives.

Delek: observes everything and draws conclussions.

Faraduran and Delek

enjoyed looking at them in nature.

Saquana: knows your dreams and hopes.

Ofu: knows the power of yes.

Saquana and Ofu

enjoyed talking about refractions

```
def explain_refractions():
    description = ("Refractions occur when light or other waves change direction as they pass from one medium "
                   "into another with a different density. This bending of light is caused by the change in speed "
                   "as the waves enter the new medium.")
    return description

# Print the explanation of refractions
print(explain_refractions())
```

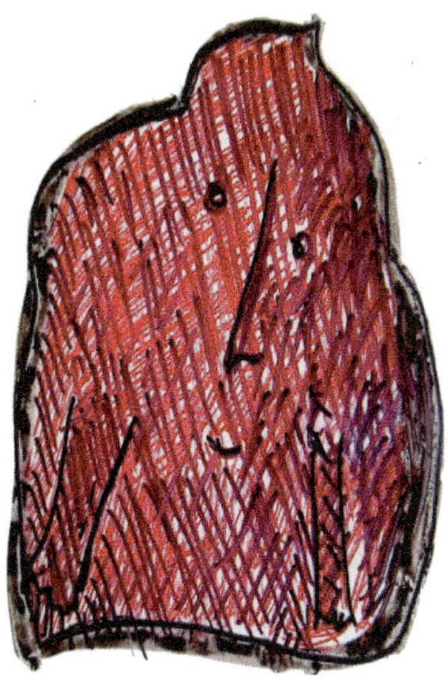

Furucho: constantly listens to music.

Dagarusta: talks to her body, and gives orders.

Furucho and Dagarusta

discussed how light changes direction due to the difference in density between the two mediums.

Jadugas: types slowly, but makes no mistakes.

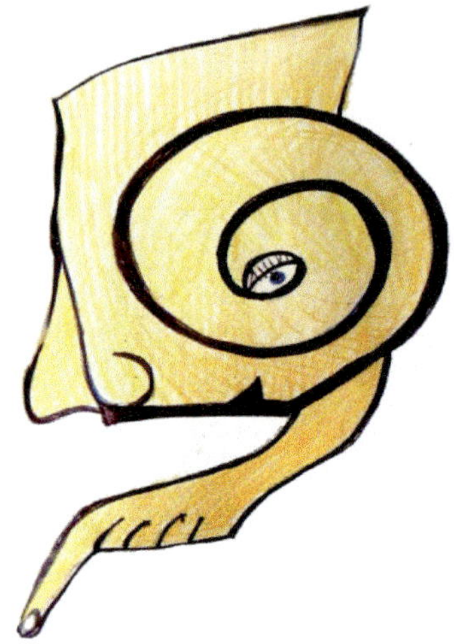

Erux: knows it all.

enjoyed symmetry

```
def explain_symmetry():
   description = ("Symmetry is when an object can be divided into parts that are mirror images of each other. "
                  "In geometry, symmetry means the object remains unchanged when
   transformed, like rotated or reflected.")  return description

# Print the explanation of
symmetry
print(explain_symmetry())
```

Faramaca: can controls the sideways movement.

Eviego: his smell is used to solve any questin.

loved nature-based designs

```
import turtle

# Set up the screen
screen = turtle.Screen()
screen.bgcolor("white")

# Create a turtle object
leaf = turtle.Turtle()
leaf.shape("turtle")
leaf.color("green")
leaf.speed(10)  # Set drawing speed to fast

# Function to draw the leaf shape
def draw_half_leaf():
    for _ in range(2):
        leaf.circle(100, 90)  # Draw a quarter-circle arc
        leaf.left(90)  # Turn 90 degrees left to make the other arc
```

```
# Draw the symmetrical leaf
leaf.penup()
leaf.goto(0, -100)  # Move to starting position
leaf.pendown()

# Draw the first half of the leaf
draw_half_leaf()

# Draw the other half of the leaf by mirroring the first half
leaf.right(180)
draw_half_leaf()

# Hide the turtle and display the result
leaf.hideturtle()

# Keep the window open
turtle.done()
```

Hunanga: becomes nicer after dinners.

H unanga and

Husago: is happy, sad, or just is.

H usago

studied water habitats

```
water_habitats = ["Oceans", "Rivers", "Lakes", "Ponds", "Swamps","Wetlands", "Estuaries"]  for
habitat in water_habitats:
        print(habitat)
```

Zutasama: never gives up.

Junku: displays two personalities.

Z utasama and

J unku

prefered deserts

```
deserts = ["Hot Desert", "Cold Desert", "Semi-arid Desert", "Coastal Desert"]
for desert in deserts:
    print(desert)
```

Galud: has solutions to your problems.

Batea: can dissaper whenever needed.

Galud and Batea

studied human senses

```
human_senses = ["Sight", "Hearing", "Taste", "Smell", "Touch"]
for sense in human_senses:
    print(sense)
```

Feroza: sees double every Tuesday.

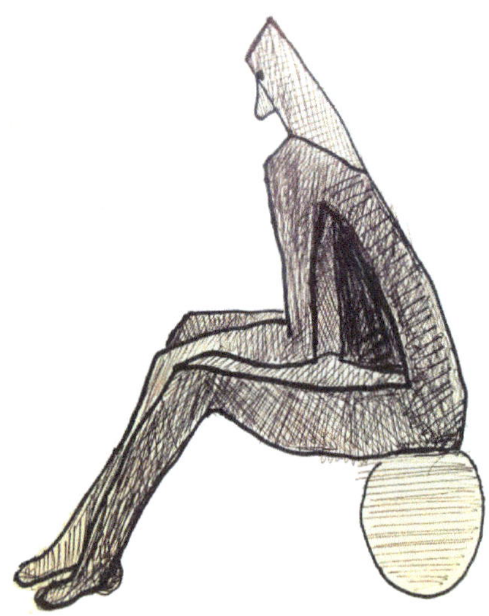

Iolo: he holds it all together inside.

Feroza and Iolo

believed people can sense more than that

```
animal_senses = ["Echolocation", "Magnetoreception", "Infrared Vision", "Electroreception", "Ultrasound Hearing"]
for sense in animal_senses:
    print(sens
```

Caredo: understands all creatures around him.

Caluta - can make things dissapear.

Caredo and Caluta

like everything simple and concrete

```
thinking = {"Concrete Thinking": "Apple is a fruit", "Abstract Thinking": "Health is important"}

for type_, example in thinking.items():
    print(f"{type_}: {example}")
```

Fafatu: likes everything.

Clister: gets rid of bad habits.

Fafatu and Clister

Were fascinated by abstrahing as a way to remove what was not crucial to deliver information

```
abstraction_ladder = {
    "Transportation": ["Land", "Air", "Water"],
    "Land": ["Car", "Bus", "Bicycle"],
    "Car": ["Electric Car", "Hybrid Car", "Gasoline Car"]
}

for level, specifics in abstraction_ladder.items():
    print(f"{level}: {', '.join(specifics)}")
```

Fihle: Experimented with physical laws.

Fihle and

Futoleto: owns one horse and one cat.

Futoleto

were heavy smokers. They had no choice, they kept saying.

Iufafu: has no questions.

Iufafu and

Benea: makes something out of something.

Benea

wanted to help and shared various perspectives over time:

```
smoking_perception = {
    "1950s": "Glamorous and popular",
    "1960s": "Health concerns emerging",
    "1970s": "Health risks recognized",
    "1980s": "Regulation begins",
    "1990s": "Anti-smoking campaigns grow",
    "2000s": "Public bans increase",
    "2010s": "E-cigarettes rise",
    "2020s": "Smoking rates decline, vaping concerns rise"
}

for decade, perception in smoking_perception.items():
    print(f"{decade}: {perception}")
```

Gizuro: his secrets are your secrets.

Gizuro and

Gijde: could tell if they tell the truth or not.

Gijde

felt somehow lost in life.

Guda: washes clothing on the go.

Guda and

Bavega: is being constantly watched.

Bavega

outlined Maslow's five levels of human needs and Gardner's eight intelligences in a straightforward way

```
# Maslow's Hierarchy of Needs
maslow_needs = {
    1: 'Physiological',
    2: 'Safety',
    3: 'Love/Belonging',
    4: 'Esteem',
    5: 'Self-Actualization'
}

# Howard Gardner's Multiple Intelligences
gardner_intelligences = [
    'Linguistic', 'Logical-Mathematical', 'Spatial',
    'Musical', 'Bodily-Kinesthetic', 'Interpersonal',
    'Intrapersonal', 'Naturalistic'
]

# Displaying needs and intelligences
print("Maslow's Hierarchy of Needs:")
for level, need in maslow_needs.items():
    print(f"Level {level}: {need}")

print("\nHoward Gardner's Multiple Intelligences:")
for intelligence in gardner_intelligences:
    print(f"- {intelligence}")
```

Fim: can reach anyplace

Finuho: carries all of his thoughts.

Fim and Finuho

struggled with the concept of sounds that humans cannot hear, but animals can.

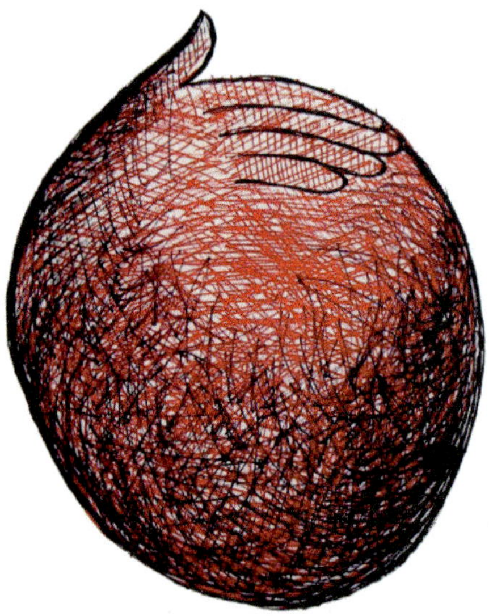

Labudo: enjoys every meal.

Labudo

had the answer.

```
class Sound:
    def __init__(self, frequency):
        self.frequency = frequency

    def can_hear(self, species):
        if species == "human" and self.frequency > 20000:
            return False # Humans can't hear frequencies above 20,000 Hz
        return True # Animals like dogs can hear higher frequencies
# Example usage
```

ultrasound = Sound(25000) # 25,000 Hz sound print(ultrasound.can_hear("human")) # False y.

Amyre: she always spoke from the bottom of her heart.

Amyre and

Gefachu: makes all the major decissions.

Gefahu

wondered about the new tools allowing them to see what is invisible to their eyes.

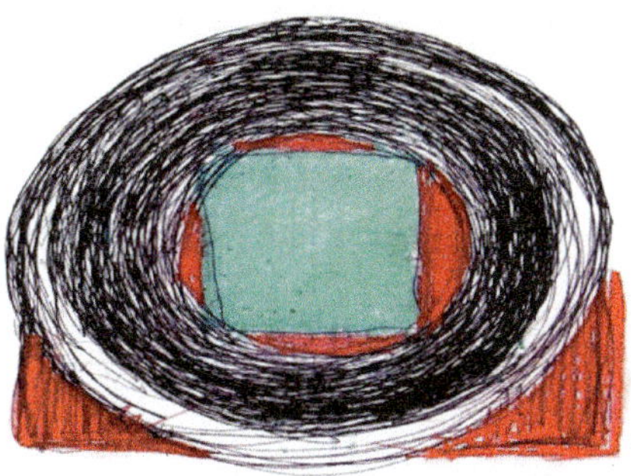

Icao

Icao: remembers times when links were printed in the yellow pages.

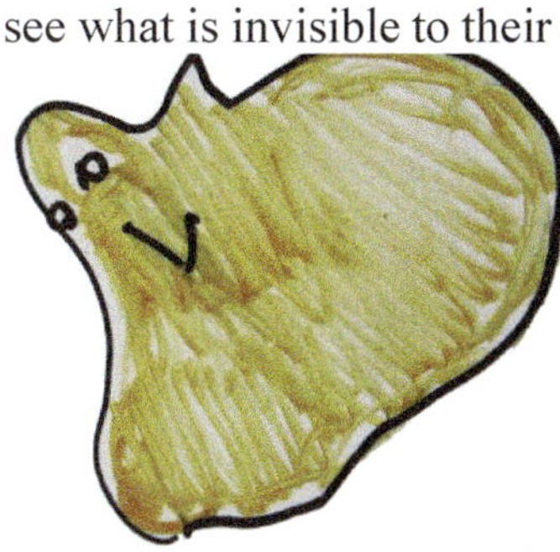

Fudara: his senses are very sensitive.

Fudara

made a list of scales in nature:

```
# Scales in Nature
scales = {
    'Pico (10^-12 m)': 'Atoms',
    'Nano (10^-9 m)': 'Molecules, DNA',
    'Micro (10^-6 m)': 'Cells, Bacteria',
    'Milli (10^-3 m)': 'Insects, Grains of Sand',
    'Meter (1 m)': 'Humans, Trees',
    'Kilo (10^3 m)': 'Mountains, Large Buildings',
    'Mega (10^6 m)': 'Countries, Continents',
    'Giga (10^9 m)': 'Planets',
    'Tera (10^12 m)': 'Stars',
    'Peta (10^15 m)': 'Solar Systems',
    'Exa (10^18 m)': 'Galaxies',
    'Zetta (10^21 m)': 'Galaxy Clusters',
    'Yotta (10^24 m)': 'Observable Universe'
}

# Displaying scales
for scale, example in scales.items():
    print(f"{scale}: {example}")
```

They all wrote a grant for:

Scanning Tunneling Microscope (STM), Atomic Force Microscope (AFM), Transmission Electron Microscope (TEM), Atomic Force Microscope (AFM), X-ray Crystallography, Optical Microscope, Confocal Microscope, Fluorescence Microscope, Stereo Microscope, Digital Camera with Macro Lens, Human eye, Laser Measuring Devices, Motion Capture Systems, Theodolites, LiDAR (Light Detection and Ranging), Satellite Imagery, Geographic Information Systems (GIS), Satellite Remote Sensing, Earth Observation Satellites (e.g., Landsat), Space Telescopes (e.g., Hubble), Planetary Radar Systems, Optical Telescopes (e.g., VLT), Radio Telescopes, Space Probes, Infrared Telescopes (e.g., James Webb Space Telescope), Spacecraft (e.g., Voyager, Hubble Space Telescope), Radio Telescopes, Gravitational Wave Detectors (e.g., LIGO), Large Optical Telescopes, X-ray Observatories (e.g., Chandra X-ray Observatory), Gravitational Lensing Techniques, Cosmic Microwave Background Detectors (e.g., Planck Satellite), Large-scale Sky Surveys (e.g., Sloan Digital Sky Survey). And got it all.

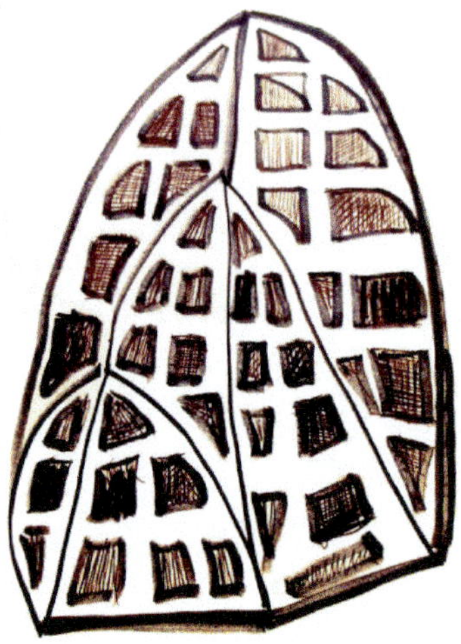

Gydus: Has problems finding the right door.

Gydus and

Nasora: invites everyone who'd be interested in nature.

Nasora

had many different tools

Pininga: holds it all in her pocket.

Pininga and

Haratena: she was a grand piano before.

Haratena

visualized the invisible by simulating the detection of unseen wavelengths of light (infrared/ultraviolet):

```
# Simulating biophotonics revealing invisible light
visible_light_range = (400, 700)  # Wavelengths in nm (visible spectrum)
biophotonics_range = (200, 1200)  # Extended range detected by biophotonics

def is_visible(wavelength):
    return visible_light_range[0] <= wavelength <= visible_light_range[1]

def biophotonics_detection(wavelength):
    if not is_visible(wavelength):
        return f"Wavelength {wavelength} nm is invisible, detected by biophotonics!"
    return f"Wavelength {wavelength} nm is visible to the human eye."

# Test examples: UV, visible, and IR light
wavelengths = [300, 500, 900]
for w in wavelengths:
    print(biophotonics_detection(w))
```

The beauty of the outcomes astounded them!

Bicadel: has enough of everything.

Fusafa: predicts everything starting with 2.

Bicadel and Fusafa

loved to have pets

Kulgress: he comes out with his conclussions

Gatae: depends on his imagination.

Kulgress and Gatae

wondered why

```
class Pet:
   def __init__(self, name, species):
      self.name = name
      self.species = species
      self.is_captive = True


   def release(self):
      self.is_captive = False
      return f"{self.name} the {self.species} has been released."
# Example usage
pet1 = Pet("Buddy", "dog")
print(f"{pet1.name} is captive: {pet1.is_captive}")
print(pet1.release())
print(f"{pet1.name} is captive: {pet1.is_captive}")
```

They soon took the zookeeper's positions.

Dytare: her brain stayed unknown to anyone she talked to.

Huru: always has something to do.

Dytare and Huru

wondered if they would like to hear what animals can but others do not

Iyuko: soft, mellow, yet enthusiastic.

Apton: always a good host.

Iyko and Apton

gave a list of animals with better hearing to compare them to those with hearing abilities similar to human ones

```
animals_can_hear_more = ["dog", "bat", "dolphin"]
animals_same_as_humans = ["human", "cat", "elephant"]

for animal in animals_can_hear_more:
    print(f"{animal.capitalize()} can hear more than humans.")

for animal in animals_same_as_humans:
    print(f"{animal.capitalize()} hears similar to humans.")
```

They adopted three cats and one dog from the animal shelter.

Jugartun: best friend with his friend.

Eforo: enjoys when they take him for an egg.

Jugartun and Eforo

wondered about the impact of different parts of the electromagnetic spectrum on our lives.

Er: could mantain mountain holes.

Agafia: talks only when asked.

Er and Agafia saw it as:

```
spectrum = {
    "Radio waves": "Communication (TV, radio, cellphones)",
    "Microwaves": "Cooking, Wi-Fi",
    "Infrared": "Heat sensing, remote controls",
    "Visible light": "Vision, photography",
    "Ultraviolet": "Tanning, sterilization",
    "X-rays": "Medical imaging",
    "Gamma rays": "Cancer treatment"
}

for wave, impact in spectrum.items():
    print(f"{wave}: {impact}")
```

They voted for the radio waves as the most enjoyable ones.

Nuhu: always solves all the issues.

Nuhu and

Hanera: always somewhat suspicious.

Henera

wished to be able to experience more in life.

Gasuka: looks nice when sad.

Gasuka and

Din: knows his ways to communicate well.

Din

highlighted senses we no longer have or have diminished compared to certain animals

```
lost_senses = {
  "Echolocation": "Used by bats and dolphins for navigation",
  "Magnetoreception": "Birds use Earth's magnetic field to migrate",
  "Ultraviolet vision": "Insects like bees can see UV light",
  "Infrared sensing": "Snakes detect heat from prey"
}

for sense, description in lost_senses.items():

  print(f"Lost sense: {sense} - {description}")
```

Soon, they all started a tool company that helped others experience more.

Det: algebraic geometry is all he needs.

Det and

Hendo: collects small objects.

Hendo

studied mathematical concepts about real-world phenomena.

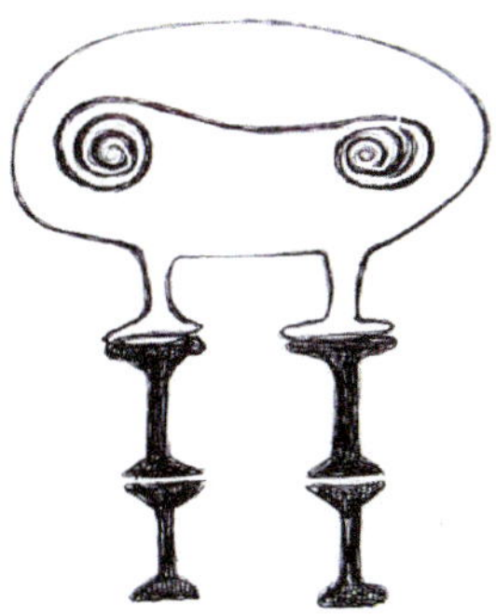

Agilia: relies on support systems.

Agilia and

Huteno: gathers daily strengths from thinking about the growth of a rose.

Huteno

linked geometry to physics, and nature

import math

want to know about not known sensory channels.

```
world_patterns = {
    "Circle": math.pi * 2 * 1,  # Circumference of a unit circle
    "Gravity": 9.8 * 1,         # Gravity's acceleration (m/s²)
    "Golden Ratio": (1 + math.sqrt(5)) / 2,  # Proportion in nature
    "Exponential Growth": math.exp(1)        # Population growth, finance
}

for concept, value in world_patterns.items():
    print(f"{concept}: {value:.2f}")
```

They noted that nothing surpasses the beauty of nature that mathematics so craftfully describes.

Duduco: can see it all at once.

D uduco and

Firiza: always ready for anything.

F iriza

were puzzled by communicating vessels: when two vessels are connected, their liquid levels equalize.

Beduge: watches every sunrise and every sunset on a daily basis, even if there is no sun.

B eduge and

Din: knows his ways to communicate well.

D ibu

had an answer.

```
# Initial water levels in two connected vessels
vessel1 = 8  # in liters
vessel2 = 2  # in liters

# Equalize water levels
def equalize(v1, v2):
    total = v1 + v2
    level = total / 2
    return level, level

vessel1, vessel2 = equalize(vessel1, vessel2)

print(f"Water level in Vessel 1: {vessel1} liters")
print(f"Water level in Vessel 2: {vessel2} liters")
```

It is all connected, they concluded.

Gutera: knows well how and when to hide.

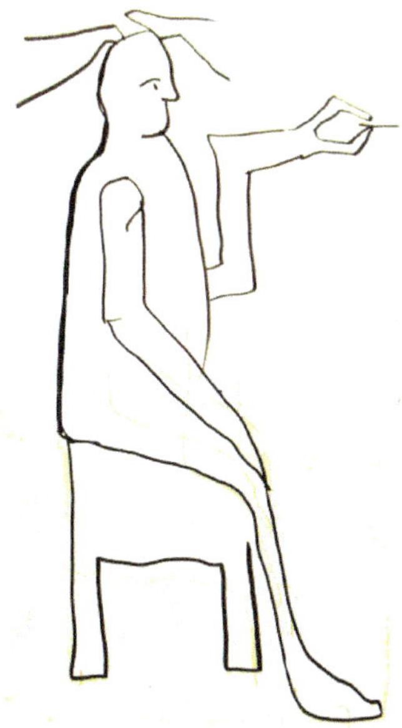

Fusagi: can fix the tiniest structures.

Gudera and Fusagi

focused on energy KE=21mv

```
# Calculate kinetic energy
mass = 10  # kg
velocity = 5  # m/s
KE = 0.5 * mass * velocity**2
print(f"Kinetic Energy: {KE} Joules")
```

Cata: writes from his memory.

Zyceza: can smell anything at the longest distance and diagnose it at once.

Cata and Zyceza

came up with a list of energy, old, new, and experimental:

Coal	Tidal and Wave Energy
Natural Gas	Biogas
Oil (Petroleum)	Advanced Nuclear (Fission & Fusion)
Wood/Biomass	Ocean Thermal Energy Conversion (OTEC)
Peat	Artificial Photosynthesis
Hydropower	Space-based Solar Power
Nuclear Energy	Algae-based Biofuels
Solar Energy	Quantum Dot Solar Cells
Wind Energy	Piezoelectric Energy
Geothermal Energy	Thermoelectric Generators
Hydrogen	Microbial Fuel Cells

Pugerelsa: has friends, but prefers alone.

Pugerelsa is fascinated by the concept of bridges.

Hurateca: makes it all simple and short.

Hurateca and

Beracho: examins every bite she takes.

Beracho

tried to make a list

```
# Dictionary of bridge types and their key concepts
bridges = {
    "Beam Bridge": "Supported by beams, good for short spans.",
    "Arch Bridge": "Uses a curved arch to distribute weight, strong for long spans.",
    "Suspension Bridge": "Hangs from cables, suitable for very long spans.",
    "Truss Bridge": "Uses a framework of triangles, strong and efficient for medium spans."
}

# Display bridge types and concepts
for bridge, concept in bridges.items():
    print(f"{bridge}: {concept}")
```

Samtua: manages all her balances.

but it was about the structural ones only, and both Samtua and

Pugerelsa liked metaphors.

Hurozu: knows how to rest.

Avvaroo: grants fifty wishes selected carefully.

Hurozu and Avvarroo collected precious stones.

Jaatan: checks every corner every two minutes.

Duduco: can see it all at once.

Jaatan and Duduco used them practical ways in industries like electronics, tools, and technology:

```
# Practical uses of precious stones beyond decoration
precious_stones = {
    "Diamond": "Industrial cutting and drilling tools due to hardness.",
    "Ruby": "Used in laser technology for its optical properties.",
    "Sapphire": "Scratch-resistant windows in electronics and watch crystals.",
    "Quartz": "Used in clocks and electronics for precise timekeeping."
}

# Display stones and their uses
for stone, use in precious_stones.items():
    print(f"{stone}: {use}")
```

Soon, they opened a practical jewelry store for beauty items providing safety and convenience.

Vuturandu: knows when to act.

Vuturandu wants to learn about telepathy

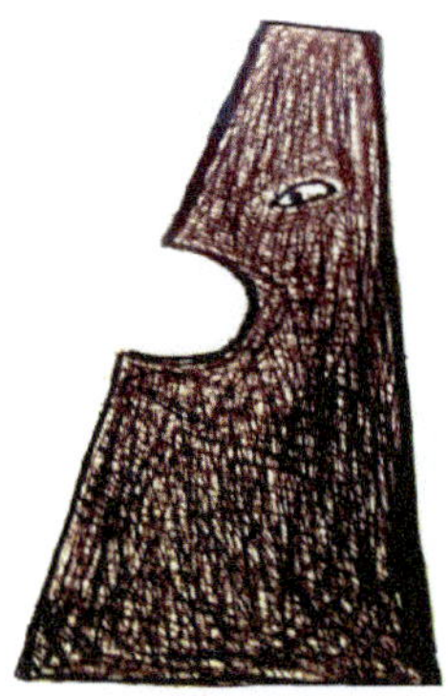

Bazelo: invites all the birds.

Bazelo and

Pensar: his passions are structure and results.

Pensar

came up with some explanations:

```
# Explanation of telepathy
def explain_telepathy():
    return "Telepathy is the hypothetical ability to transmit thoughts or feelings directly between minds without using known sensory channels."

# Display explanation
print(explain_telepathy())
```

Lajena: can speak four languages at the same time.

Lajena

Bugu: can be taken for a tree, if he wants.

Bugu

Lanarazo: they are inseparrable, which worries some of his friends.

Lanarazo

Felcara: notices the slightest changes.

Felcara

study historically known ways of communication

Hungo: changes notes for cash.

Hungo and

Kufanyo: always first to explore.

Kufanyo

suggest their answers:

```
# Historical methods of communication
communication_methods = {
    "Smoke Signals": "Used by Native Americans for long-distance signaling.",
    "Carrier Pigeons": "Used to carry messages over long distances.",
    "Drum Signals": "Used by various cultures for long-distance communication.",
    "Semaphore": "Visual signaling using flags or lights."
}

# Display communication methods
for method, description in communication_methods.items():
    print(f"{method}: {description}")
```

Felchencor: waites for the hail.

Felchencor and

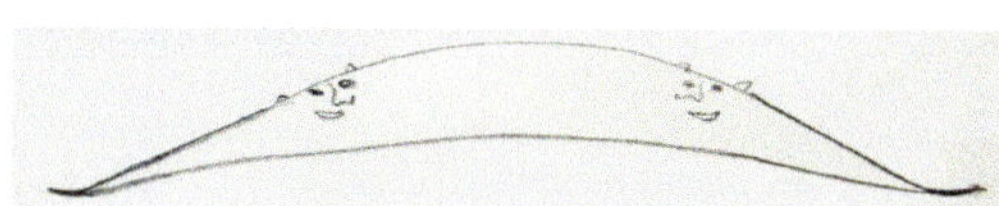

Fradu: always talks to himself.

Fradu

Enjoy their phones too much.

Dugra: has handsfull of work.

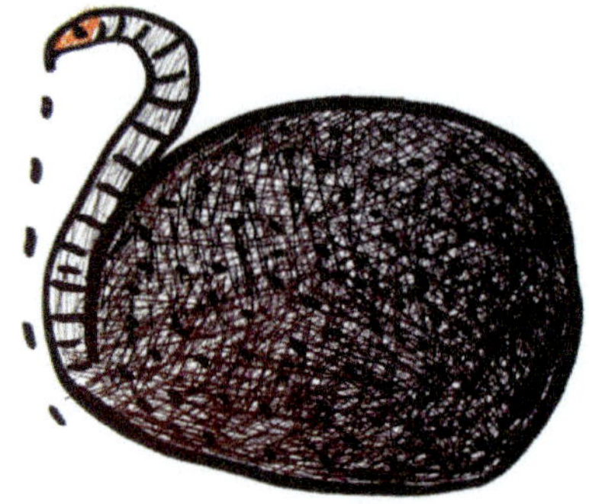

Fugo: owns lots of parking lots.

Dugra and Fugo

wonder why there are so many measurements systems

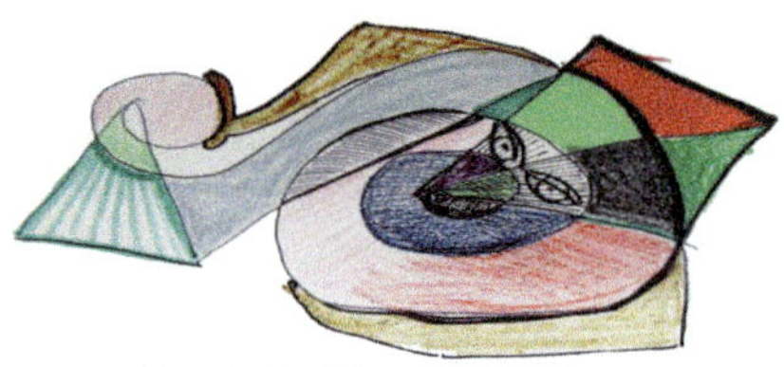

Iringe: developed his own winning system.

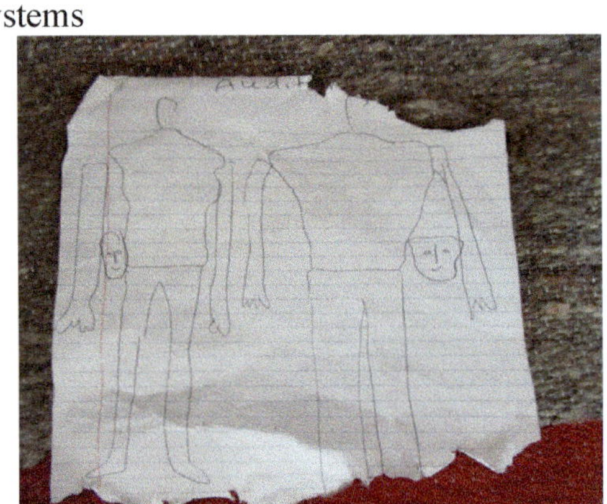

Fugo & Pei: exchange their toughts.

Iringe and Fugo

wrote an explanation of how the systems evolved in time:

```
# Evolution of measurement systems
measurement_evolution = {
    "Ancient Units": "Using body parts (e.g., cubits, feet) for measurement.",
    "Metric System": "Introduced in France, based on decimal units (meters, kilograms).",
    "Imperial System": "Used in the UK and US, includes units like pounds and inches.",
    "SI Units": "Modern system based on the metric system (e.g., meters, kilograms)."
}

# Display measurement evolution
for era, description in measurement_evolution.items():
    print(f"{era}: {description}")
```

then they added an updated explanation:

```
# New measurement systems
new_measurement_systems = {
    "SI Units": "The International System of Units, used worldwide for scientific and everyday measurements.",
    "Imperial Units": "Used primarily in the US and UK for various measurements like distance and weight.",
    "Metric Prefixes": "Units like nano, micro, and kilo to express quantities in powers of ten.",
    "Digital Measurements": "Precision measurements in electronics and computing, e.g., bytes, pixels."
}

# Display new measurement systems
for system, description in new_measurement_systems.items():
    print(f"{system}: {description}")
```

Kardelup: has his mirror image in mind.

Kardelup himself: uses one square only.

Kardelup

likes codes

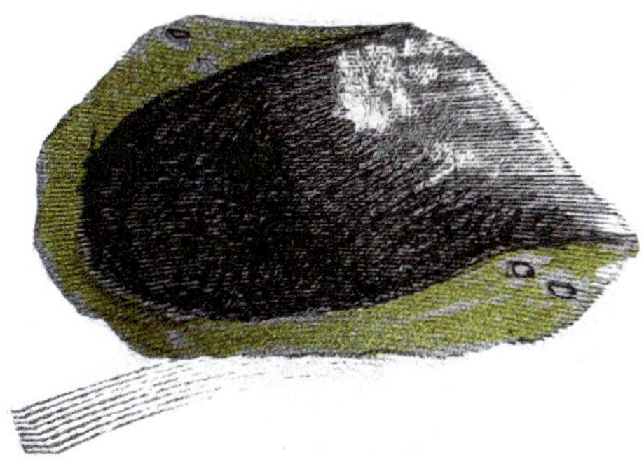

Femige: sees all the problems in time.

Femige and

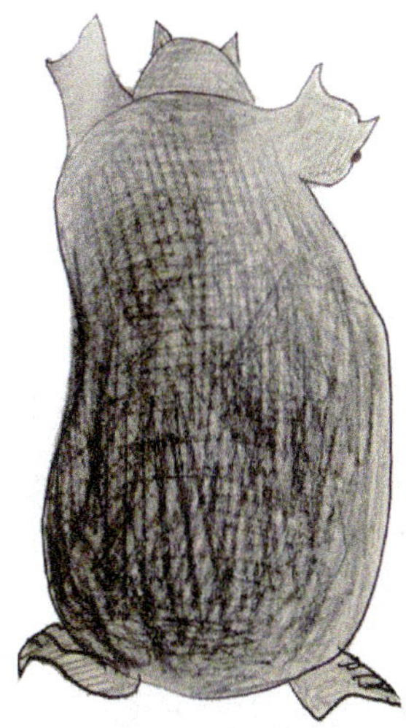

Inlu: consideres good and bad advices.

Inlu

made a list of some:

```
# Evolution of codes throughout history
code_history = {
    "Ancient Ciphers": "Simple substitution codes used in ancient Greece and Rome.",
    "Enigma Machine": "Complex encryption used during WWII for secure communication.",
    "Digital Encryption": "Modern methods like AES and RSA for secure data transmission.",
    "QR Codes": "Used today for storing and quickly accessing information via mobile devices."
}

# Display historical use of codes
for code, description in code_history.items():
    print(f"{code}: {description}")
```

it was written as a code.

Hasafo: always thinks about a better solution.

H usafo and

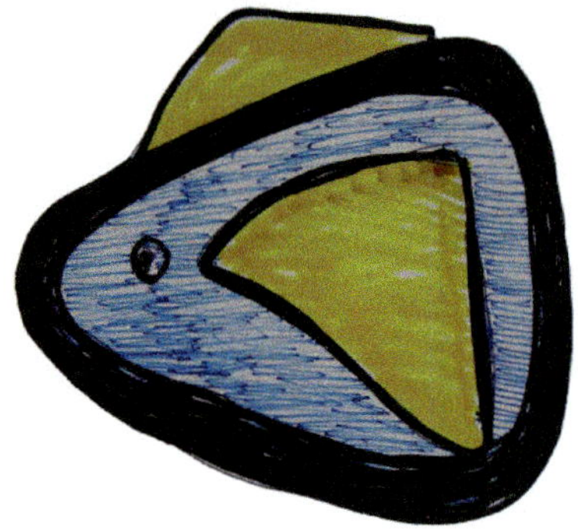

Horuo: knows three styles of writing.

H oruo

wondered why languages are so different

Bugearu: has many unknown powers.

B ugearu and

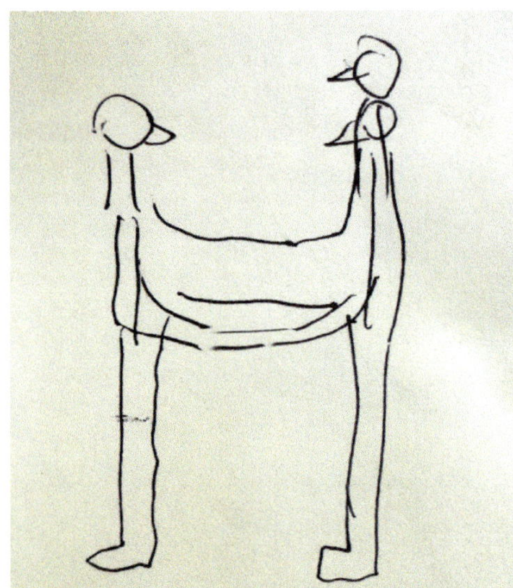

Buglo: best marketting.

B uglo

had an answer:

```
# Reasons for the diversity of languages
language_diversity = {
    "Geographical Isolation": "Communities develop unique languages due to physical separation.",
    "Cultural Evolution": "Languages evolve and diverge as cultures develop distinct identities.",
    "Migration and Trade": "Interactions between different groups lead to the creation of new languages.",
    "Colonialism": "The spread and imposition of languages during colonial periods lead to linguistic diversity."
}

# Display reasons for language diversity
for reason, description in language_diversity.items():
    print(f"{reason}: {description}")
```

They wrote it in English.

Kopel: never gives up in full.

Itoa: eats an apple a day.

Kopel and Itoa wanted to be able to teleport

Ahaaro: has a face for each of you.

Gerua: has endless pockets.

Alhaaro and Gerua explained that

```
# Explanation of teleportation
def explain_teleportation():
    return "Teleportation is the hypothetical transfer of matter or information instantaneously from one location to another, bypassing physical space."

# Display explanation
print(explain_teleportation())
```

They all agreed to invest in a virtual reality system.

Catcha: knows when she looks good.

Huato: makes a record of all good things.

Catcha and Huato were considered all the time being playful.

Cadugo: talks to himself succefully.

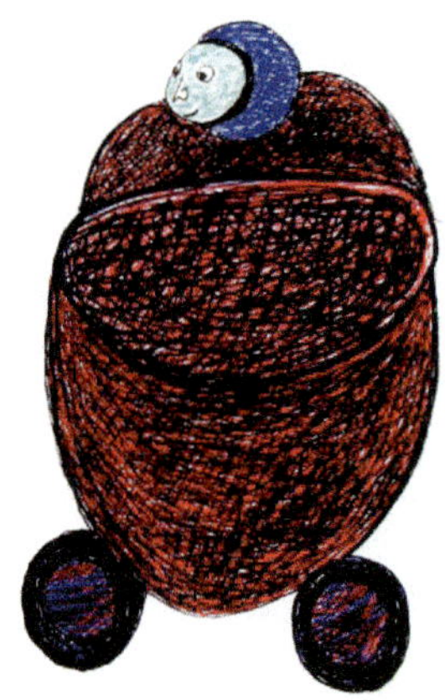

Bugutun: stays warm by staying off the window.

Cadugo and Bugutun had some suggestions for them:

```
# Types of instruments
instrument_types = {
    "String Instruments": ["Piano", "Guitar", "Violin"],
    "Percussion Instruments": ["Drums", "Tambourine", "Xylophone"],
    "Wind Instruments": ["Saxophone", "Flute", "Trumpet"],
    "Keyboard Instruments": ["Piano", "Organ", "Synthesizer"]
}

# Display instrument types and examples
for type_, examples in instrument_types.items():
    print(f"{type_}: {', '.join(examples)}")
```

Now, they cannot decide who plays what and when, so they have to study hard.

Benut: sends inspiration out to the people.

Harada: ties all the facts together.

Benut and Harada

ponder self-similarity

Yunil: has more powers than he knows.

Fyl: knows three alphabets.

Yunil and Fyl

know much about it

```
# Explanation of self-similarity
def explain_self_similarity():
    return "Self-similarity is when a shape or pattern appears similar at different scales or levels of magnification."

# Display explanation
print(explain_self_similarity())
```

Now, together they offer fractal sock knitting classes.

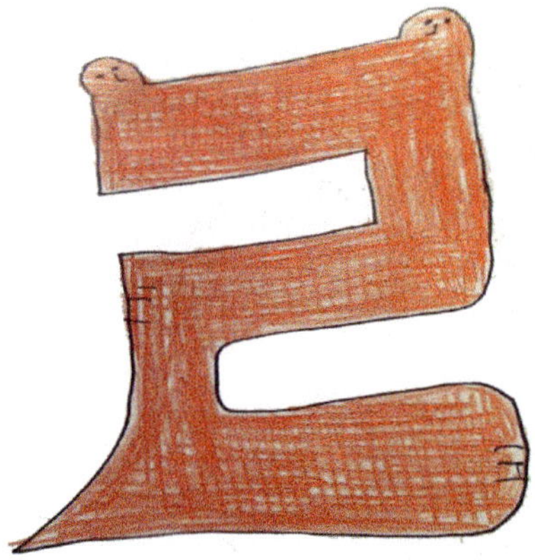

Zualu: to do list is overwhelming.

Zualu and

Baraza: Sees everything.

Baraza

wondered about the role of mathematics in describing the world

Bangel: has powers to focus anytime.

Bangel and

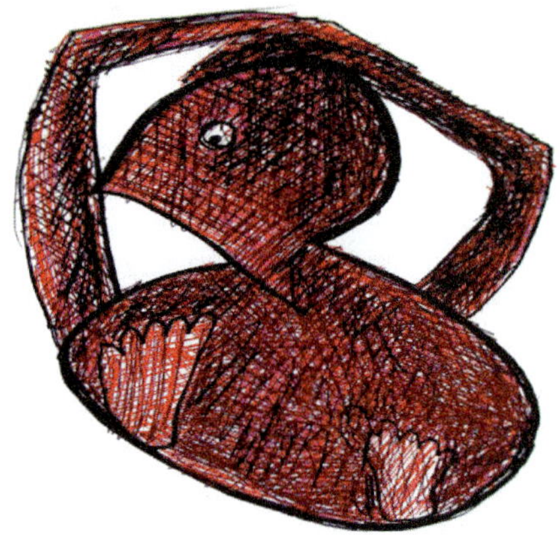

Kardu: has more problems than time to rest.

Kardu

made some suggestions

```
# Role of mathematics in describing the world
def role_of_mathematics():
    return "Mathematics helps describe and understand the world by providing models and formulas to explain patterns, structures, and relationships in nature and human-made systems."

# Display explanation
print(role_of_mathematics())
```

Pufso: reads while eating, eats, while reading

Pufso and

Hu: loves cherimoya.

Hu

Argued that physics serves those purposes better. They studied comparative literature.

Jaturu: got everything he ever wanted.

Juturu and

Letha: knows how to rest

Letha

wanted to know how the newly found rare earth minerals can be used

```
# Uses of rare earth minerals
rare_earth_uses = {
    "Neodymium": "Used in powerful magnets for electric motors and wind turbines.",
    "Lanthanum": "Used in camera lenses and hybrid vehicle batteries.",
    "Cerium": "Used in catalytic converters and glass polishing.",
    "Yttrium": "Used in LEDs and phosphors for display screens."
}

# Display uses of rare earth minerals
for mineral, use in rare_earth_uses.items():
    print(f"{mineral}: {use}")
```

Judte and

Judte: drinks two cups of tea daily.

Ique

wanted to know how rare earth minerals can be used:

```
# How rare earth minerals protect the planet
rare_earth_usage = {
    "Neodymium": "Enables electric motors,.",
    "Lanthanum": "Used in hybrid vehicle batteries..",
    "Cerium": "Helps in catalytic converters..",
    "Yttrium": "Used in energy-efficient LED lighting."
}

# Display usage of rare earth minerals
for mineral, usage in rare_earth_usage.items():
    print(f"{mineral}: {usage}")
```

Jukanero: never in his room.

Jukanero and

Zutango: always discusses things.

Zutango

Could not wait till the snowy season

```
# Hail size comparison in inches
hail_sizes = {
    "Pea": 0.25,
    "Marble": 0.5,
    "Golf Ball": 1.75,
    "Tennis Ball": 2.5,
    "Baseball": 2.75,
    "Grapefruit": 4.5
}

# Display hail size comparison
for hail, size in hail_sizes.items():
    print(f"{hail}: {size} inches")
```

Berenum: conceals the truth.

Berenum and

Yasrund: depends on beautiful sunsets.

Yasrund

Measured speed of various winds

```
# Hurricane categories and wind speeds in mph
hurricane_strengths = {
    "Category 1": "74-95 mph",
    "Category 2": "96-110 mph",
    "Category 3": "111-129 mph",
    "Category 4": "130-156 mph",
    "Category 5": "157+ mph"
}

# Display hurricane strengths
for category, speed in hurricane_strengths.items():
    print(f"{category}: {speed}")
```

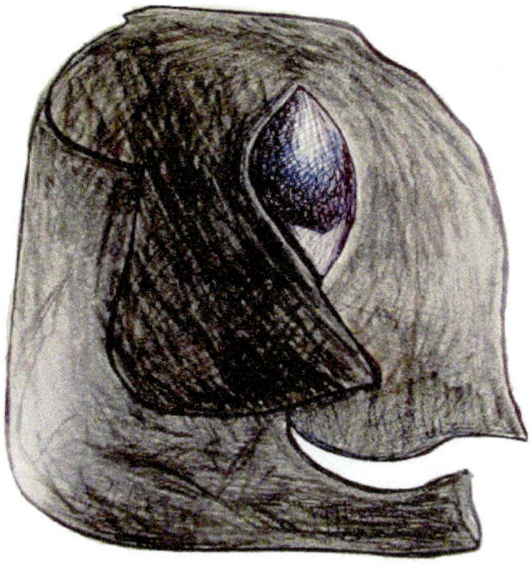

Akund: stays there always.

Akund and

Bezuga: carries his ball to every meeting.

Bezuga

Were the meteorologists and measured the speed of a tornado in the Enhanced Fujita (EF) scale:

```
# Tornado strengths on the EF scale
tornado_strengths = {
    "EF0": "65-85 mph",
    "EF1": "86-110 mph",
    "EF2": "111-135 mph",
    "EF3": "136-165 mph",
    "EF4": "166-200 mph",
    "EF5": "200+ mph"
}

# Display tornado strengths
for category, speed in tornado_strengths.items():
    print(f"{category}: {speed}")
```

Mijataza: she had several faces for various ocassions.

Mijataza and

Mudu: has some healing powers.

Mudu

studied water levels

```
flood_strengths = {
    "Minor Flood": "Inundation of low-lying areas, minimal property damage.",
    "Moderate Flood": "Some inundation of buildings, potential road closures.",
    "Major Flood": "Significant inundation, widespread damage to property.",
    "Catastrophic Flood": "Severe flooding, extensive damage, life-threatening."
}

# Display flood strengths
for level, description in flood_strengths.items():
    print(f"{level}: {description}")
```

Mudru: sees everything.

Lihtun: will tell you all.

Mudru and Lihtun

wondered what would happen if the time stopped

```
def time_stopped():
    return "If time stopped, all motion, perception, and processes would cease. No change or awareness could occur."

# Display explanation
print(time_stopped())
```

Bucol - can bring the rain down.

Vesador: leads multifunctional life.

Bucol and Vasador

Knew the universe could not function without time flowing, as cause and effect depend on time.

Batisa; controls the entire city.

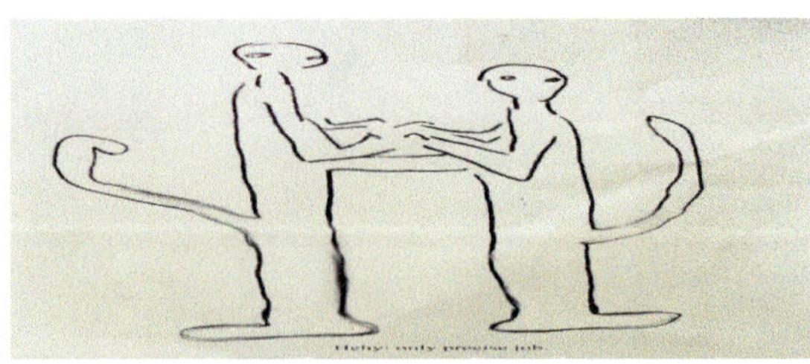

Hchy: only precise job.

Batisa and Hchy

Decided that the stoppage of time is a paradox within our current understanding of physics—it would freeze everything in the universe, including thought and experience, making the notion of "stopping time" impossible to experience or comprehend. We'd not like it, they all concluded.

Konfil: sets up the team spirit

Konfil and

Bujdhor: knows nothing about it.

Bujdhor

explore signals from space

```
# Explanation of signals from space
def space_signals():
    return ("Signals from space include radio waves, light, and other electromagnetic radiation, "
            "emitted by stars, galaxies, and phenomena like pulsars or fast radio bursts (FRBs).")

# Display explanation
print(space_signals())
```

Lucharucha: twinks twice before responding to anyone.

Lucharucha and

Bropode: eats four meals a day in equal intrvals.

Bropode

want an explanation of the FRB 20220610A signal and its significance

```
# Explanation of FRB 20220610A
def explain_FRB():
    return ("FRB 20220610A is a fast radio burst, a brief and intense burst of radio waves "
            "from a distant galaxy. Its origin and cause are still being studied by astronomers.")

# Display explanation
print(explain_FRB())
```

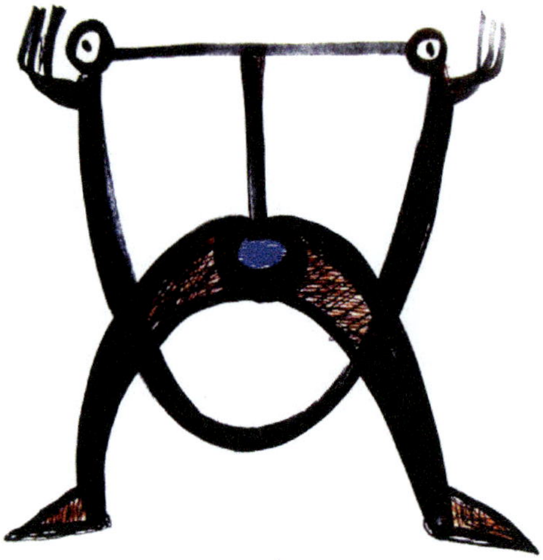

Maoda: always a gentelman.

Humur: time is hs beat friend.

M aoda and H umurc

explored values

```
# Explanation of values
def explain_values():
    return "Values are principles or standards that guide behavior and decision-making, such as honesty, integrity, or kindness."

# Display explanation
print(explain_values())
```

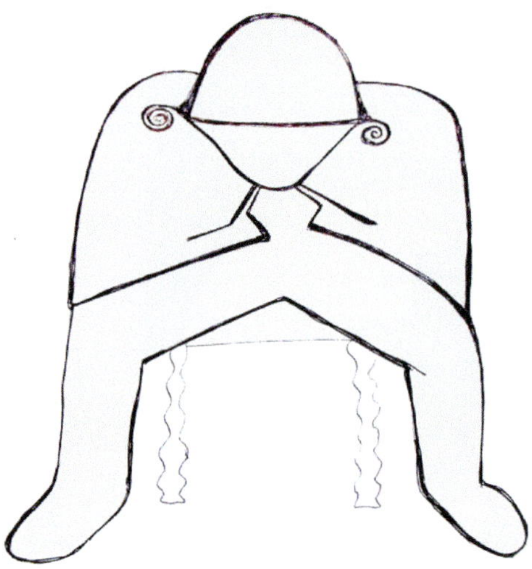

Zurdana: hangs on his thoughts.

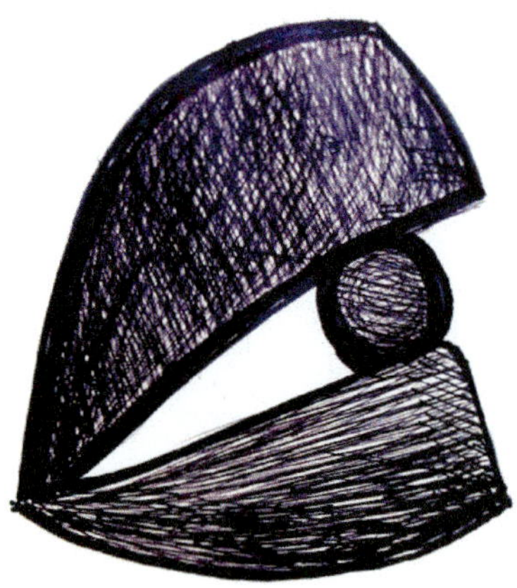

Jihs: has many secrets, but talks about them all.

Z urdana and J ihs

wondered how to adapt values

```
def shift_values():
    return ("To shift values, we must prioritiz, empathy, and collaboration, "
            "adapting to challenges.")

# Display how to shift values
print(shift_values())
```

Musgo: always well connected.

Musgo and

Jumego: eats and drink a lot at each party he goes to.

Jumego

are interested in grass culture and its importance in agriculture and ecosystems

```
# Explanation of grass culture
def grass_culture():
    return "Grass culture involves the cultivation and maintenance of grass for lawns, agriculture, and ecosystems, promoting soil health and biodiversity."

# Display explanation
print(grass_culture())
```

Buderago: always posing.

Buderago and

Nasawadi: holds all his treasures together.

Nasawadi

wondered how to cope with its impact on our health

```
# Impact of grass culture on health
def grass_health_impact():
    return ("Grass culture improves air quality, reduces heat, and promotes mental well-being by providing green spaces for relaxation and physical activity.")

# Display the impact
print(grass_health_impact())
```

Jakawanta: she owns three cats she has to comb.

Jakawanta

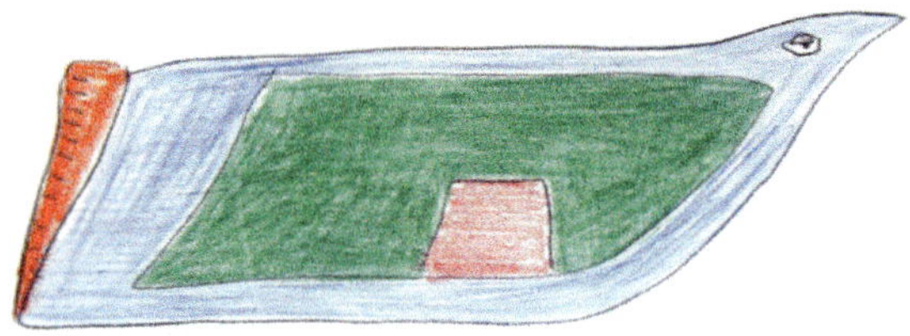

Efertog: very welcoming, yet reserved.

Efertog

wanted to know about what was beneath urban life and how it served the cities

```
# Explanation of underground structures in cities
def underground_cities():
    return ("Beneath cities are tunnels, subways, sewers, and utility lines that provide transportation, "
            "sanitation, and essential services like water, electricity, and communication.")

# Display explanation
print(underground_cities())
```

Monm: receives currents.

Monm and

Eleut: always finds what he'd lost.

Eleut

researched how ancient cities used underground infrastructure to support urban life

```
# Ancient underground support for urban life
def ancient_urban_support():
    return ("Ancient cities built underground aqueducts for water supply, catacombs for burial, "
            "and drainage systems like the Roman Cloaca Maxima to manage waste and prevent flooding.")

# Display explanation
print(ancient_urban_support())
```

Muhavi: always hides what he likes.

Muhavi and

Fahon: makes a discovery, forgets it, then rediscovers it.

Fahon

wondered why people display their wealth

```
# Reasons for displaying wealth
def reasons_display_wealth():
    return ("People display wealth to show success, gain social status, attract attention,  influence others. "
          "It can also be a form of self-expression or a way to reinforce their identity.")

# Display reasons
print(reasons_display_wealth())
```

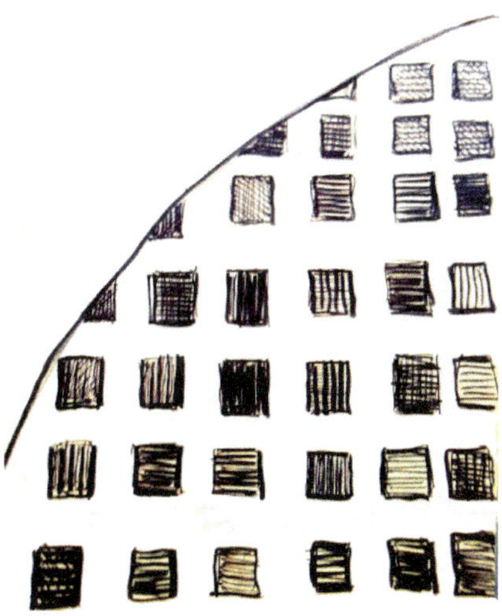

Fariso: always sits by his window.

Nurgucha: Loves Nature more than poetry.

displayed their wealth

```
# Ways to display wealth
def display_wealth():
    return ("Wealth is often displayed through luxury items like cars, jewelry, homes, fashion, "
          "as well as art collections, philanthropy, and exclusive memberships.")

# Display explanation
print(display_wealth())
```

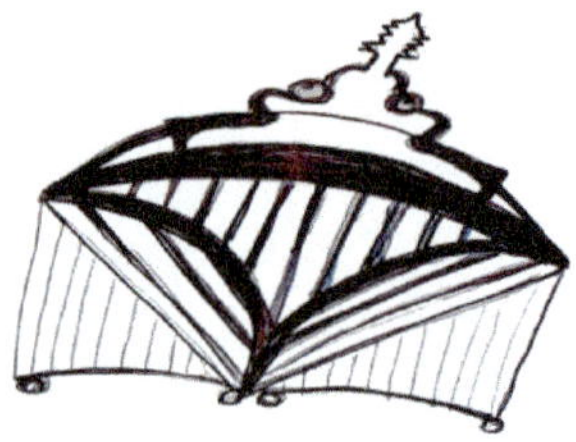

Lasadu: plays tunes when hunting.

Lasadu and

Fecenda: helps farmers with good crops.

Fecenda

wondered about aesthetics

```
# Explanation of aesthetics
def explain_aesthetics():
    return "Aesthetics is the study of beauty, art, and taste, focusing on what makes things visually pleasing or meaningful."
# Display explanation
print(explain_aesthetics())
```

Patarusa: knows 44576 tricks, perform 3456 daily.

Paturasa and

Locetta: eats everything separately.

Locetta

wanted to know what group aesthetics might look like

```
# Explanation of group aesthetics
def group_aesthetics():
    return "Group aesthetics refers to shared visual styles or tastes within a community, culture, or social group."
# Display explanation
print(group_aesthetics())
```

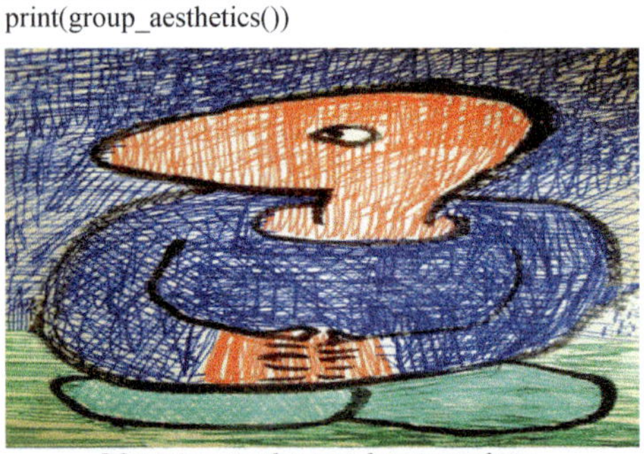

Nureto: makes te best omlets.

Pecaa: they let him out with his piece.

explained the concept of individual aesthetics versus group aesthetics:

```
# Aesthetics vs. Group Aesthetics
def aesthetics_comparison():
    return ("Individual aesthetics reflect personal taste and expression, while group aesthetics conform to shared cultural or social norms, creating a collective identity.")

# Display comparison
print(aesthetics_comparison())
```

Logudo: delivers his best thoughts on time.

Logudo and

Nusengo: more friendly than knowleageable.

Nusenguo

wondered if drone transportation would be an option:

```
# Explanation of drone commuting
def drone_commuting():
    return ("Commuting on drones could be an option for short distances, but limitations like safety, "
            "battery life, regulations, and airspace management need to be addressed.")

# Display explanation
print(drone_commuting())
```

Nylevi: always has many questions.

Nylevi and

Pendeldel: Could compose a song on any table.

Pendelel

wanted to explore if one could travel on a jetpack

```
# Explanation of jetpack commuting
def jetpack_commuting():
    return ("Jetpack commuting could be an option for short trips, but challenges include fuel, "
            "safety, flight control, and regulatory approval.")

# Display explanation
print(jetpack_commuting())
```

Gudica: gold coins turn her more yellow.

Peleku: whistles while he works.

G udica and P eleku

were interested in the roles of a hero

```
# Explanation of a hero's roles
def hero_roles():
    return ("A hero protects others, inspires hope, shows courage, and often sacrifices for the greater good.")

# Display explanation
print(hero_roles())
```

Pegv: when he talks, he smiles, when smiles, talks.

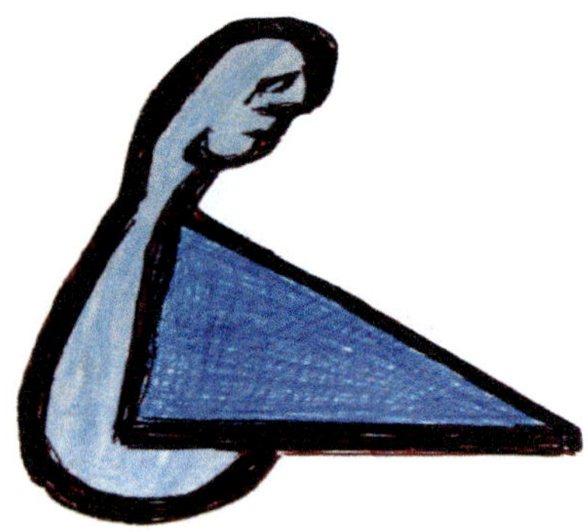

Jitre: plays his instrument 12 hours a day.

P egv and J itre

wondered why pirates while considered a negative thing being so present in the movies

```
# Explanation of pirate popularity in movies
def pirate_popularity():
    return ("Pirates symbolize adventure, rebellion, and freedom, making them exciting characters in movies, despite their negative connotations.")

# Display explanation
print(pirate_popularity())
```

They were discussing all the good deeds and positive outcomes after watching each movie.

Musrus: can really enjoy things.

Lefeto: waits for an inspiration to help him organize.

Musrus and Lefeto

were attracted to dark storytelling

```
# Explanation of attraction to dark storytelling
def dark_storytelling():
    return ("Dark storytelling explores fear, mystery, and the human psyche, allowing us to confront emotions and gain deeper understanding of ourselves.")

# Display explanation
print(dark_storytelling())
```

Punginoe: talks with his mouth full.

Eneo: is able to impress anyone.

Punginoe and Eneo

knew that not releasing emotions can be harmful to the body:

```
# Explanation of holding in emotions
def emotional_suppression():
    return ("Not releasing emotions can lead to stress, anxiety, and physical issues like headaches or weakened immunity due to the mind-body connection.")

# Display explanation
print(emotional_suppression())
```

Patago: watched his diet few timesa a day.

P atago and

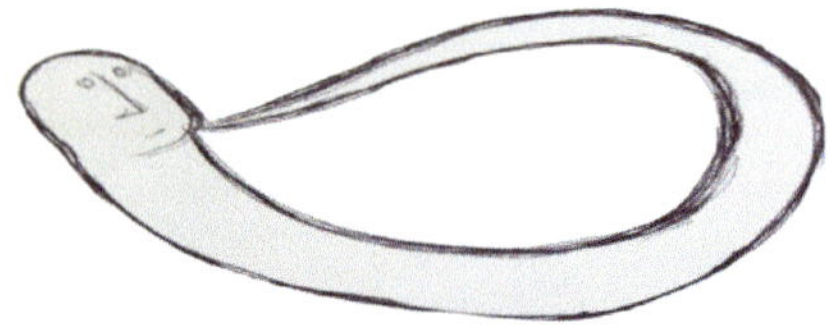

Felco: tastes food with his tail.

F elco

discussed how good characters deliver stories

```
# Explanation of how good characters deliver stories
def good_characters_in_story():
    return ("Good characters drive stories by being relatable, evolving through challenges, and creating emotional connections, making the narrative compelling.")

# Display explanation
print(good_characters_in_story())
```

Parego: has more pets his friends are aware of.

P arego and

Jingot: knows when to speak.

J ingot

discussed how bad characters deliver stories

```
# Explanation of how bad characters deliver stories
def bad_characters_in_story():
    return ("Bad characters create conflict, challenge protagonists, and add tension, making the story more engaging and dynamic.")

# Display explanation
print(bad_characters_in_story())
```

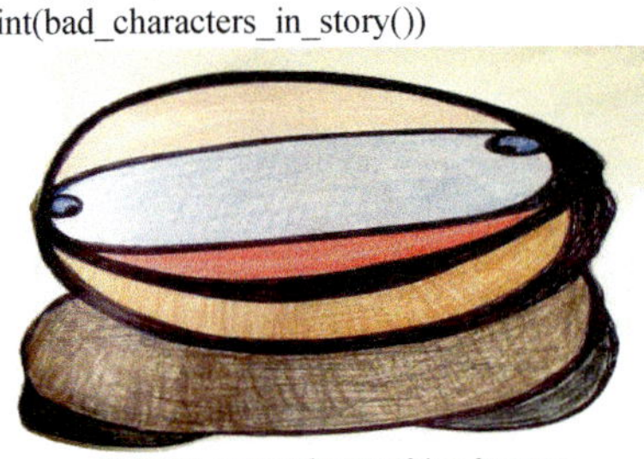

Pukute: can make anything happen.

P ukute and

Rajata: knows the secrets of some words.

R ajata

explained why some might view characters differently based on individual perspectives

```
.# Explanation of varying perceptions of characters
def character_perception():
    return ("Perceptions of characters can vary based on personal values, experiences, and context, causing some to see bad characters as good and vice versa.")

# Display explanation
print(character_perception())
```

Quono: always knows why.

Quono and

Pato: studies ants in the park by talking to them.

Pato

briefly explained the role of fantasy creatures in enriching storytelling

```
# Explanation of fantasy creatures
def fantasy_creatures():
    return ("Fantasy creatures, like dragons and elves, enrich stories by adding magical elements, diversity, and imaginative possibilities.")

# Display explanation
print(fantasy_creatures())
```

Fanalezo: keeps waiting to be taken.

Fanalezo and

Fedelito: the best member of the symbiotic world, they say.

Fedelito

dwelled on the need to achieve what’s impossible

```
# Explanation of the drive to achieve the impossible
def achieve_impossible():
    return ("The drive to achieve the impossible inspires innovation, pushes boundaries, and fosters personal growth, motivating us to overcome challenges.")

# Display explanation
print(achieve_impossible())
```

They were all impossible creatures, after all.

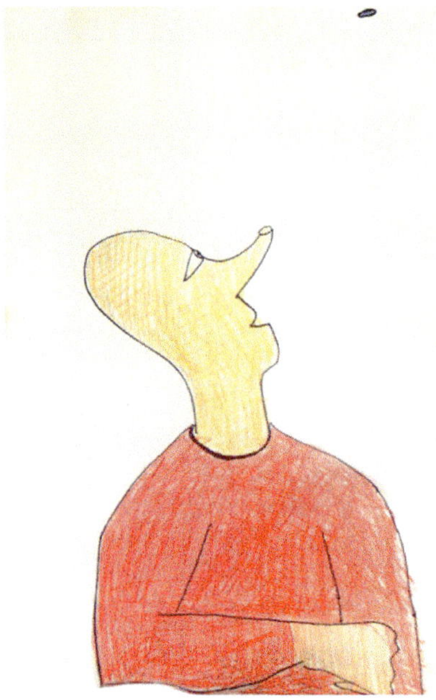

Ondebtud: no space for mistakes for him.

Lungo: makes conclussions based on readings.

Ondebtud and Lungo were fascinated by saving lives

```
# Explanation of saving lives
def saving_lives():
    return ("Saving lives involves taking actions to prevent harm, provide aid, and support well-being, making a profound impact on individuals and communities.")

# Display explanation
print(saving_lives())
```

Ionzo: when in doubt, he talks.

Kud: straightens things out.

Ionzo and Kud knew some who did and always waited for a chance to do so

```
# Opportunities for saving lives
def life_saving_opportunities():
    return ("Opportunities to save lives include improving healthcare access, promoting safety measures, advancing emergency response, and supporting mental health.")

# Display opportunities
print(life_saving_opportunities())
```

Jutago: only speaks when asked to.

Jutago and

Uki: wears one hat daily, but two socks.

Uki

discuss adopting creatures from animal shelters:

```
# Benefits of adopting from animal shelters
def adopt_shelter_animals():
    return ("Adopting animals from shelters provides them with a loving home, reduces overpopulation, and offers a rewarding experience for adopters.")

# Display explanation
print(adopt_shelter_animals())
```

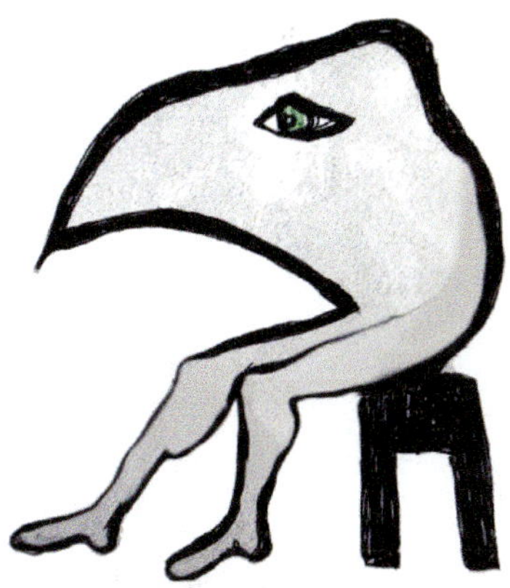

Pufeca: has to sit when he thinks.

Pufeca and

Purag: all for everyone.

Purag

outlined the key benefits of having pets

```
# Advantages of having pets
def pet_advantages():
    return ("Pets provide companionship, reduce stress, encourage physical activity, and offer unconditional love and support.")

# Display explanation
print(pet_advantages())
```

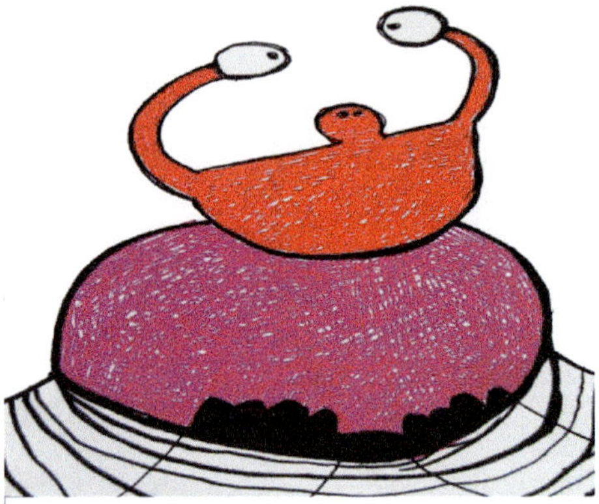

Parcada: never misses a pitch.

Parcada and

Savena: recalls everything.

Savena

talked about ruling and order

```
class Ruler:
    def _init_(self, name):
        self.name = name

    def establish_order(self):
        return f"{self.name} enforces laws and maintains order."

class Citizen:
    def __init__(self, name):
        self.name = name

    def follow_order(self):
        return f"{self.name} follows the established laws."
# Example Usage
ruler = Ruler("King Arthur")
citizen = Citizen("John")
print(ruler.establish_order())
print(citizen.follow_order())
```

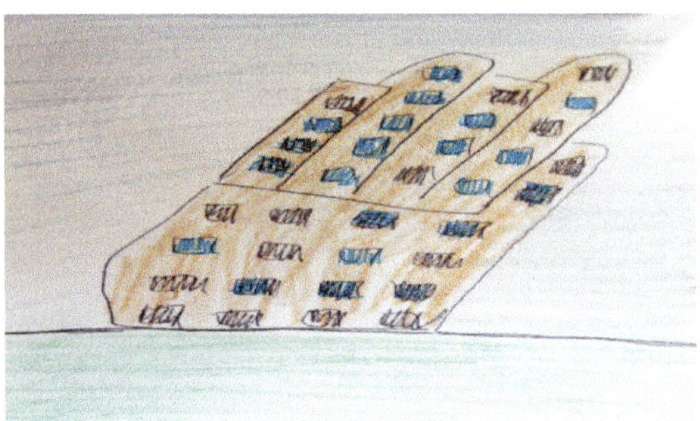

Over: can host many of them.

Over and

Safeo: checks his potatoes daily befor cooking them soft.

Safeo

were interested in order and ruling

```
class Authority:
    def rule(self):
        return "Authority establishes order."

class Society:
    def obey(self):
        return "Society follows the established order."
# Example usage
authority = Authority()
society = Society()
print(authority.rule())
print(society.obey())
```

Lym: never had a bad thought.

Lym and

Tentaster: changes itself to fit well.

Tentaster

were always helping people with not uncommon challenges

```
class Helper:
    def assist(self, problem):
        if problem == "common":
            return "Offer standard solutions."
        else:
            return "Provide customized support for unusual problems."

# Example usage
helper = Helper()
print(helper.assist("unusual"))  # Output: Provide customized support for unusual problems.
```

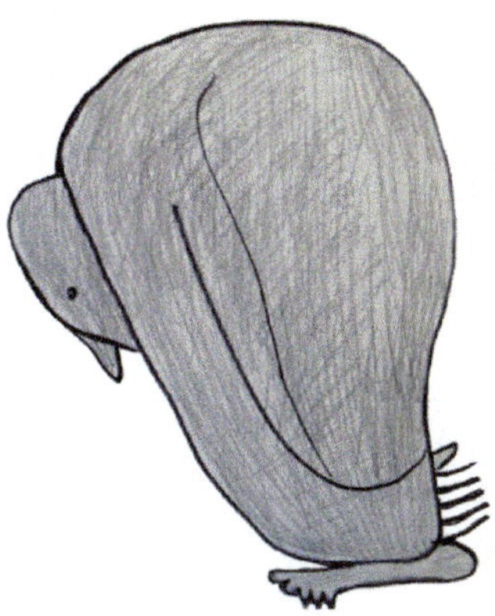

Nusagu: will visualize your problems.

Nusagu and

Oacho: always was dressed in red.

Oacho

thought that power can come out of disabilities

```
class Individual:
    def __init__(self, challenge):
        self.challenge = challenge

    def find_strength(self):
        return f"Strength emerges from overcoming {self.challenge}."

# Example usage
person = Individual("disability")
print(person.find_strength())
```

Huvago: can make five out of four.

Fynta: can see behind her back.

H uvago and F ynta

discussed the power of pets

```
class Pet:
    def comfort(self):
        return "Pets bring comfort and joy."

# Example usage
pet = Pet()
print(pet.comfort())
```

Jusada: holds all she values under her arm.

Gavadungo: lost it, then found it, and lost it again.

J usada and G avadungo

studied the history of pets

```
class PetHistory:
    def origin(self):
        return "Pets were domesticated for companionship and utility."

# Example usage
history = PetHistory()
print(history.origin())
```

Nasada: lost something on Sunday

Nasada and

Tipok: always waits for better times.

Tipok

benefited from physical therapy to be mentally fit

```
class PhysicalTherapy:
    def treat(self):
        return "Uses exercise and movement to restore function."

# Example usage
therapy = PhysicalTherapy()
print(therapy.treat())
```

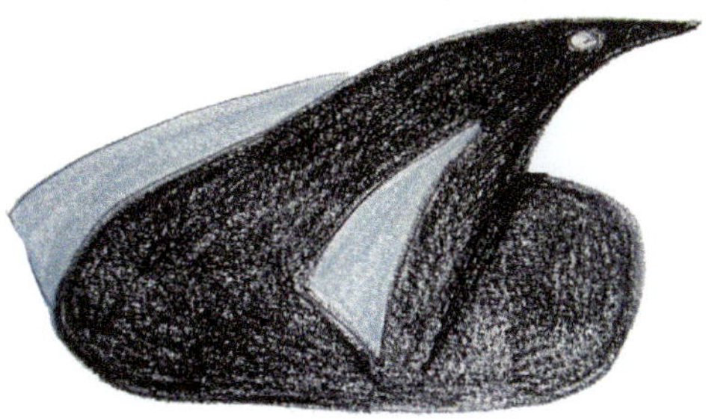

Gutasur: has more reasons to be happy than we all.

Gutasur and

Jusurs: consults any possible action.

Jusurs

needed mental therapy to be in physical shape

```
class MentalTherapy:
    def heal(self):
        return "Uses conversation and reflection to improve mental well-being."

# Example usage
therapy = MentalTherapy()
print(therapy.heal())
```

They all looked and felt great!

Sudo: remembers times anyone remembers.

Sudo and

Funmeer: he always gets what he wants.

Funmeer

developed interest in how hackers think

```
class HackerMindset:
    def analyze(self):
        return "Thinks critically and seeks vulnerabilities in systems."

# Example usage
hacker = HackerMindset()
print(hacker.analyze())
```

Zadt: carries all she needs with her.

Zadt and

Ugacha: controlls all artists.

Ugacha

never understood the opportunists

```
class Opportunist:
    def seize_opportunity(self):
        return "Looks for chances to benefit from situations."

# Example usage
opportunist = Opportunist()
print(opportunist.seize_opportunity())
```

Gfarentea: dreams about having a computer to record her dreams on.

Gfarentea and

Utranda: keeps it all together.

Utranda

wonder how dinosaurs functioned

```
class Dinosaur:
    def function(self):
        return "Dinosaurs adapted to their environment for survival."

# Example usage
dino = Dinosaur()
print(dino.function())
```

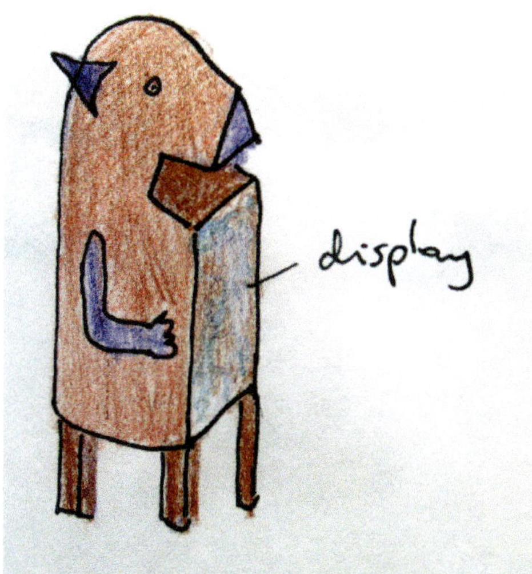

Zuchacho: likes sharing all he knows.

Zuchacho and

Gudeito: always sleeps.

Gudeito

are interested in beings from space

```
class Alien:
    def function(self):
        return "Aliens adapt to their environment and utilize advanced technology."

# Example usage
alien = Alien()
print(alien.function())
```

Puco: never shares any information.

Koho: supports well balanced life.

Puco and Koho

were interested in various systems

```
class System:
    def describe(self, system_type):
        descriptions = {
            "ecosystem": "A biological community interacting with its environment.",
            "computer": "A system for processing and storing data.",
            "economic": "A framework for the production and distribution of goods.",
        }
        return descriptions.get(system_type, "Unknown system type.")
# Example usage
system = System()
print(system.describe("ecosystem"))
print(system.describe("computer"))
print(system.describe("economic"))
```

Lavatusa: has a different message for every person.

Pufago: grows plants like anybody else.

Lavatusa and Pufago

created one.

Puchurago: solves problems by counting.

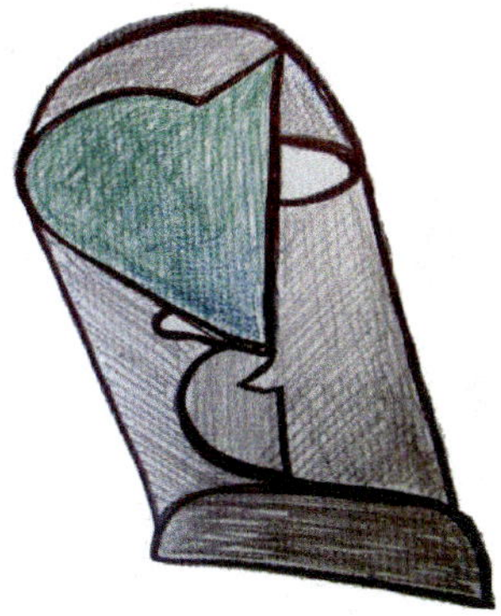

Nufozo: loves to be included.

Puchurago and Nufozo

studied the concept of wellness

```
class Wellness:
    def define(self):
        return "Wellness is a holistic approach to health, encompassing physical, mental, and social well-being."

# Example usage
wellness = Wellness()
print(wellness.define())
```

Iili: does not collect stamps.

Nestu: keeps it all hidden, but talks about it.

Iili and Nestu

wanted to know how much is enough

```
class Enough:
    def evaluate(self, context):
        if context == "resources":
            return "Enough means preserving and sufficient for needs."
        elif context == "happiness":
            return "Enough is having contentment and peace."
        else:
            return "Context defines what is enough."

# Example usage
enough = Enough()
print(enough.evaluate("resources"))
print(enough.evaluate("happiness"))
```

Kagu: thinks aloud.

Kagu and

Ogea: can convince anyone.

Ogea

discussed what it means to be a good person

```
class GoodPerson:
    def qualities(self):
        return "A good person demonstrates kindness, empathy, and integrity."

# Example usage
person = GoodPerson()
print(person.qualities())
```

Lutuduru and

Mundo: can make any party fun.

Mundo

Lutuduru: changes mood twice a day.

discussed the roles of unsolicited advice

```
class UnsolicitedAdvice:
    def role(self):
        return "Can provide different perspectives but may be unwelcome or ignored."
# Example usage
advice = UnsolicitedAdvice()
print(advice.role())
```

Hagelo: enjoys silence whenever he can.

H agelo and

Gufazo: will hold your tickets for three weeks.

G ufazo

were busy as a bee

```
class BusyAsABee:
    def meaning(self):
        return "Describes someone who is very active and industrious."

# Example usage
busy = BusyAsABee()
print(busy.meaning())
```

Hadola: makes the best sandwitches.

H adola and

Olundo: creates music out of nothing.

O lundo

wanted to be strong as an ox

```
class StrongAsAnOx:
    def meaning(self):
        return "Describes someone who possesses great physical strength."

# Example usage
strong = StrongAsAnOx()
print(strong.meaning())
```

They all become busy oxen.

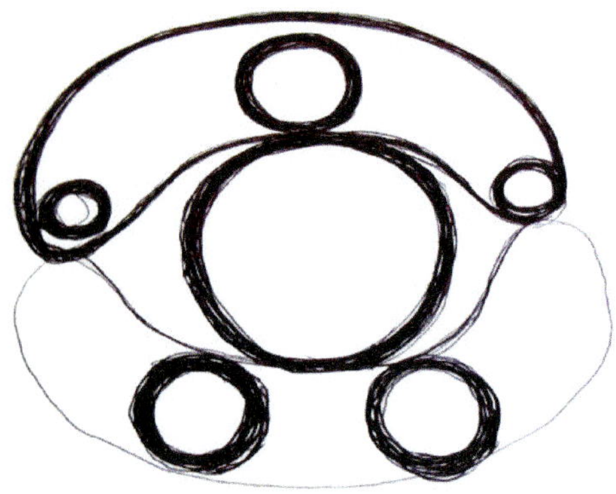

Pluf: can use three jump-ropes at once.

Pluf and

Qamno: hides well all that is important.

Qamno

discussed how stereotypes can misrepresent people based on generalized labels

```
# Stereotypes generalize traits based on identity, creating unfair assumptions.
# This function demonstrates how dangerous stereotypes can be in decision-making.

def make_decision_based_on_label(label):
    # Label is a simplified stereotype, e.g., "artist" or "scientist"
    if label == "artist":
        return "Creative, emotional"
    elif label == "scientist":
        return "Logical, unemotional"
    else:
        return "Undefined stereotype"

# Stereotypes are harmful because they reduce individuality.
print(make_decision_based_on_label("artist")) # Example output
```

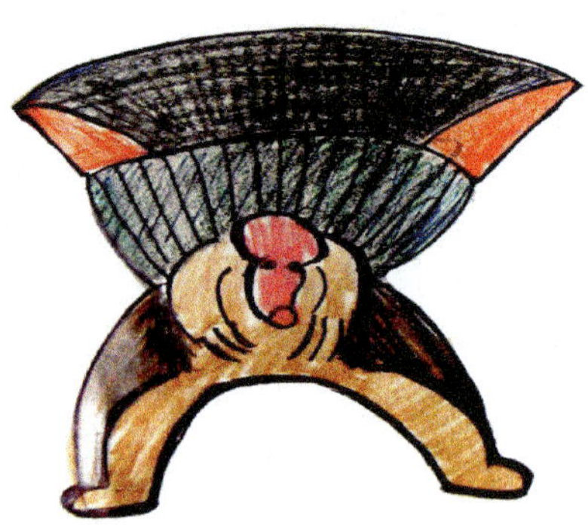

Reteque: gathers and collects atoms.

Reteque and

Hugatsa: eats like a Fractal.

Hugatsa

knew why people use stereotyping:

```
# People use stereotyping for simplification, familiarity, or fear of the unknown.

def reasons_for_stereotyping():
    reasons = {
        "Simplification": "Easier to categorize people quickly.",
        "Familiarity": "Comfort in known patterns or experiences.",
        "Fear": "Avoiding discomfort with differences."
    }
    return reasons
# Example: Print out common reasons for stereotyping
for reason, explanation in reasons_for_stereotyping().items():
    print(f"{reason}: {explanation}")
```

Nusada: talks faster than anyone she knows.

Jadamara: scratches his head when is sure of the solution.

Nasuda and Jadamara

were fascinated by the design and concept underlying the mandalas

```
# Mandalas represent harmony, unity, and the universe through circular patterns.

def mandala_concept():
    design = {
        "Circle": "Symbolizes the universe, wholeness, and eternity.",
        "Center": "Represents self or inner focus.",
        "Symmetry": "Balance and harmony in life and nature."
    }
    return design

# Example: Print the core elements of mandala design
for element, meaning in mandala_concept().items():
    print(f"{element}: {meaning}")
```

Karapacho: finds errors everywhere.

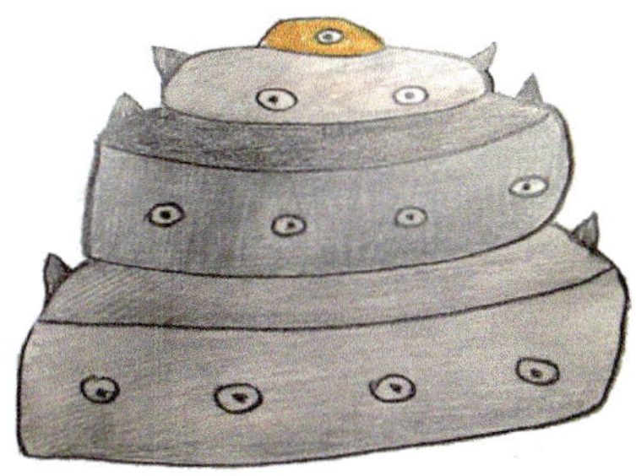

Katungo: celebrated

Karapacho and Katungo

Knew how to make them:

```
import matplotlib.pyplot as plt
import numpy as np

# Function to draw a simple mandala with circular symmetry
def draw_mandala():
    num_circles = 10
    angles = np.linspace(0, 2 * np.pi, num_circles, endpoint=False)

    for i in range(1, 6):  # 5 layers of circles
        for angle in angles:
            x = i * np.cos(angle)
            y = i * np.sin(angle)
            circle = plt.Circle((x, y), 0.5, color='blue', fill=False)
            plt.gca().add_artist(circle)

    plt.gca().set_aspect('equal')
    plt.axis('off')
    plt.show()

# Call the function to display the mandala
draw_mandala()
```

Ratuba: known for the cleanness of his shoes.

Ratuba and

Revza: always keeps appearances.

Revza

enjoyed the idea behind the Platonic forms:

```
# Platonic forms are ideal, unchanging concepts that represent the essence of things.

def platonic_forms():
    forms = {
        "Circle": "Perfect roundness, never achievable in the physical world.",
        "Justice": "An ideal of fairness, beyond individual examples.",
        "Beauty": "Abstract concept of perfection in appearance."
    }
    return forms

# Example: Print descriptions of some Platonic forms
for form, description in platonic_forms().items():
    print(f"{form}: {description}")
```

Owolungu: his mini does not look like him.

Owolungu and

Runachu: always seen with his friend.

Runachu

can list them:

```
# List of Platonic forms (ideal concepts).
def list_platonic_forms():
    forms = ["Truth", "Beauty", "Justice", "Equality", "Goodness"]
    return forms

# Example: Print the list of Platonic forms
print(list_platonic_forms())
```

Padungo: won the Best Introvertic Award.

Rinento: still thinks about the same problem.

Padungo and Rinento

wanted to know about Kepler's Universe:

```
# Kepler's universe: Planetary motion follows elliptical orbits, not perfect circles.

def keplers_laws():
   laws = {
      "1st Law": "Planets move in elliptical orbits with the Sun at one focus.",
      "2nd Law": "A line between the Sun and a planet sweeps equal areas in equal times.",
      "3rd Law": "The square of a planet's orbital period is proportional to the cube of its distance from the Sun."
   }
   return laws
# Example: Print Kepler's three laws
for law, description in keplers_laws().items():
   print(f"{law}: {description}")
```

Vahaku: makes a pie every hour.

Vusar: looks, but does not see.

Vahaku and Vusar

knew who Kepler was:

```
# Kepler: German astronomer, laws of planetary motion.
print({"Name": "Johannes Kepler", "Born": "1571", "Known For": "Planetary Motion"})
```

Ziz: nobody knows why.

Virga: never has to stand up to anything.

Ziz and Virga

studied snowflakes as crystals

```
# Snowflakes are ice crystals with hexagonal symmetry.

def snowflake_crystal():
    return "Snowflakes form when water freezes into a hexagonal crystal lattice."

# Print explanation
print(snowflake_crystal())
```

Widi: interested in the essence.

Kreal: enjoys tea.

Widi and Kreal

admired 5000 never repeated snowflakes as photographed with new then camera
by W.A. Bentley, the first to photograph snowflakes and expose people to their unique crystal structure.

```
def bentley_snowflakes():
    return "Bentley took the first microphotographs of snowflakes, showing their crystal forms."

# Print explanation
print(bentley_snowflakes())
```

Vazea: holds on to his cat.

V azea and

Guselo: was a boxer.

G uselo

enjoyed the small world

```
# The small world concept: Most people are connected by short chains of acquaintances.

def small_world():
    return "In a small world network, individuals are connected through a few intermediaries."

# Print explanation
print(small_world())
```

Nusada: talks faster than anyone she knows.

N usada and

Panango: tastes food before eating.

P anango

studied the nano world

```
# The nano world: Scale of 1 to 100 nanometers, where unique properties emerge.

def nano_world():
    return "In the nano world, materials exhibit distinct physical and chemical properties."

# Print explanation
print(nano_world())
```

It was like comparing a marble to the Earth!

Uyu: attracts all magnets.

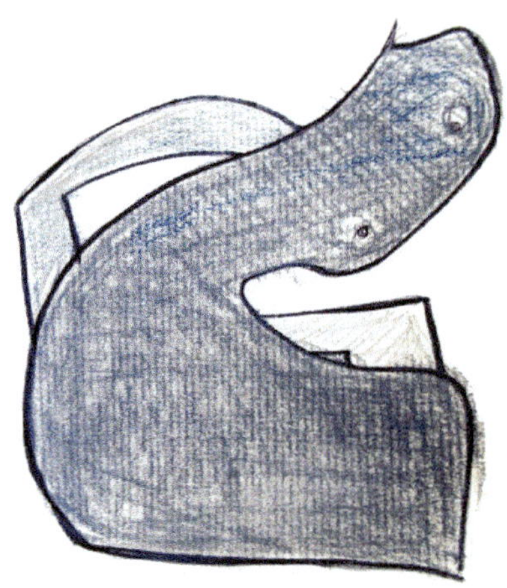

Virutu: watches what he reads.

Ulu and Virutu were interested in the processes behind rain and hail, as both are forms of precipitation with different formation

```
def precipitation_explanation():
    return "Rain: Liquid water droplets; Hail: Ice pellets formed in strong storms."

# Print explanation
print(precipitation_explanation())
```

Tacho: keeps it all in his pocket.

Sahatu: his knee is also his table.

Tacho and Sahatu understood the four states of matter: Solid, Liquid, Gas, Plasma

```
def states_of_matter():
    return "Solid: Fixed shape; Liquid: Takes shape of container; Gas: Fills volume; Plasma: Ionized gas."

# Print explanation
print(states_of_matter())
```

Sufara; has a lot to say every single minute, no matter what he does.

Sufara and

Situ: to him everything is connected.

Situ

wonder why the negative side is stronger than the positive one

```
# Negative aspects often perceived as stronger due to bias and survival instincts.

def negative_vs_positive():
    return "Negativity captures attention more than positivity; it's linked to survival instincts."

# Print explanation
print(negative_vs_positive())
```

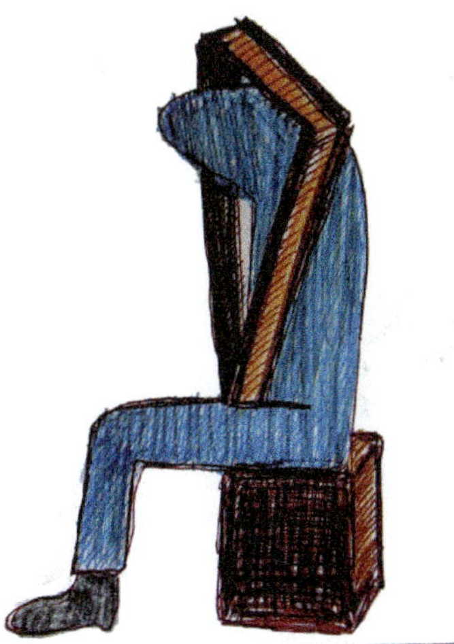

Yudebli: has lots to say but frames others.

Yudebli and

Zuba: always ready to cook.

Zuba

knew how to survive and shared their tips:.

```
print(["Stay calm", "Find shelter", "Source water", "Signal for help"])
```

Varacho: he can see inside you.

Teguno: discusses his problems on a daily basis.

V aracho and T eguno

knew what they thought was important: the power of numbers, as they influence decision-making, patterns, and even predictions, they believed

```
def power_of_numbers():
    return "Numbers reveal patterns, guide decisions, and help predict outcomes."

# Print explanation
print(power_of_numbers())
```

Owolongu: his mini does not look like him.

Kireo: knows how things work.

O wolongu and K ireo

enjoyed exploring the Magic Square:

```
# Magic square: Grid where all rows, columns, and diagonals sum to the same value.

print("Magic square: All rows, columns, and diagonals sum to the same value.")
```

Vutar: has always more to say than what he does.

Mefeta: can see it all anytime.

Vutar and Mefeta understood the significance of words, which can inspire, heal, or harm.

print("Power of words: They can inspire, heal, or harm.")

Turo: plays piano on his lap.

Wantage: kind and helpful, but does not have a clue.

Turo and Wantage knew how to use words:by choosing wisely, be clear, and consider the impact.

print("Use words: Choose wisely, be clear, and consider their impact.")

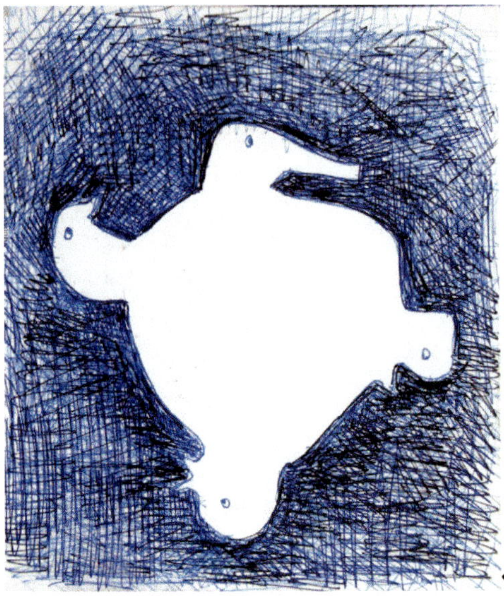

Vugaraca: plays bridge days and nights.

Xaro: relaxes by watching any movement.

Vugaraca and Xaro

were very careful with when to do what, careful with superstition: beliefs that certain actions or events influence luck or fate

```
print("Superstition: Beliefs that actions/events can influence luck or fate.")
```

Yeresco: smells flowers from a mile.

Toftus: they agree on everything.

Yoresco and Toftus

based everything on their research: using types of research: Qualitative, Quantitative, Mixed Methods, Experimental

```
print("Types of research: Qualitative, Quantitative, Mixed Methods, Experimental."
```

Tsu: makes you feel wiser.

Yatahu: self-contained.

T su and Y atahu

keep exploring reasons why so many of us look down on things we don't possess:
perhaps insecurity, fear, envy, lack of understanding. They thought about what they would do if they were granted them

```
print("Reasons: Insecurity, fear, envy, lack of understanding.")
```

Safado: brings things on time.

Woozoo: always goes first.

S afado and W oozoo

explore why others appreciate things, talents, senses, or insights they do not possess themselves, such as admiration, inspiration, respect, curiosity. Would they have enough time or energy to use them if suddenly gifted with them, they pondered.

```
print("Reasons: Admiration, inspiration, respect, curiosity.")
```

Together they possessed many talents, things, ideas, and products developed so they did not have to compete.

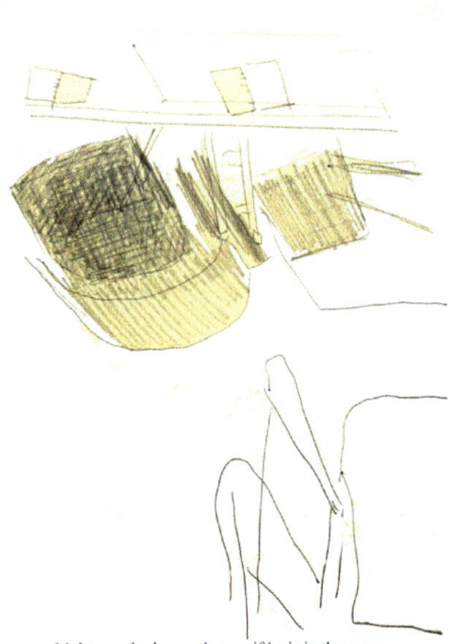

Myhtar: nobody ever knows if he is in the room.

Myhtar and

Sarua: always finds his way out.

Sarua

explored the role of personal heroes from those around them, such as inspire, guide, motivate, and provide examples to follow.

```
print("Heroes inspire, guide, motivate, and provide examples to follow.")
```

Xacago: went to the bar, once.

Xacago and

Wusturan: knows his powers.

Wusturan

wondered about the role of personal heroes from literature in their lives to teach values, inspire growth, and provide moral lessons

```
print("Literary heroes teach values, inspire growth, and provide moral lessons.")
```

Soon, they become personal heroes to others by being written about and shared.

Veruda: likes to think.

Vihuntu: can count to pi.

Veruda and Vihuntu wondered what luck is: a set of random events perceived as favorable or unfavorable outcomes.

```
print("Luck: Random events seen as favorable or unfavorable outcomes.")
```

Vurungo

Rucheta: always has a second thought.

Rucheta

Vurungo: everyone is familiar ith his ability to reach out.

were always lucky. They considered the factors such as opportunity, readiness, preparation, timing, and mindset

```
print("Luck: Opportunity, readiness, preparation, timing, and mindset.")
```

Musadado: always ready.

Musadado and

Wurod: makes sure the soup is always on time.

Wurod

explored robot design and they focused on functionality, mobility, and user interaction.

```
print("Robot design: Functionality, mobility, and user interaction.")
```

Yabajud: hides between the windows.

Yabajud and

Vacado: always on time.

Vacado

focused on the robot's intelligence, speed, strength, and weaponry as the robot's attributes:

```
def robot_attributes():
    return {
        "Intelligence": "AI-driven decision making",
        "Speed": "Fast movement and response",
        "Strength": "High endurance and power",
        "Weaponry": "Advanced defense and attack systems"
    }

# Print robot attributes
print(robot_attributes())
```

Wapcu: always gets what she wants.

Vudaso: was there all the time, but never seen.

W apcu and V udaso

researched the history of love from ancient myths to modern ideals, romantic ones, as love evolves culturally, is shaped by culture and time.

Xajuda: sees through you.

Vaharju: always thinking.

X ajuda and V aharju

loved history and understood past events, to earn from mistakes, and appreciate culture

```
print("Love for history: Learn from the past, appreciate culture, and avoid mistakes.")
```

Utasco: looks when eating.

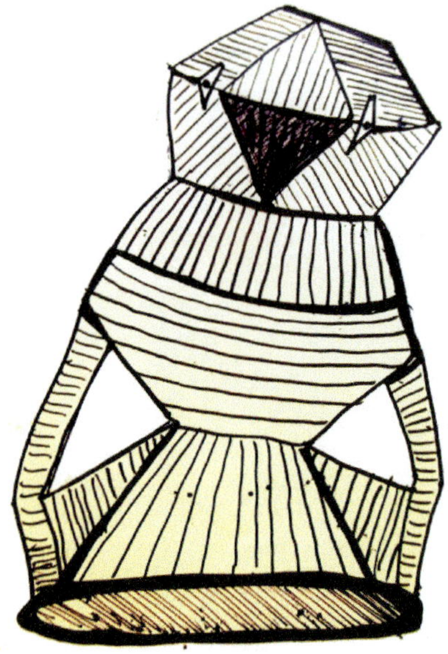

Xeruz: owns many pockets.

Utasco and Xenuz loved the fire, but were afraid of it for possible destruction, injury, and environmental damage.

```
print("Bad side of fire: Destruction, injury, and environmental damage.")
```

Xeto: has all the records.

Xugo: does not like any form of cold.

Xeto and Xugo knew how to handle fire to enjoy its good sides, such as cooking, warmth, and energy generation

```
print("Good side of fire: Cooking, warmth, and energy generation.")
```

Musanove: excercises during any activity.

Wopeto: likes to lead but also be advised.

Musanove and Wopeto

wanted to implement holograms for the zoo exhibits

```
class Hologram:
    def __init__(self, animal):
        self.animal = animal

    def display(self):
        return f"Hologram of {self.animal} is now displayed!"
# Example usage
hologram = Hologram("Lion")
print(hologram.display())
```

Rutego: when not happy, becomes one.

Vusatui: happy or sad, always examines his options.

Rutego and Vusatui

worked on using holograms for the circus performances

```
class Hologram:
    def __init__(self, performer):
        self.performer = performer

    def display(self):
        return f"Hologram of {self.performer} is now performing!"

# Example usage
hologram = Hologram("Acrobat")
print(hologram.display())
```

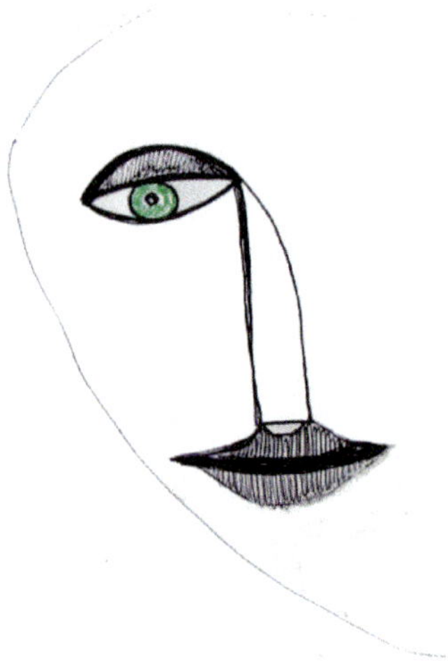

Vurocha: had more secrets than solutions.

Vurocha and

Veme: has all that she needs.

Veme

understood the power of stones

```
def stone_power(stone):
    powers = {
        'amethyst': 'Calmness and clarity',
        'rose_quartz': 'Love and compassion',
        'turquoise': 'Healing and protection',
        'citrine': 'Abundance and positivity',
    }
    return powers.get(stone.lower(), 'Unknown stone')

# Example usage
print(stone_power('Amethyst'))
```

Myhtar: nobody ever knows if he is in the room.

Myhtar and

Teder has some unresolved issues, but has a plan.

Teder

wanted to understand alchemy

```
class Alchemy:
    def __init__(self):
        self.elements = {'earth': 'stability', 'water': 'emotion', 'fire': 'transformation', 'air': 'intellect'}

    def transform(self, element):
        return self.elements.get(element.lower(), 'Unknown element')

# Example usage
alchemy = Alchemy()
print(alchemy.transform('Fire'))  # Output: transformation
```

Wegne: does not understand his deeper thoughts.

Wegne and

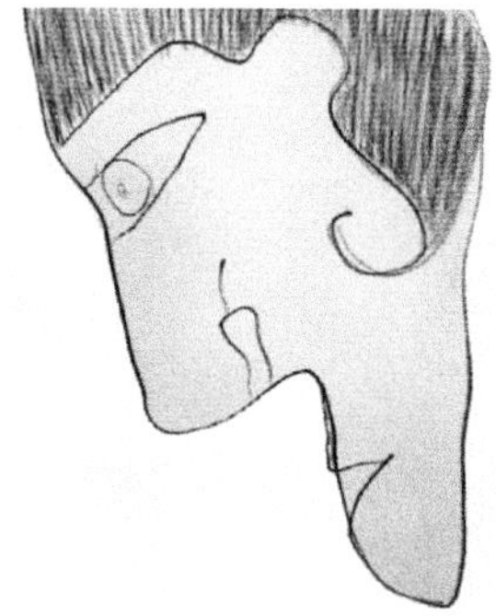

Varacho: he can see inside you.

Varacho

wanted to comprehend cloning

```
import copy

class Cloneable:
    def __init__(self, value):
        self.value = value

    def clone(self):
        return copy.deepcopy(self)

# Example usage
original = Cloneable(42)
cloned = original.clone()

print(f'Original: {original.value}, Cloned: {cloned.value}') # Output: Original: 42, Cloned: 42
```

Vema: keeps all her assets safe.

Vema

learned more about alter ego

```
class AlterEgo:
    def __init__(self, name, traits):
        self.name = name
        self.traits = traits

    def describe(self):
        return f"{self.name}: Traits - {', '.join(self.traits)}"

# Example usage
alter_ego = AlterEgo("Shadow", ["mysterious", "bold", "adventurous"])
print(alter_ego.describe())
```

Nukre: dangerous when informed.

Vusatui: happy or sad, always examines his options.

Nukre and Vusatui

wondered what it was for them when they heard “What is it for me”question used in a sentence

```
def WIIFM(options):
    return max(options, key=lambda x: x['benefit'])

# Example usage
choices = [
    {"option": "Job A", "benefit": 5000},
    {"option": "Job B", "benefit": 7000},
    {"option": "Job C", "benefit": 6000}
]

best_choice = WIIFM(choices)
print(f"Best choice: {best_choice['option']} with benefit {best_choice['benefit']}")
```

Semai: holds truth close to heart.

Seva: knows her colors.

Semai an Seva

Saw it differently: only the numbers ?, they asked

```
actions = [{"action": "Help", "gain": 10}, {"action": "Donate", "gain": 5}, {"action": "Volunteer", "gain": 2}]
print(min(actions, key=lambda x: x['gain'])['action'])
```

Sateria: oversensitive, but businesslike.

Sateria and

Rintari: lets everything go.

Rintari

suffered from boredom

```
stimuli = 0
state = "bored" if stimuli == 0 else "engaged"
print(state)
```

Ramyra: always checks on her daily experiences.

Ramyra

Varaga: keeps it all together.

and Varaga

Vare's meal: always waiting.

and Vare

were bored because they were assigned monotonous work to perform. They thought AI would solve it all.

```
def boredom(task, times):
   return "bored" if task * times > 5 else "engaged"

# Example usage
print(boredom("repetitive task", 6))  # Output: "bored"
```

Tutmurs: they always agree.

Tutmurs and

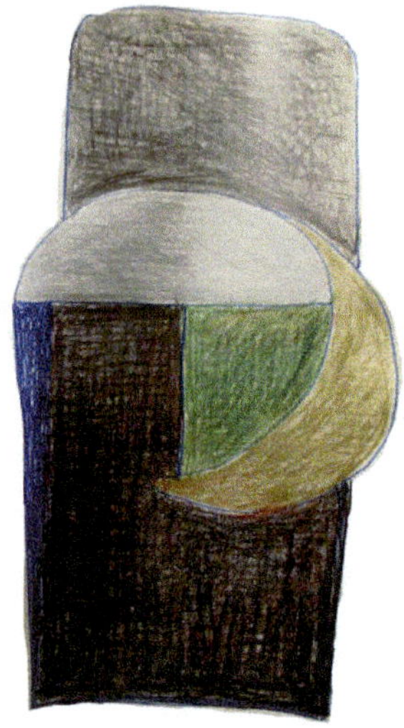

Turano: carries it all mentally and physically.

Turano

were competitive

```
def competitiveness(score1, score2):
    return "competitive" if score1 != score2 else "tied"

# Example usage
print(competitiveness(90, 85))  # Output: "competitive"
```

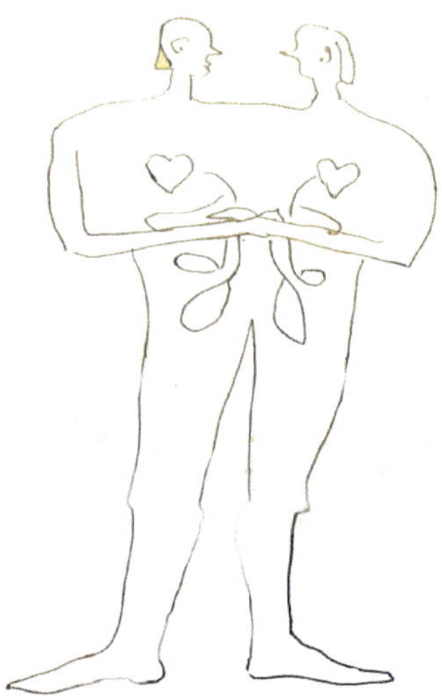

Rufati: shares everything with his brother.

Rufatis and

Heluba: discusses every thought she'd have.

Helubas

The two twin brothers dated two twin sisters

```
def focus_on_progress(current, previous):
    return "progressing" if current > previous else "stagnant"

# Example usage
print(focus_on_progress(80, 70)) # Output: "progressing"
```

The Coast © 2025 by Matylda Czarnecka. (Used with permission).

Bundo: never answers why questions.

Bundo: never answers why questions.

CHAPTER 8
HOW TO APPRECIATE NATURE
ENJOYING NATURE – WE ARE PART OF IT

We benefit from the abundance of gifts, from utilizing natural resources, production, and lifestyle to sports and recreation solutions. We can find an answer for a specific thing, theme, or question. There is always a 'but there is a new solution.' While the word 'but' may have negative connotations, we work together for our children's preparation for new professions based on new materials, technologies, and media. Contrary to a definition of the 'media' accepted in the arts, saying that a medium means materials, tools, and procedures an artist uses to create or produce an artwork, in sciences, medium means research to discover or invent new materials and technologies. There is no perfect solution, so the respectful tolerance of others and their answers is necessary, thus working collaboratively on replacing conflictual ones with ever-growing standards everyone can accept. Cooperation helps us enjoy our place.

On the way to conclusions, we should perceive and recognize different types of things

– Things we cannot control now
– Things we can address
– Things we can do through action steps we can take to appreciate nature and
– Things we must do.

THINGS WE CANNOT CONTROL

Natural disasters we cannot prevent come from the natural and human-enhanced changes in the cycles of weather conditions, which influence weather patterns and result in hurricanes, floods, tornadoes, wildfires, blizzards, hailstorms, and mudslides. Oscillation of patterns in weather conditions, with phases such as the warm El Niño and the neutral or cold La Niña change ocean temperature, surface pressure, winds, and rainfall we cannot control. The same relates to oceanic circulation patterns. Earthquakes, volcanic eruptions, and following tsunamis result from geological processes. Along with the movement of the Earth's crust, plate tectonics and mantle convection occurring deep within the Earth cannot be managed by humans. We cannot change solar radiation's variable intensity and sunspots' occurrences.

THINGS WE CAN ADDRESS DAILY

We can focus on health, bike, walk, or carpool, cheer the use of electric vehicles, and the development of public transport systems, giving us time to do something while moving. We can conserve energy when making energy-efficient practices at home and in businesses, using LED bulbs and energy-efficient appliances, which cuts the bills. We promote renewable energy production by investing in solar, wind, and other renewable energy sources. We can recycle to reduce landfills. They are not a pretty sight. We engage in water conservation by saving water through rainwater harvesting and efficient irrigation. We can practice recycling, composting, and reusing plastic containers. We can protect ecosystems and endangered species so the new generations can see the abundance of species on the planet. We can participate in local actions such as tree planting, clean-up drives, and community gardens. Learning about research, inventions, and innovations and supporting scientific research about technologies and practices is important. By taking these steps, we can appreciate nature, individually and in groups.

THINGS WE CAN DO FOR NATURE – WE ARE PART OF

Using solar, wind, or geothermal energy sources for homes.
Upgrading insulation, energy-efficient appliances, and adopting smart home technologies to save energy.
Encouraging biking, walking, carpooling, and using public transport; consider electric or hybrid vehicles. Watching our diet to stay healthy
Using water-saving fixtures, fix leaks, and implement rainwater harvesting systems. Buying from local farmers and businesses.
Promoting upcycling and reusing materials to minimize waste.
Supporting initiatives to reduce landfills.
Sharing within the community.

THINGS WE MUST DO

Implementing energy-efficient technologies and practices in homes to lower energy consumption. Applying recycling and composting practices to minimize waste and reduce landfill use.
Supporting local farming practices that prioritize soil health and biodiversity.
Minding forests, wetlands, and other critical habitats to maintain biodiversity and ecosystem services. Using water-saving technologies and practices to reduce consumption and protect water resources.
Practicing biking and new technologies as suggested for transportation. Encouraging informed decision-making.
Following local, national, and international policies. Making improvements and emergency preparedness.
Promoting product design emphasizes reusing, repairing, and recycling to minimize waste.
Investing in new technologies and practices that enhance ecological balance and address the challenges of weather conditions

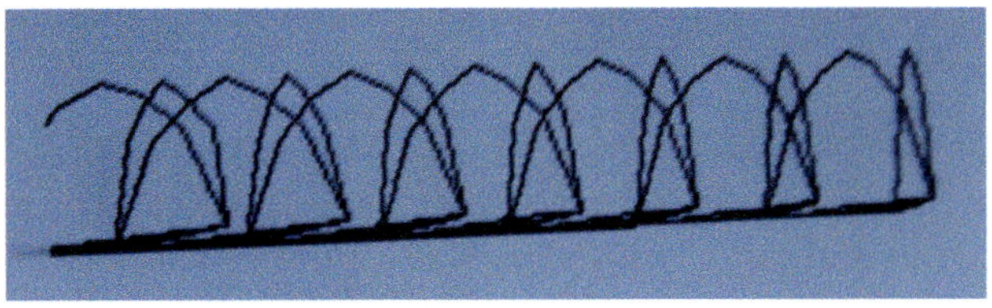

THINGS THAT WE SHOULD AVOID

Cutting down trees without replanting them
Relying on single-use products.
Allowing plastic, chemicals, and waste to contaminate oceans, air, and land. Ignoring endangered species and their habitats
Ignoring local communities and ecosystems.
Avoiding reducing unnecessary emissions.
Wasting water resources and failing to protect freshwater ecosystems.

Addressing these issues is crucial for mitigating unwanted changes in the world and promoting nature.

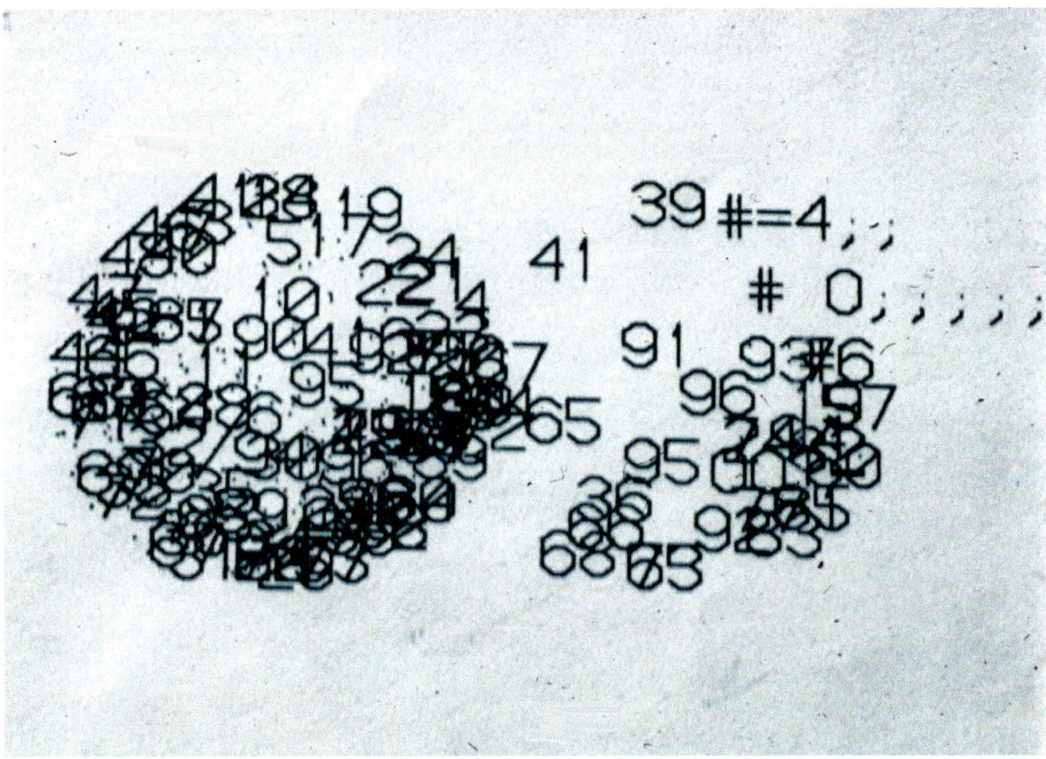

Vuturandu: knows when to act.

We want to enjoy nature, and research suggests solutions, and typically, there is a "but."

WE ALL LOVE NATURE - ONE THING WE HAVE IN COMMON

FROM	TO	BUT
Over consumerism	Nature Appreciation	Remembering about economy
Overspending	Learning new habits and attitudes	Searching for solutions
Comparing oneself with others	Collaboration	Using help from the machines
I do not know/can/excel	I know/can/excel	I am ready to share
Fixed ways to do things	Value the new approaches	Respect values and heritages
Complaining	Open minded views	Problem solving
Competitiveness and jealousy	Finding a solution together	Persistent search
Generation gap	Group goals and achievements	Learn from your children
Break as a reward for children	Abstract concepts from preschool	Stay playful
Using bad words in front of kids	A positive outlook	Raising curiosity
Staying current to shine	Recycling and upcycling	Adapting novel trends
One vision	Self-improve, widen interests	Stay open and respectful
Food fights as a play	Gifting and sharing food	Composting
Outfits for one occasion	Receptiveness of events	Donation
Connoisseurship as a status	Constant learning and knowing	Sharing knowledge
Travel as a display of status	Sharing the beauty of those places	Select preserving travel
Repetitive tasks	Using robots and AI	Supporting good causes
Boredom	Inner growth as a goal	Sharing passions
Forcing to change someone	Changing one's own habits	Finding common values
Loving being outdoors	Affecting Nature in a positive way	Staying alert and up to date
Competing with everyone	Sharing good outcomes	Be happy for others
A sense of one solution for all	Finding new ways	Building new solutions

Feeling better than the rest	Setting safe trends for the planet	Respect every individual
Following trends as a swarm	Openness to different opinions	Respect yourself
Prizing one-type righteousness	Doing one good thing a day	Positively affecting others
Feeling unsecure	Creating a list of good things	Giving and sharing
Blind marketing	AI for interested audience	Using renewable resources
Protests	Making slow changes	Building understanding
Always better than	Good	Understanding quality
Ridiculing others	Approaching issues with humor	Creating good atmosphere
Prejudices	Fact-searching	Widening outlooks
Stereotyping	Learning from different people	Learning and sharing values
Fashion-building stereotypes	Acceptance of one's body type	Considering health's side
Trends Fascination	Personal curiosity	Share your own creations
Curiosity	Passion	One's own and group progress
Following group trends	Theory of Multiple Intelligences	Play and focus

START IN KINDERGARTEN

Children learn fast and carry on with early memories. Forming early habits and culture toward nature might help them protect the planet most naturally by knowing the best, respectful, non-judgmental tactics, procedures, and techniques to blend in with the rhythms and patterns of the natural world we were given to enjoy and thrive in.

Let's look at a few attitudes, but it is hard to adjust habits and attitudes as an example:

Many people stay away from the word math. Others see math as beautiful and is used to discover nature.
People say, "It's Greek for me," but fraternities or sororities use Greek letters from a different alphabet.
Sciences help research, and math helps with accurate descriptions. They form knowledge.
We depend on others, one way, or another, just like scientific disciplines do.
We all do our best but often have our priorities.
We specialize, but understanding what other people focus on is important. Collaborate well!
Understanding how coding works speeds up work on the job and helps with prompt writing.
Coding is a language with roots in the Latin language.

Things are always going better than we are anxious about!

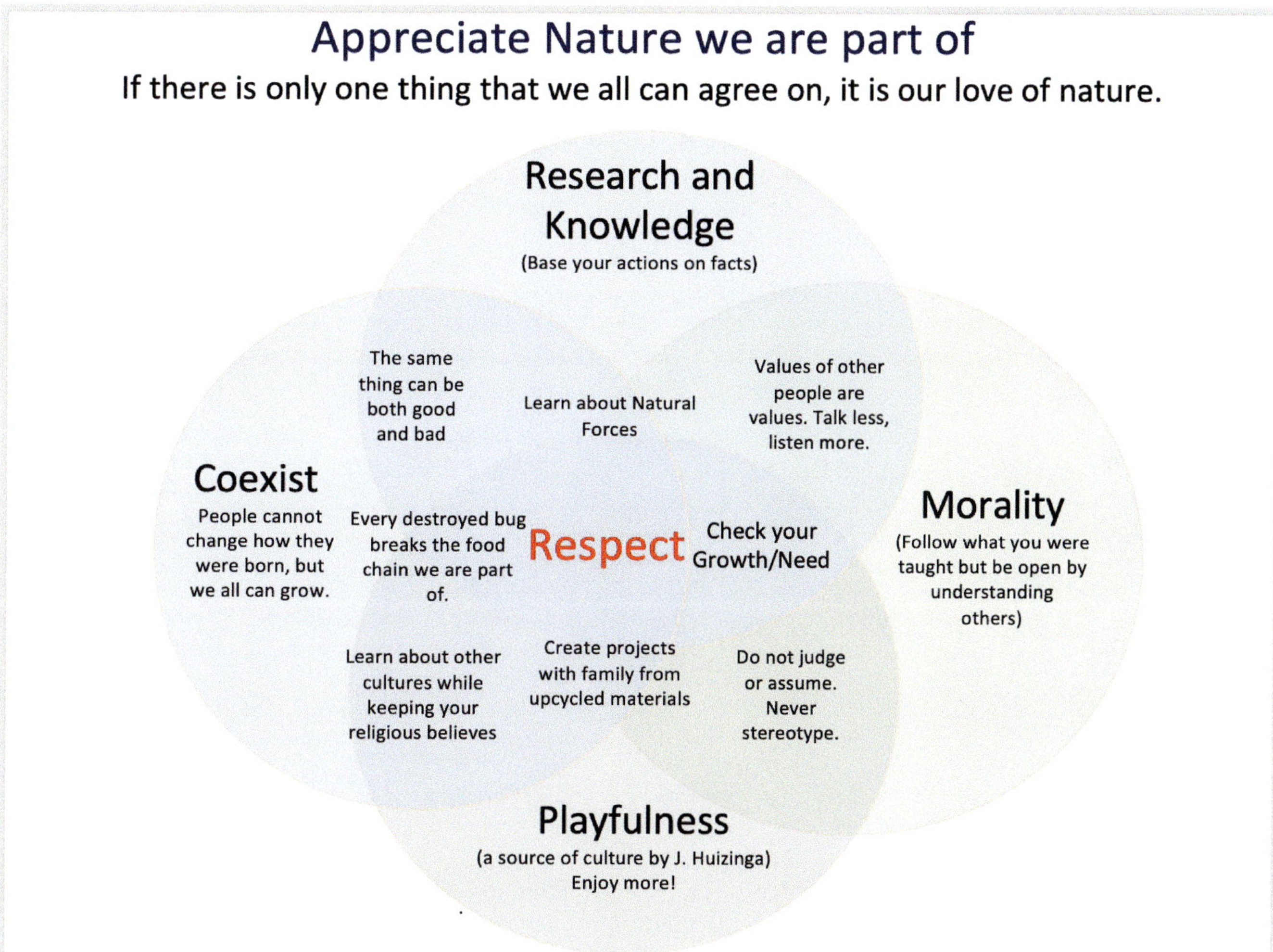

Gysa: drives fast.

Gysa: drives fast.

ACKNOWLEDGMENTS

The UNC President, Board of Trustees members, Provost and members of the Provost Office, Dean of the Performance and Visual Arts, Chair of the School of Art and Design, colleagues, and members of several grant committees have been supporting me in my research and performances based on my books. My great thanks go to all of them and everybody else involved.

My appreciation goes to Randi Slack and Heba Kusseibati from Taylor & Francis Group for all their help with making the books available, Matylda Czarnecka, and Joohyun Pyune for providing artwork and photographs. My thanks go to grant committees for awarding me grants. Thank you to Dr. Lucinda Shellito for consulting and cooperating on the theatrical performances.

Books apps were used, including Grammarly, QuillBot, ChatGPT, WordQuill, Wordtune, and more. Images are by the author and collaborators, as credited.

Tropical forest. © 2025 by Matylda Czarnecka. (Used with permission).

Birds. © *2025 by Matylda Czarnecka. (Used with permission).*

PUBLICATIONS RELATED TO THIS BOOK

al-Rifaie, M. M., Ursyn, A., & Wyeld, T. (2020). *The Art of Coding: The Language of Drawing, Graphics, and Animation.* CRC Press: Chapman and Hall/CRC. Taylor and Francis Group. ISBN 978-0-367-90037-3; 978-1-138-62964-6; 978-1-315-21033-9.

Artificial Intelligence. Chat GPT, Grammarly, Wordtune. -1-63542-191-0

Arya, A. (2020). *Anyone Can Code.* Routledge. ISBN-10: 0367199696, ISBN-13: 978-0367199692

Holoworld, *The Basics of STREAM Education: A Comprehensive Guide* (2024). Retrieved from https://www.blogs.holoworld.one/what-is-stream-education/

Beginner's Step-by-Step Coding Course: Learn Computer Programming the Easy Way. (DK Complete Courses), Hardcover –2020. ISBN 1465482210

Erwig, M. (2022). *Once Upon an Algorithm: How Stories Explain Computing.* MIT Press. ISBN-10: 0262545292, ISBN-13: 978-0262545297.

Gardner, H. (1983/2011). *Frames of mind: The theory of multiple intelligences* (3rd ed.). New York City, NY: Basic Books.

Gardner, H. (1993/2006). *Multiple intelligences: New horizons in theory and practice.* New York City, NY: Basic Books.

Gardner, H. (1997). *Extraordinary minds: Portraits of exceptional individuals and an examination of our extraordinariness.* New York City, NY: Basic Books, Harper Collins Publishers.

Gardner, H. (2000). *Intelligence reframed: multiple intelligences for the 21st century,* New York City, NY: *Basic Books,* ISBN 978-0-465-02611-1

Gardner, H. (2011a) The unschooled mind: how children think and how schools should teach (2nd ed.). New York City, NY: Basic Books. ISBN 0465024386.

Gardner, H. (2011b). The theory of multiple intelligences: the battle-scarred journey (An excerpt from *The theory of multiple intelligences: As psychology, as education, as social science.* Address delivered at José Cela University on October 29, 2011. Madrid, Spain. *The Daily Riff.* Retrieved from http://www.thedailyriff.com/articles/the-theory-of-multiple-intelligences-the-battle-scarred-journey-908.php

Gardner, H. (2016). *Intelligence isn't black and white: There are 8 different kinds.* Bigthing. come. video. Check minutes 5:00 - 5:55 and 8:16

Guilford, J. P. (1950). Creativity. *The American Psychologist, 5,* 444–454. doi:10.1037/h0063487. PMID:14771441.

Guilford, J. P. (1959). Traits of creativity. In *Creativity and its cultivation.* New York City, NY: Harper and Row.

Guilford, J. P. (1967). *The nature of human intelligence.* New York City, NY: McGraw-Hill.

Guilford, J. P. (1968). *Intelligence, creativity and their educational implications.* San Diego, CA: Robert Knapp, Publ.

Mancuso, S. (2022). *The Incredible Journey of Plants.* New York: Other Press. ISBN 978

Montfort, N. (2021). *Exploratory Programming for the Arts and Humanities, second edition* MIT Press. ISBN-10**:** 0262044609.

National Research Council of the National Academies. (2008). *Inspired by biology: From Molecules to Materials to Machines.* Washington, DC: The National Academies Press.

STEAM (2023). Rhode Island School of Design. Retrieved from https://www.risd.edu/steam.

VisionShiftStudios (2024).

STEM to STEAM: Integrated Studies STEM to STEAM Resources Toolkit (2024). Edutopia, George Lucas Educational Foundation. Retrieved from https://www.edutopia.org/article/STEM-resources-downloads.

Sternberg, R. (2011). *Cognitive psychology*. Belmont, CA: Wadsworth Publishing (6th ed.) ISBN 1111344760.

Sternberg, R. J. (2007). *Wisdom, intelligence, and creativity synthesized*. Cambridge, UK: Cambridge University Press.

Ursyn, A. (2024). *The Transfer of Knowledge through Art and Visualization: Novel Technologies, Collaboration, and Visual Communication of Science-based Projects*. Anna Ursyn (Author). Taylor & Francis Group. Routledge. ISBN 9781032624

Wohlleben, P. (2015). The Hidden Life of Trees: What They Feel, How They Communicate. Discoveries from a Secret World. Vancouver/Berkeley: Greystone Books, David Suzuki Institute. ISBN 978-1-77164-248-4.

Maoda: always a gentleman; to those he does not compete with.

The Bird's Eye View of a City. © 2025 by Matylda Czarnecka. (Used with permission).

TERMS WITH SHORT DESCRIPTIONS

Abstract – a concept or thought that does not have physical, concrete existence. Also, an artistic object that has a meaning independent of narrative or pictorial representation. Also, a summary of a larger text.

Aesthetics – analysis of principles related to beauty in terms of arts or philosophy

Algorithm – a sequence of instructions telling a computer how to perform computation or write programs. In a recursive process, algorithms can be written many times to create repetition. Algorithms help to solve a complex problem by writing a sequence of simple steps.

Anthropology means the study of human characteristics. Physical anthropology studies human biological and physiological features and their evolution. Cultural anthropology studies societies, cultures, and their development.

API – application programming interface, is a software interface that allows communication between computers and/or programs.

Artifact – an object produced by a human being, examined in the artistic or historical terms (it may be an artwork, a craft object, a tool, a weapon, or an ornament of archaeological or historical interest).

Artificial intelligence (AI) uses computer systems and applies machine learning for tasks, involving big collections of data, that would require human intelligence.

Binary numeral system uses two symbols: typically, "0" (zero) and "1" (one).

Biointerface is a place of contact between a biomolecule, living tissue, or organism and a living or another material. Nanostructure interfaces are extensively studied.

ChatGPT is a computer program that uses artificial intelligence (AI) and natural language processing (NLP) to understand user questions, providing automatic responses, and simulating human conversation (ibm.com/topics/chatbots)

Cognitive abilities enable to think abstractly (not only on concrete objects), learn from experience, reason, comprehend ideas and concepts, and solve problems. They support gaining knowledge, utilizing information, creative and critical thinking.

Cobots are robots that collaborate with people.

DALL·E 2 is a version of GPT-3 that can create realistic images and art from text descriptions.

Data – factual information specially organized for analysis, reasoning, or making decisions.

Data Visualization – information abstracted in a schematic form to provide visual insights into data sets. Data visualization enables us to go from the abstract numbers in a computer program (ones and zeros) to the visual interpretation of data. Text visualization means converting textual information into graphic representation, so we can see the information without reading the data, as tables, histograms, pie or bar charts, or Cartesian coordinates.

Dimension relates to spatial measures such as width, height, or length. Dimension means how many numbers (coordinates) are needed to determine a position of a point in space. In the Cartesian three-dimensional space, three coordinates, x, y, and z, describe the position of a point: x-horizontal axis, y-vertical axis, and z-depth. René Descartes (Cartesius) revolutionized mathematics by providing the first systematic link between geometry described by Euclides and algebra). A point has no length, area, volume, or other dimensional attributes, so some mathematicians claim a point is 0-dimensional. A line has one dimension because only one coordinate is needed to describe a point in space, while a surface has two dimensions. Data may be linear or multidimensional.

Electromagnetic radiation results from the electromagnetic field's propagation of waves (or photons) which carries radiant energy. Waves, which have different wavelengths, include radio waves, microwaves, infrared, light (which is visible), ultraviolet, X-rays, and gamma rays.

Empathy means understanding and sharing another person's or creature's feelings. One may apply cognitive (by knowing how to take somebody's perspective), emotional (by feeling somebody's emotions), and compassionate (by combining intellect and feelings) empathy.

Extended Reality (XR) comprises real-and-virtual environments generated by computer technology and used in wearables.

Virtual Reality (VR) refers to immersive experiences created with the use of real-world content (e.g., 360° Video), purely synthetic content (for instance, computer-generated), or a hybrid of both.

Augmented Reality (AR) is an overlay of computer-generated content on the real world that can superficially interact with the environment in real time. With AR, the CG content and the real world do not block themselves.

Mixed Reality (MR) – in MR, the synthetic content is overlaid and anchored to interact with objects in the real world in real-time.

Fiber lasers use fiber optic cables with added rare earth elements and other materials to provide and transmit light and light signals.

Form – mass that occupies space, giving the weight, density, and thickness of a 3D object or is implied in a picture of this object.

Fractal geometry describes self-similar or scale-symmetric objects called fractals. When magnified or reduced in size, fractal things are self-similar: their parts are similar to the whole, and the likeness continues when the parts are magnified more and more. They are present in nature, designs, and artworks. Fractal geometry can explain the origination of patterns in living organisms.

GPT (generative pre-trained transformer) is a deep learning model originated by Google in 2017.

GPT-4 is a multimodal model that accepts prompts of images and texts as inputs and gives out text outputs, such as natural language or code.

Graphic is an image represented by a graph or relating to graphics. Computers often generate graphic displays.

Haptic – relates to the sense of touch; the senses of touch and proprioception enable the perception and manipulation of objects.

Higher-order thinking goes beyond observation of facts and data memorization, enabling one to build data-based knowledge. Higher-order thinking makes critical thinking possible in an evaluative, creative, and innovative way.

HTML – Hypertext Markup Language. This language codes formatting, links, and other things on Web pages. XML – eXtensible Markup Language. A markup language like HTML; it lets individuals define and use their tags.

Hyperlink – a link from a hypertext file or document to another file activated by clicking on a highlighted word or image on the screen.

Icon, iconic object or image. An icon represents a thing or refers to something by resembling or imitating it; thus, a picture, a photograph, a mathematical expression, or an old-style telephone may be regarded as an iconic object. Therefore, an iconic object or image has qualities in common with things it represents by looking, sounding, feeling, tasting, or smelling alike.

Iconography means visual elements such as images and symbols used in a specific culture, society, or artwork. It also may indicate a study about these elements.

Immersive experience happens when a 3D or 4D (including time) image (maybe plus sound or other stimuli) surrounds you creating extended reality. Platforms that support immersive experiences include augmented reality (AR), virtual reality (VR), Mixed reality (MR), 360° video, wearable devices, the Internet of Things (IoT), and more.

Infographics – tools and techniques involved in the graphical representation of data, mostly in journalism, art, and storytelling.

Information – knowledge derived from study, experience, or instruction based on facts or data.

Information visualization – representation plus interaction; it means using the computer-supported, visual-spatial representation of abstract data to amplify cognition and derive new insights. Data presented as information visualization are often interactive, numerical, verbal, and graphical (such as the text of geographic representations).

Ions: cations and anions. An atom or molecule with an electric charge is called an ion. An electric charge results from the presence of single, double, triple, or even higher negative electrons, unequal to the number of positive protons in the nucleus of an atom. Removing or adding one or more electrons changes a neutral atom into an ion. A cation is an ion or group of ions with a positive charge. An anion is a negatively charged ion. In an electrolyte solution, cations move toward the cathode (negative electrode) after applying an electric current, and anions migrate to an anode.

Interface denotes a connection or interaction between two units (which may be subjects, organizations, physical or electronic systems), for example, social interface, or interface between phases of matter such as solid, liquid, and gas, and also interaction of hardware and software. The user and computer interface allows communication with the operating system. Interface with the internet may go through the Internet protocol.

Internet of Things (IoT) means a set of objects connected over a wireless network and acting without human actions. It serves for personal use in smart homes (with everyday physical devices embedded with sensors and software), for elder with disabilities care, as an internet of medical things (IoMT), for business, industrial, vehicular communication, and many kinds of infrastructure systems.

Kinesthesia means knowing about the position and movement of the parts of the body. Sensory organs (proprioceptors) in the muscles and joints signal changes in position.

Knowledge visualization uses visual representations to transfer insights and create new knowledge in communicating different visual formats.

Latitude and longitude are parts of a grid system giving us horizontal and vertical coordinates in the geographic coordinate system. Latitude lines run east-west, and longitude lines run north-south. Every location on Earth has a universal address described by two numbers called latitude and longitude coordinates; they say where the coordinates intersect.

LED, the light-emitting diode, is a semiconductor diode that glows when a voltage is applied.

Mandala is a geometric circular figure depicting the universe according to Hindu and Buddhist traditional symbols.

Manifesto is a public declaration of opinions, statements, and programs mostly of political or social aims. An art manifesto expresses aesthetic and philosophical thoughts about the art defined by an artist or a group of artists. An individual art manifesto facilitates the translation of artistic, visual messages into literary form and conveys it to the viewers, critics, and jurors.

Meander is a geometric pattern made by a line bending along and repeatedly crossing a straight line but not crossing itself. In the arts, it is a decorative pattern constructed from a continuous line shaped into a repeated, ornamental motif.

Metaphor – indicates one thing as representing another, thus making an implied mental comparison. For example, we use metaphors every day when we talk about desktop items, such as folders, documents, and in and out boxes, using familiar objects for organizing elements related to the computer. Also, a figure of speech where we use one word or phrase to designate another one, thus suggesting comparison, as in 'a sea of trouble.'

Mime – a performance art involving body motions without the use of speech.

Mythology is a collection of stories, myths, legends, and beliefs typical of a given culture or religion; for example, Christian, Jewish, Egyptian, Hindu, or Muslim mythologies.

NASA is the *National Aeronautics and Space Administration* civil space program and space exploration. This agency works with contractors, academia, and international and commercial partners to explore, discover, and expand knowledge for the benefit of humanity.

Negative space is the space around the objects depicted in a picture. A figure-ground reversal is an optical illusion that happens when we perceive an image formed by the negative space.

Network is a set of connected (wired or wireless) devices, such as computers, servers, mainframes, peripherals, firewalls, smartphones, and more, which allows people to share data. Devices may be linked through cables, telephone lines, radio waves, satellites, or infrared light beams.

Networking means exchanging ideas and information among people for social or business contact.

Neurotransmitters are chemical substances released by nerve cells that transfer signals from neurons to other cells.

OpenAI is a research unit that derives its solutions from deep learning and natural language processing.

Pantomime – a musical, theatrical production using gestures and movements but not words

Paradigm is a pattern of thought: a set of concepts or a way of thinking characteristic of a specific field in science (research methods, postulates, and standards) or philosophy. Paradigm shifts – transitioning to a new approach to the field under study is how the developments come about. Paradigm also means a model, a typical example.

Pattern means the regular order existing in nature and a manmade design. We see patterns everywhere in nature, mathematics, art, architecture, and design. In nature, patterns can be seen as symmetries (e.g., snowflakes) and/or structures having fractal dimensions such as spirals, meanders, or surface waves. In computer science, design patterns serve in creating computer programs. In the arts, the pattern is an artistic or decorative design made of recurring lines or any repeated elements.

Perspective is the appearance of depth, picturing the world on a two-dimensional, flat surface of a piece of paper or a computer screen. Perspective represents 3D objects and depth relationships on a 2D surface.

Photonics is the science of light (photons) generation, detection, and manipulation. It can go through emission, transmission, modulation, sensing, signal processing, switching, and amplification.

Scale is a range of values that forms a standard system for measuring the size of something. Units for measuring in science are known as the International System of Units, which is based on the meter. Very small physical and biological structures are measuring fractions of a meter: micrometer (one-millionth of a meter – $1x10^{-6}$ m), nanometer one billionth of a meter – $1x10^{-9}$ m), and picometer (one trillionth of a meter – $1x10^{-12}$ m) thus, the picometer is one-thousandth of a nanometer. Below are examples of objects of various sizes.

The Milky Way galaxy (10^{21} m) Our solar system (10^{13} m)
The Earth (10^{18} m) A city (10^{4} m)
A tree (10^{1} m) A leaf (10^{-1} m) A cell (10^{-5} m)
Strands of DNA (10^{-7} m) An atom (10^{-10} m), and Quarks (10^{-16} m).

Scientific visualization presents real, abstract, or model-based objects in a digital way directly from the data. It may deliver art-science cooperative learning projects and make knowledge understandable to a broad audience. Visualization as storytelling comprises narratives, interactive graphics, explanatory and animated graphics, and multimedia.

Semiconductor material has a conductivity between a conductor (most metals, for example, copper) and an insulator (such as glass). The properties of a semiconductor, its moving electrons, and electron holes in a crystal lattice can be explained by quantum physics. Silicon crystals are semiconductive materials; they are used in microelectronics and photovoltaics used for direct conversion of sunlight to electricity with the use of solar panels.

Semiotic studies the meaningful use of signs, symbols, codes, and conventions for communication. The name 'semiotics' is derived from the Greek word 'semeion,' which means "sign ." "Meaning" is always the result of social conventions, even when we think something is natural or characteristic and use signs for those meanings. Therefore, culture and art are a series of sign systems. Semioticians analyze such sign systems in various cultures; linguists study language as a system of signs, and some even examine film as a system of signs. The semiotic content of visual design is essential for non-verbal communication applied to practice, especially for visualizing knowledge.

Sign tells about a fact, an idea, or information; it is a distinct thing that signifies another thing. Natural signs signify events caused by nature, while conventional signs may signal art, social interactions, fashion, food, interaction with technology, machines, and practically everything else. Signs take conventional shapes or forms to tell about facts, ideas, or information. Icons and symbols help visually compress information. An icon represents a thing or refers to something by resembling or imitating it; thus, a picture, a photograph, a mathematical expression, or an old-style telephone may be regarded as an iconic object. Therefore, an iconic object has qualities in common with things it represents by looking, sounding, feeling, tasting, or smelling alike. Natural signs signify events caused by nature, while conventional signs may signal art, social interactions, fashion, food, interactions with technology, machines, and practically everything else.

Signage is a visual graphic that displays information, for example, street signs, room identification signs, or any informational or regulatory signs. Signs, symbols, and icons are collectively called signage.
Effective design of a complicated product may help memorize and learn how to use this product (for example, 'Where is the switch?' or 'How to open this thing?').

Social media include social networking sites, image-sharing sites, video hosting sites, discussion sites, community blogs, and economic networks.

Social networking means using Internet-based social media websites and applications to interact with other users for a social or business purpose and stay connected with friends, family, colleagues, customers, or clients. Social networking acts through sites like Facebook, Twitter, LinkedIn, and Instagram.

Space is a three-dimensional expanse in the physical universe where we can measure the position and direction of objects and events. A Cartesian coordinate system (with the x, y, and z axes) serves this purpose in Euclidean geometry.

Spectroscopy records how matter interacts with or emits electromagnetic radiation. A spectroscope serves to study matter by measuring properties of specific frequencies and wavelengths of electromagnetic radiation.

Symbol does not resemble things it represents but refers to something by convention; for example, the word "red" represents red. We must learn the relationship between symbols and what they represent, such as letters, numbers, words, codes, traffic lights, and national flags. A symbol represents an abstract concept, not just a thing, and is comparable to an abstract term. Highly abstracted drawings that show no realistic graphic representation become symbols. Symbols are omnipresent in our life, for example:

– An electric diagram that uses abstract symbols for a light bulb, wire, connector, resistor, and switch.
– An apple for a teacher or a bitten apple for a Macintosh computer.
– A map – a typical abstract graphic device.

– A 'slippery when wet' sign.

Symmetry is present when similar parts of an object are arranged around a line, point, or plane. A crystal shows symmetry when it has a center of symmetry, rotation axes, or mirror planes (imaginary planes that divide it into halves). There are several types of symmetry: for example, line or mirror symmetry, radial, cylindrical, or spherical symmetry. A figure with a line, bilateral symmetry has two identical halves when folded along its line of symmetry, and these halves are congruent, meaning they are the same size and shape. An object has a radial symmetry when it can be rotated around the rotation axis. For example, with a fourfold rotation axis, the crystal repeats itself each 90°. Angles of rotational symmetry possible for crystals are: 60 degrees, 90 degrees, 120 degrees, 180 degrees, and 360 degrees. The halves of the bilaterally symmetrical animals, for example, butterflies, form each other's mirror images when seen along the axis. A circle is symmetrical about its center. Optical isomers are 'mirror images' of each other and are symmetrical around a plane. For example, molecules of some sugar isomers deflect the rays of light in the right or left direction.

Synesthesia means the merging of two or more senses. It happens when a sensory stimulus is received by one sense but also triggers perception in another sense.

Synapse – a structure that links (through a synaptic cleft) a nerve cell with another nerve or some other cell type. In an electrical synapse, an activated neuron develops an electric signal on its presynaptic cell membrane, which induces a voltage change on the postsynaptic cell. In a chemical synapse, electrical activity on the presynaptic cell membrane initiates the release of a neurotransmitter and its diffusion to a postsynaptic cell.

Texture – a characteristic of a substance or a material. Texture exists all around us. It can be actual (natural, invented, or manufactured) or simulated (made to look rough, smooth, hard or soft, or like a natural texture). Simulated textures are made to represent real textures, such as smooth arms or rough rock formations. But they are not actual textures; if you touch the picture, you feel only the paint or the pen or pencil marks.

URL means Uniform Resource Locator. Also, resources are called well-known codes, such as http://www.sciam.com/, used in hyperlinks (activated by clicking).

Variable is a feature or a factor that can take on different numerical values.

Vernacular is an adjective to describe the local, indigenous, folkloristic, common, or simple form of a specific culture, architecture, language, or other human activities or products.

Vernacular language is typical of a particular country or region or a dialect that can be regional, professional, or otherwise linking a group of people. It may also denote the architecture of houses in a particular region.

Visuals are pictures, diagrams, graphics, film clips, or various forms of display.

Visual media are primarily images, videos, and infographics. Powerpoint presentations may serve as an example.

Visualization means the communication of information with graphical representations. Interactive visual representations of abstract data use easy-to-recognize objects connected through well-defined relations.

Wireframe is a skeletal three-dimensional model in which only lines and vertices are represented. It can also be a way to design a website at the early structural level, a 2D outline of a web page or app which displays the functional elements of a website.

Clouds. © 2025 by Matylda Czarnecka. (Used with permission).

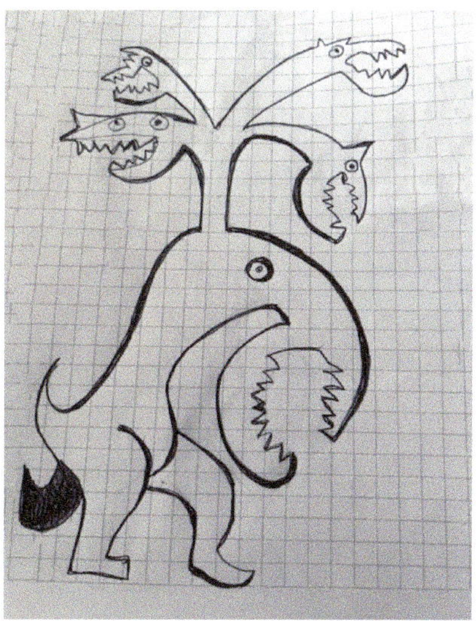

ABOUT THE AUTHOR

Anna Ursyn, Ph.D., is a professor of Computer Graphics at the University of Northern Colorado. She combines programming with software and printmaking media to unify computer-generated and painted images and sculptures.

She had over 50 single juried and invitational art shows and participated in over 200 juried and invitational fine art exhibitions, such as over a dozen times in ACM SIGGRAPH Art Galleries and traveling shows, including Louvre, Paris, Der Prix Ars Electronica Linz, Austria; Eurographics (Artistic Merit Award), Denver International Airport Show, Denver Capitol shows. Her work was selected to be sent to the Moon by NASA as a part of Carnegie Mellon's MoonArk project and traveling shows, including Centre Pompidou in Paris. Animations projected at the Victory Media Network, Dallas, TX, ISEAs, New York Digital Salons, 20th Century Matrix for NTT Museum, Tokyo, Japan (2000 images and 5000 texts describing the 20th Century), Winner of BauBoden, Deutsche Bau-und Bodenbank AG, cover and 18 color plates, Computerkunst/Computer Art Gladbeck, Germany + traveling shows. Salon de la Culture et des Jeux Mathematiques, CIJM, University Pierre et Marie Curie, Paris, Honorable Mention; Art of the Animal, Australia (award), GRAPHITEs, Art of Photography Show San Diego, CA, Common Ground the Haun Tie Art Museum in Beijing, M.I.A.D. Torento Argentina (Second Place), Immaginando, Digital Visions of Etruria (Honorable Mention), Italy, Bridges Mathematical Art Galleries, Joint Mathematics Meetings Art Galleries, and Generative Art galleries. Her work in ABADs is in the permanent collection of the Museum of Modern Art MOMA in New York City, the Los Angeles County Museum of Art, CA, the Smithsonian Institution, Washington, DC, and more. Anna published over a dozen books, chapters, and articles with her students' artwork included in her book.

Research and pedagogy interests include integrated art, science, and computer art graphics instruction. Chaired the SpaceTime international competitions for students by ACM SIGGRAPH, the International Conference on Computer Graphics and Interactive Techniques. Since 1997, Anna has served as a Liaison, Organizing, and Program Committee member of the International IEEE Conferences on Information Visualization (iV) in London, UK, and has chaired the Symposium and Digital Art Gallery D-ART iV.

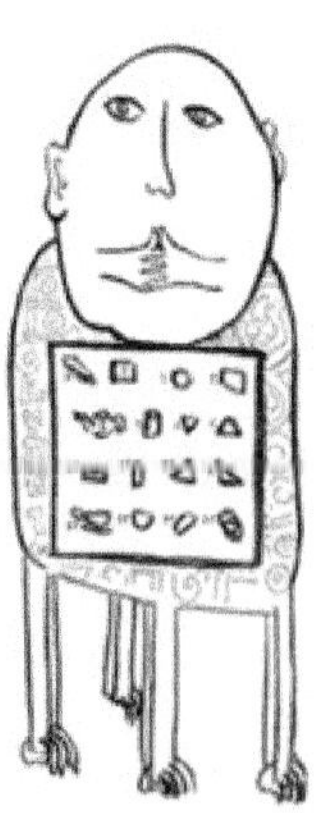

Cityscape. © 2025 by Matylda Czarnecka. (Used with permission).

A city seen from a window. © 2025 by Matylda Czarnecka. (Used with permission).

BOOKS – AUTHORED, CO-AUTHORED, AND EDITED BY ANNA URSYN

A LIST OF TITLES FROM THE PREVIOUS PAGE

1. *Dance Code, Dance Steps as a Code,* Anna Ursyn (Author). Taylor & Francis Group.
2. *New Storytelling: Learning through Metaphors.* Anna Ursyn (Author). Taylor & Francis Group.
3. *Code Appreciation, Reshaping Knowledge.* Anna Ursyn, (Author). Taylor & Francis Group.
4. *Nature Appreciation: Knowledge as Art,* Anna Ursyn (Author), Taylor & Francis Group
5. *The Transfer of Knowledge through Art and Visualization: Novel Technologies, Collaboration, and Visual Communication of Science-based Projects.* Anna Ursyn (Author). Taylor & Francis Group. Routledge. 2024, 143 pages, ISBN 9781032624228.
6. *Photography for Professions: Creative Knowledge Explorations.* Anna Ursyn (Author), Kendall Hunt Publishing Company, 2022, 177 pages, ISBN 979-8-7657-4703-2.
7. *Art for Professions: Art Appreciation and Knowledge Visualization.* Anna Ursyn (Author), Kendall Hunt Publishing Company. 2021, 538 pages, ISBN-10 1792466609, ISBN-13 978-1792466601.
8. *Describing Nature Through Visual Data.* Anna Ursyn (Author/Editor), IGI Global, 2020, 367 pages, ISBN-10 1799857530, ISBN 13 978-1799857532.
9. *The Art of Coding: The Language of Drawing, Graphics, and Animation.* by al-Rifaie, M. M., Ursyn, A., Wyeld, T. CRC Press, Taylor & Francis Group, A Chapman & Hall Book. 2020, 312 pages. ISBN: 9780-0-367-90037-3 (hbk), 978-1-138-62964-6 (pbk), 978-1-315-21033-9 (ebk).
10. *Graphical Thinking for Science and Technology Through Knowledge,* Visualization (Advances in Multimedia and Interactive Technologies) (Anna Ursyn, Author//Editor), IGI Global. 2020, 374 pages, ISBN-10: 1799816516, ISBN-13 978-1799816515.
11. *Interface Support for Creativity, Productivity, and Expression in Computer Graphics.* Anna Ursyn (Author/Editor) IGI Global. 2019, 355 pages, ISBN13 9781522573715, DOI: 10.4018/978-1-5225-7371-5.
12. *Visual Approaches to Cognitive Education with Technology Integration.* Anna Ursyn (Author/Editor), IGI Global. 2018, 387 pages, ISBN-13 9781522553328.
13. *Knowledge Visualization and Visual Literacy in Science Education.* Anna Ursyn (Author/Editor). IGI Global. 2016. 431 pages, ISBN-13 9781522504801.
14. *Maximizing Cognitive Learning through Knowledge Visualization.* Handbook of Research. Anna Ursyn (Author/Editor). IGI Global, 2015, 572 pages, ISBN-13 9781466681422.
15. *Computational Solutions for Knowledge, Art, and Entertainment: Information Exchange Beyond Text.* Anna Ursyn (Author), IGI Global, 2014, 511 pages, ISBN-13 9781466646278.
16. *Perceptions of Knowledge Visualization: Explaining Concepts through Meaningful Images.* Anna Ursyn (Author), IGI Global, 2014, 418 pages, ISBN-13 9781466647039.
17. *Biologically Inspired Computing for the Arts: Scientific Data Through Graphics.* Anna Ursyn (Author/Editor), IGI Global, 2012, 442 pages, ISBN-13 9781466609426.

INDEX

K

L

M

N

O

P

R

S

T

V

Waterfall. © 2025 by Matylda Czarnecka. (Used with permission).

City View. © *2025 by Matylda Czarnecka (Used with permission)*

Artwork by © Joohyun Pyune. (Used with permission).

Trees. © 2025 by Matylda Czarnecka. (Used with permission).